Obama and the New Left in Latin America

Obama and the New Left in Latin America

Clara Nieto

Translation by Gabriel Ponce de León

Originally published as:

Obama y la nueva izquierda latinoamericana
First edition, December 2011
Ediciones B, Colombia, S.A.
www.edicionesb.com.co

Contents

Prologue

CELEBRATING CHANGE

In the first decade of the 21st century, two coinciding developments signal a fundamental shift in the geopolitical panorama within Latin America as well as hemispheric relations. For the first time, a majority of Latin American and Caribbean nations are led by progressive and nationalistic governments determined to free themselves from the political and economic hegemony of the United States, and assert their independence through organizations for regional integration that exclude it. This "New Left" comes to power supported by popular and indigenous movements, traditionally marginalized sectors of society that now surge into the political arena, displacing traditional, discredited parties. These newly empowered groups fight in defense of national sovereignty, and the environment, and against policies supporting foreign mining and resource extraction, as well as neoliberal programs implemented under previous governments. They are the agents of the change now sweeping the region.

Meanwhile, in the United States, the Democratic candidate, Barack Obama, triumphs in the presidential election, overcoming racial barriers to become the first African-American president of the global superpower. Many in his country hope this historic event portends the beginning of the end of still unresolved racial divides the candidate himself described in eloquent campaign speeches. These concurrent events—the political rise of Barack Obama and the New Left—are tied together by the domination exerted for decades by the United States on Latin America, its so-called "sphere of influence." Since gaining independence from its colonial powers, the hegemon to the north has imposed upon Latin America asymmetrical relations marked by exploitation and abuse. Throughout the region the U.S. callously supports military dictatorships, viewed as allies in the fight against Communism, and protectors of its economic interests. In one notably grim remark, John Foster Dulles, secretary of state under President Eisenhower, affirms: "The U.S. has no friends, only interests" (Aguilar, 1968: 108). In defense of those interests, the U.S. proceeds to topple—often through covert actions—inconvenient governments. In the 1950's, President Jacobo Arbenz of Guatemala is overthrown—for having dared to expropriate lands belonging to the United Fruit Company—and in his stead a brutal, corrupt and submissive coronel installed.

Upon taking office, President Obama encounters a different Latin America than the one Washington has traditionally sought to shape. The region is in the process of consolidating its independence, trying to free itself from the political and economic control his country has exerted in the past. Many people and governments now oppose neoliberal policies, such as privatizations and Free Trade Agreements (FTA's), imposed by the "Washington Consensus." Some countries have settled or renegotiated their debts with the International Monetary Fund (IMF) and World Bank, and begun to expand their markets, broadening diplomatic and commercial ties to other continents. Some countries no longer depend on the U.S. as their primary trading partner; the super power has lost ground in its historic sphere of influence.

Obama's campaign slogan—one of the most memorable in U.S. history—is "Change We Can Believe In." Indeed, the multitudes that supported his candidacy yearn for transformational change. The country is reeling from the ill-fated Bush-Cheney years, which thrust a skeptical nation into bloody and ruinous wars in Afghanistan and Iraq, and left behind the worst economic crisis in seven decades, a financial meltdown resulting in bankruptcies, millions of people unemployed and families left without homes. The Bush administration's unilateral, domineering foreign policy, moreover, has diminished American prestige around the world. Relations between the United States and Latin America have sunken to a new low.

In the diplomatic arena, Obama commits to a more multilateral foreign policy, pledging his support for the UN, which the Bush administration had repeatedly sought to undermine, while showing greater respect for international agreements and conventions previously abandoned or branded "obsolete" by his predecessor. The new president expresses a willingness to build bridges towards Russia and the Muslim world, offering to engage not only friendly nations but also rivals, such as Iran, whom he hopes to persuade, through increased cooperation, to halt its nuclear program that the West has long opposed. This conciliatory spirit—virtually absent during the previous eight years—is cause for hope among friends and enemies alike. At his first meeting with Latin American and Caribbean heads of state, in April 2009, President Obama offers to dialogue on equal terms, speaking of a "new beginning," even in dealing with Cuba, despite announcing the continuation of the embargo.

On the home front, the majority that supported Obama hopes for miracles, a complete fix to all the disasters left behind by his predecessor. They want a clean break from the previous administration, considered by many to be the worst in the history of the country. Upon taking office, Obama bans the use of torture, and other brutal interrogation techniques employed against suspected terrorists in overseas prisons, authorized by President Bush. Yet to the dismay of many, in security matters there are unsettling continuities. Many questions remain. What, exactly, has Obama inherited? Which policies will he reject? And which will continue?

This book opens with the capitalist "tsunami" of 2008: the collapse of the financial system that breaks out in the United

States and quickly spreads across the globe. According to many analysts, its primary cause was market deregulation, coupled with Wall Street excesses. Meanwhile, President Bush's lack of attention to Latin America has widened the gulf between his country and the region, giving rise to antagonistic policies detrimental to Washington's interests. As a candidate, Obama unveils his policy towards the region before an anti-Castro audience in Miami. Yet for all his lavish rhetoric, Obama fails to propose any concrete changes: in the drug war he will continue to support the security apparatuses of Colombia—the epicenter of the cocaine trade—as well as Mexico, a principle route through which drugs transit on their way to the U.S.; despite offering to broaden dialogue with Cuba, he pledges to maintain the embargo. Some observers wonder if Obama's policy towards the region will amount to just more of the same.

Chapter II studies the leadership, politics and ideology of the New Left; the movement toward regional integration effectively marginalizing the U.S.; the growing influence of indigenous movements and organizations as agents for change; regional backlash against the World Bank, IMF and FTAs; and the struggle to defend scarce water supplies, which the aforementioned credit institutions seem intent on privatizing.

Chapter III analyses the influence of the Cuban Revolution on the rise of this New Left, how its half century of resistance to American aggression serves as an example, or point of reference for these recent movements; and how influential business and political groups attempt to push the candidate Obama toward a change in Cuban policy, the lifting of the embargo, as well as general rapprochement with Latin America.

Chapter IV focuses on the leadership of the New Left, particularly the heads of state who have brought about profound transformations to their countries, including those who have adopted new constitutions embracing certain socialist principles; the leaders of regional integration and those who have clashed with the United States, such as Lula da Silva from Brazil, and Hugo Chavez, from Venezuela; Evo Morales, the first indigenous president of Bolivia. This chapter will examine their domestic and foreign policies, and frequent confrontations with Washington, including the expulsion of American ambassadors, DEA agents, and public rebukes of U.S. intervention. It also covers the clash between Colombia and Ecuador over the 2008military operation by the Colombian army in that country to kill a FARC chief and the ensuing continental reaction: namely, Ecuador and Venezuela breaking diplomatic relations with Colombia, and the subsequent confrontation between Colombia and UNASUR.

Chapter V explores the world of Barack Obama: his rise through national politics and presidential campaign, the magisterial power of his oratory, including his historic speech on racism—"The Perfect Union"—in Philadelphia. Bridging the partisan divide is a central theme of his campaign, yet from the beginning of his presidency Obama faces a Republican opposition bent on derailing his political agenda. This chapter analyses the impact of the Obama presidency in the international arena, his first encounter with Latin American leaders, as well as his handling of the military coup in Honduras—the first regional crisis confronting his administration. In the second year of his presidency, Obama is forced to respond to the passage of Arizona SB 1070, a divisive bill imposing harsh measures against undocumented immigrants; the administration ultimately challenges the legislation in court. Other thorny issues defining Obama's first term are Iran's controversial nuclear program—and Washington's conflict with Latin American governments that voice support for Iran—and climate change, which also brings hemispheric divisions to the surface.

Chapter VI covers the war on drugs and military expansion of the United States under the pretext of this conflict; the U.S. acquisition of new overseas bases after losing those held for nearly a hundred years in Panama. This chapter also examines the signing of Plan Colombia, an agreement permitting 800 members of the American military as well as 600 private contractors to be permanently stationed in that country; the new FOL bases (Forward Operation Locations) in Central American and the Caribbean and, most controversial of all, the Center for Advanced Operations in Ecuador. In October 2009, under the umbrella of the war on drugs, the U.S. and Colombia sign a pact granting the former use of seven air and naval bases inside the territory of the latter. That the two governments negotiated behind the backs of their respective congresses sparks international outrage. Colombia is now the primary military enclave of the U.S. in the Americas, the greatest threat to neighboring countries, and the region as a whole. Hugo Chávez rails against the growing military presence of the United States in Colombia, which he considers a threat to Venezuela. The agreement becomes yet another source of friction, recrimination, and rupture between Presidents Uribe and Chavez. Accusing his nemesis of harboring FARC fighters in his territory, Uribe threatens to bring Venezuela before the International Criminal Court.

Considering that the changes pledged in his first meeting with Latin America's heads of states—a new beginning, broadened dialogue with Cuba—are yet to materialize, Chapter VII poses the question: "Obama, more of the same?" It examines his dubious handling of the military coup in Honduras. Turning a blind eye on prevailing regional sentiment, the president ultimately supports the perpetrators of the coup, and their illegitimate government that most Latin American leaders refuse to recognize. President Lula suggests that the White House has set a dangerous precedent, leaving the door open for future military coups. This chapter also scrutinizes the "phenomenon" that is Álvaro Uribe, a right-winger viewed by many as a Trojan horse against regional integration and unity, a Teflon president who somehow manages to emerge unscathed from the frequent scandal enveloping his administration.

Obama's record in Latin America thus far has been disappointing. According to President Lula, the continental superstar, the American leader has done "nothing" for the region. For the most part, he has remained distant, and on the issue of immigration reform, which concerns several Latin American countries, the president has failed to deliver.

Chapter VIII opens with the Republican landslide victory in the 2010 midterm elections and its political implications, both at home and abroad. Meanwhile, Latin America continues to drift leftward as the integration movement consolidates, yet not without setbacks; we witness the region's old nemesis—the illegitimate removal of democratically elected heads of state—rear its ugly head again, albeit behind a veneer of democracy. Notable instances of this new phenomenon—or "institutional" coup—include the ousting of President Fernando Lugo in Paraguay and Manuel Zelaya in Honduras. This final chapter also covers the myriad challenges facing President Obama at the onset of his second term, in particular the Edward Snowden NSA revelations and their impact on relations with Latin America. And yet, despite a polarized electorate and vehement Republican obstructionism, the president manages to notch several significant political victories, none larger than the implementation of his monumental healthcare reform law. Finally, recent developments in Latin America are examined, including the initiation of peace negotiations in Colombia, Venezuela's downward spiral following the death of Hugo Chávez, and the triumph of leftist presidential candidates in Central America.

The epilogue delivers a final verdict on Obama's foreign policy in Latin America, with a particular focus on the interminable, divisive war on drugs, and evolving attitudes in Latin America regarding how the crisis should be confronted. Washington's bilateral relationship with Mexico and the vexed question of immigration reform are also examined here.

1

THE CAPITALIST TSUNAMI

In September 2008, the world watches in disbelief as an economic tsunami crashes through the global super power. The U.S. real estate market plummets under the weight of bad mortgages. Some of the country's leading financial institutions—Lehman Brothers, Merrill Lynch, Goldman Sachs, Bear Sterns and AIG—fall flat on the ground; the stock market collapses like a castle of cards; large banks, including Citigroup and J.P. Morgan, teeter on the brink of insolvency; smaller banks go under. In November, the iconic automobile industry declares itself bankrupt; more than half a million jobs vanish. By the end of the year, that jobless figure approaches 3 million. In a hyper-connected, globalized economy, mere seconds is all it takes for the contagion to spread: European and Asian markets tank; tens of millions lose their jobs. The world shudders at the prospect of a global recession.

So who is to blame? The finger pointing, and recriminations, begin. Among the first to call out George W. Bush is former President Carter, who accuses the current office holder of causing "the worst global financial crisis since the Great Depression in the 1930s, with atrocious economic policies adopted since his arrival in the White House;" Carter cites wasteful spending, gargantuan debts and dramatic tax cuts geared toward the affluent, as the principle causes. Eight years earlier, he adds, the nation enjoyed budget surpluses, a robust economy and low inflation (*Reuters*, 2008, October 10).

Despite a budget surplus carrying over from the previous administration, President Bush runs the external debt up to 6.3 trillion dollars. Obligations to China alone, the country's leading creditor, rise to around one trillion dollars. Other creditors, such as Saudi Arabia, Russia and Japan, acquire large volumes of its treasury bonds. For eight years, the Bush administration has managed the country as if it were a corporation of tycoons exempt from taxation and regulatory oversight. "How Wall Street Sold Out America," reads *Time* Magazine's September 29 cover.

In the years preceding the crisis, South American nations create new bodies for regional integration, such as the Union of South American Nationals (UNSASUR) and the Council of South American Defense. Some nations reject outright neoliberal policies imposed by Washington; they nationalize industries that were privatized under previous governments, retake control of national resources, such as petroleum, gas, and minerals, and settle or renegotiate outstanding IMF and

World Bank debts to free themselves from the stringent terms of those lenders. Since their creation, these institutions have been the cause of much conflict in the region, and higher levels of poverty. In 2005, during the 4th Summit of the Americas, a forum for regional dialogue initiated by President Clinton, the Free Trade Area of the Americas (FTAA) fails to garner the support necessary for ratification. In the FTAA, President Clinton had envisioned a single market extending from Alaska to Patagonia. Brazilian President Lula da Silva, however, saw it as an "annexation" attempt.

President Hugo Chávez of Venezuela plays a pivotal role in the creation of the Bolivarian Alliance for the Peoples of Our America (ALBA) as an alternative to the FTAA. Questioning the IMF "dictatorship," he advocates joint negotiations of foreign debts, which he characterizes as "immoral," and repays his own country's outstanding debt to the IMF. For more than 60 years, he claims, that institution has imposed unfair conditions on weak and vulnerable nations, obligating them to privatize public industries and natural resources in order to gain access to foreign credit.

In the past, the IMF has held up Argentina as a shining model for neoliberal policy, but between 1999 and 2002 the nation plummets into the gravest economic crisis in its history—a financial meltdown of unprecedented proportions on the continent—when its banking system collapses, spreading mayhem throughout the country. The people rise against the government: massive protests break out, with businesses and warehouses looted, and dozens of deaths, forcing the resignation of President Fernando de la Rúa. A long, ungovernable period ensues. According to some economists, the crisis can be blamed on the IMF's own faulty projections (Tracinski, 2002, January 7). Brazil, its largest regional trading partner, is also affected by the Argentinean crisis. There is nationwide resentment against the World Bank and IMF. Several countries settle their debts to the fund. To help facilitate repayments, Hugo Chávez purchases their government bonds. Another Chávez initiative, the Bank of the South, aims to offer the region an alternative to these credit institutions, which are controlled by the United States.

Leaders of the "New Left," who are eager to liberate their countries from the control of the IMF and World Bank, initially believe that the financial calamity only afflicts the "Empire." Riding high from his own country's boom, President Lula da Silva asks: "What crisis? Go and ask Bush about that," when questioned about the financial collapse, and misidentifies the economic tsunami as a "little wave." Nicaraguan President Daniel Ortega characterizes the crisis as "God's punishment" against the U.S. for attempting to impose its own economic ideology on poorer nations. (*Reuters*, 2008, October 11). But like the rest of the world, Latin America is not immune to financial contagion, and President Lula himself soon backtracks, informing Brazilians that "a recessionary crisis in a country like the United States can bring problems to all countries" (*The New York Times*, Barrionuevo and Romero, 2008, October 2).

On October 2, 2008, in an article titled "From Gleeful to Fearful in Latin America," *The New York Times* reports a prevailing mood shift in the region: while certain leaders may have initially derived some measure satisfaction from the financial collapse now embroiling the unpopular American president, they soon must face the harsh reality that no country is immune (*The New York Times*, Barrionuevo and Romero, 2008, October 2). Those who believed they had broken with neoliberalism now have to grapple with their continued dependence on Washington, and vulnerability to the ills of economic contagion.

Alarm over the scope of the crisis can be heard from various quarters. In Caracas, Hugo Chávez, George Bush's indefatigable gainsayer, proclaims the "economic catastrophe has the strength of a hundred hurricanes," and Ignacio Ramonet, editor of *Le Monde Diplomatique*, characterizes its scale as "apocalyptic," contending that "Wall Street's collapse is comparable, in what it represents to the financial sector, to what the fall of the Berlin Wall meant to geopolitics." He cites Paul Samuelson, winner of the 1970 Nobel Prize in Economics, who likens the current crisis to the one that precipitated the fall of the USSR. "Market fundamentalists repeated that it was also true, that globalization was synonymous with happiness, and financial capitalism built a paradise on earth for all. They were wrong," he concludes (Ramonet, 2008, September 30).

SPEAKING OF THE CRISIS

Four months after the bubble bursts, the 39th World Economic Forum Annual Meeting in Davos, Switzerland is without a doubt among the most somber in its history. Many attendees call out the United States for its role in the crisis. Russian Prime Minister Vladimir Putin describes the crisis as a "perfect storm" ravaging every corner of the global economy, and reminds those in attendance that the previous year American representatives had extolled the "soundness of their economy" while "today the leading Wall Street investment banks have virtually ceased to exist, a statement more eloquent than any public rebuke," he adds. Wen Jiabao, the Chinese premier, characterizes the U.S. economic system, with its low savings, high consumption, and "blind pursuit of wealth" as "unsustainable." *Time* grimly declares "for years the financial markets roared along as if there were nothing to fear. Now it's payback time and all of us will be feeling the pain (Serwer and Sloan, 2008, September 18).

Though the theme of the 18th Ibero-American Summit in San Salvador, held from October 29-31 2008, and convening heads of government and state of Spanish- and Portuguese-speaking nations of Europe and the Americas, is the "Rights of Youth," it is the spreading economic crisis that monopolizes the dialogue. Citing security concerns, President Chávez skips the meeting, traveling to China instead. Uruguay is represented by its vice president, and Cuba by its ambassador to Brazil. In general the commentary is bitter, with harsh criticism leveled against the global economic system. President Evo Morales blames the crisis on a capitalist system that is "speculative and miserly"; for Daniel Ortega capitalism has "failed since its inception," and Argentinean President Cristina Fernández suggests that they are now "confronting the failure of the neoliberal model." In the summit's final communiqué, attendees demand increased state vigilance of financial markets, and call for active participation from the Ibero-American community in the global response to the crisis *(Granma,* 2008, October 31).

Around the world it comes as a surprise to some that President Bush, just two days before the election to determine his successor, calls a summit to discuss the crisis. With one foot out the door, the lame duck president will not be around to implement any of the solutions agreed upon; his call for action is seen by some as damage control, a desperate measure to save face in the wake of his administration's political and economic debacles. Some analysts suggest that the President is seeking to demonstrate, both at home and abroad, that he continues to be in control, despite the severity of the crisis for which he continues to deflect all blame. The summit, which convenes in Washington from November 14-17, brings together heads of state and government, the presidents of the IMF and World Bank, the Financial Stability Forum, and the secretary-general of the United Nations. Owing to the gravity of the crisis, the G8 is expanded to include 12 key emerging economies, among those Brazil, India, China, Argentina, and Mexico, which form the new G20. President-elect Obama sends former Secretary of State Madeleine

Albright, and Jim Leach, former chairman of the House Committee on Banking and Financial Services (and a leading figure in "Republicans for Obama"), as emissaries. The summit incites protest in front of World Bank headquarters, and around the world. In Spain, 600 NGOs coordinate protests in 75 cities against this "elitist and exclusionary" summit, with the number of demonstrators rising into the millions. These protests, however, lack both the scope and impact of those staged in Seattle against the WTO, which represent a milestone in the history of popular protest.

The G20 agenda is sweeping and complex and adds up to a firm defense of the capitalist system. Its final communiqué—drafted in advance by neoliberal economic advisors, according to Fidel Castro—amounts to a renewed commitment to neoliberal principals, free trade, respect for private property, and the requisite elimination of commercial and regulatory barriers for such a system to function. On a positive note, a compromise is reached on regulating world financial markets, and pushing forward reforms to the Bretton-Woods institutions (World Bank and IMF), despite opposition from President Bush and some of his allies; at the same time, those institutions are also reinforced, even though they have been, in large part, the cause of the crisis. The communiqué is unanimously endorsed. India and Brazil, despite opposing positions on regulation and how to confront the crisis, find themselves obligated to accept it. Certain issues divide the U.S. and Europe as well. President Lula rejoices in the eclipse of the G8, and the prominent role of emerging nations in an increasingly multipolar world. Some Third World leaders find the defense of capitalism in the final communiqué to be absurd; was it not the unfettered excesses of that system, after all, which spawned the current crisis? With their customary optimism—however detached from reality—President Bush and his agents laud the summit as a "success." The final communiqué is, in essence, an ode to capitalism, its grandest resolution to "continue speaking" (Landler and Meyers, 2008, November 15).

In *Granma*, Fidel Castro writes: "Anybody would have thought [the summit] would produce an in-depth debate on this thorny subject," but a mere six hours is dedicated to the discussion of the crisis and "the problems of the planet and human race"; he calls out the "unbelievable" unanimous acceptance of the communiqué, the public reading of which lasted half an hour, and which amounts to a full acceptance of Bush's demands, before and during the summit, while "the United States receives no criticism for its abusive practices." The Cuban leader finds the communiqué to be tedious, and ridden with banalities and technocratic jargon that say "absolutely nothing" (*Granma*, 2008, November 16).

While the G20 summit convenes in Washington, world stock markets, already depressed since the onset of the financial crisis, continue their downward spiral (Canwest News Service, 2008, November 17). The summit's tepid resolutions, devoid of concrete measures, do little to allay investor fears. Still, some participants leave Washington optimistic, believing a foundation for joint action has been laid. For workers, though, it's another story. "Millions of frustrated union members face the loss of their jobs or are close to losing them on account of the greed and irresponsibility of the world's financial markets," comments Ken Georgetti, President of the Canadian Labour Congress, one of thousands of trade unionists to attend the summit. He sets forth the concerns of labor to the World Bank and IMF, asking for measures to protect workers from losing their jobs, and protect the economies of developing nations. Georgetti complains: "Our governments sat by while this crisis was in the making, and ignored our arguments [...] for new international rules to regulate global finance, as advocated by the global labor movement and some European and developing-country leaders (*Canwest News Service*, 2008, November 17).

Addressing the UN General Assembly that same month, Evo Morales accuses the capitalist system of causing the crisis; the Bolivian President advocates breaking with neoliberalism, and reformulating the rules of the WTO, IMF, and World Bank under UN—rather than G20—guidance. Morales, moreover, laments that "in 15 days [G20 members] have contributed 30 times more money to Wall Street banks than to the UN Millennium Development Goals, one of which"—he points out—"is the eradication of poverty" (*Cuba Información*, 2008, November 19).

The day after the G20 summit ends, President Bush travels to Lima, Peru to participate in the 16th Annual Asia-Pacific

Economic Cooperation (APEC) Leaders Meeting, which convenes from November 17-20. Among the 21 members in attendance are the Chinese Premier Wen Jintao and Russian President Dimitry Medvedev, both of whom exhibit renewed interest in building bridges to Latin America. They arrive at commercial agreements in Lima, followed by visits to Brazil, Costa Rica, and Cuba, where they carry out similar agendas—to fill space previously occupied by the United States. President Bush manages to garner a declaration of support for the G20 agreement. Some countries with Pacific coasts, such as Colombia, Ecuador, Panama, and the Central American nations, are not members of APEC. Since 1993, Colombia has attempted to enter the organization, but has to submit to a moratorium on new membership that ends in 2010. The Colombian President, Álvaro Uribe, nonetheless manages an invitation, arriving at the meeting with several ministers and signing cooperation agreements with Canada, China, and Peru.

AGAINST CAPITALISM

The groundswell of animosity towards the neoliberal policies endorsed by the Washington Consensus—a package of policies prescribed for developing countries by institutions such as the IMF and World Bank, through which the U.S. imposes its economic agenda on the Third World—does not originate in any political party or trade union but rather, according to some analysts, in the Zapatista uprising of January 1994, which inspires other progressive movements in the region, such as the Landless Workers' Movement in Brazil, the Piqueteros in Argentina, and various populist, labor, and indigenous movements and organizations—rural as well as urban—in Bolivia, Ecuador and Peru. The Zapatista rebellion breaks out on January 1, the day in which the North American Free Trade Agreement (NAFTA)—between the United States, Canada and Mexico—enters into force. An indigenous political-military organization from Chiapas, led by the eloquent Subcomandante Marcos, the EZLN—Zapatista Army of National Liberation—declares war on NAFTA, and the neoliberal principles on which it's conceived. According to many analysts, this uprising marks the beginning of the regional backlash against neoliberalism, a symbol of the rise of the New Left. The implementation of NAFTA proves to be disastrous for agriculture and labor markets in Mexico, raising already high levels of unemployment, and leading to land abandonment by farmers unable to compete with the flood of subsidized imports from up north. NAFTA increases poverty levels and migration of undocumented workers to the United States. (Years later, President Calderón asks to revise the agreement, advocating the inclusion of labor and environmental standards). To the Clinton administration, however, NAFTA represents a first step toward the creation of the Free Trade Area of the Americas (FTAA), whose goal is to control hemispheric commerce from Alaska to Patagonia. Indeed, the proposal for the broadened free trade agreement is initially introduced at the First Summit of the Americas in December of the same year.

Populist movements and citizen organizations from numerous countries begin organizing demonstrations against the institutional pillars of capitalism. The first mass protest, against the WTO, staged in Seattle in 1999, draws activists and grassroots organizations from many developing countries. The first protest of its kind and scale in the post-Cold War Era, the demonstration gives rise to others, some equally impressive in size, between 2000 and 2006 in Prague, Washington, New York, Quebec, Geneva, Gothenburg (where there are fatalities), Paris, among other European cities. Protesters boycott meetings of the WTO, IMF, and World Bank, and G8 summits at Davos. Despite police and military deployments designed to impede their access to these conferences, activists manage to unsettle the discussions, and on more than one occasion are able to influence their outcomes.

To counterbalance the enormous influence of the aforementioned institutions, parallel forums to debate the same issues from dissenting viewpoints arise around the Third World. The first World Social Forum in Porto Alegre, Brazil, in 2001—and those held every year since in this and other cities—is attended by many thousands of populist, indigenous and citizen organizations, from all corners of the developing world, and gives rise to new forums for national and regional dialogue. It is through these forums Latin America is able to project itself into the worldwide debate against neoliberalism, the Washington Consensus, and controversial elements of U.S. foreign policy, such as the global war on terror.

THE BUSH DEBACLES

Looking for answers to the 2008 crisis, many analysts turn to Franklin Roosevelt's New Deal. They liken the ravaged economic landscape Barack Obama inherits to that which FDR navigated in the 1930's. "In 2008, as in 1932," writes *The New York Times* columnist and Nobel laureate Paul Krugman, "a long era of Republican political dominance came to an end in the face of an economic and financial crisis that, in voters' minds, both discredited the G.O.P.'s free-market ideology and undermined its claims of competence." (Krugman, *The New York Times*, 2008, November 21). Hard economic times, he adds, can stir the hopes of progressives.

By the end of President Bush's second term in office, the country is mired in one of the worst economic crises in its history, in addition to a pair of bloody and polarizing wars. The unilateral heavy-handedness of his administration has eroded its credibility around the world. The U.S. does not ratify the Kyoto Protocol on greenhouse gas emissions, and withdraws from the International Criminal Court established by the Rome Statute, and disavows the Geneva Conventions, which President Bush characterizes as "obsolete."

The Bush administration pressures NATO and allied nations into joining its war on terror. Under false premises, and despite widespread protest, it launches an invasion of Iraq. Many believe that Washington intends to seize the oil production of that country, whose reserves are among the largest on earth. "No Blood For Oil," reads the ubiquitous placard slogan at anti-war protests around the world. Bush pushes NATO into its war in Afghanistan, the country responsible for sheltering Osama Bin Laden prior to September 11. NATO forces oust the Taliban government. Eight years later, a resurgent Taliban once again controls the majority of the country. Hamid Karzai, the Afghani president, installed by Washington, complains of the interminable war, the poor NATO results, and CIA drone strikes in Afghanistan that leave thousands of civilians dead. President Karzai laments not being able to stop them, and unleashes some harsh criticism of Washington.

Latin America has no soldiers in this war Afghanistan; only the Colombian government, in August 2008, offers to send a battalion of troops, though under Spanish command. Faced with a wary public, the government pledges that its contingent will aid only in dismantling land mines and poppy eradication efforts (despite the limited success of eradication programs in its own country, where coca production has risen 27% in 2008) (*Associated Press*, 2008, November 2).

Other than Great Britain, its major European allies decline to join the U.S. in the invasion of Iraq. From Latin America, only Central America joins the "Coalition of the Willing," sending a handful of soldiers to Iraq. Mostly a symbolic gesture, the meager force little by little disbands. The last Central American government to withdraw, El Salvador, led by a right wing government friendly to President Bush, does so two months before the American president leaves the White

House. In December 2008, as President Bush winds down his second term, the situation in Iraq is heating up. Furious demonstrations protest a military agreement being negotiated between the U.S. and Iraqi governments to maintain the former's troops an additional three years. *Time* magazine comments on the improbable union of Shiites and Sunnis, who have been warring with each other since the start of the occupation. "Friends and enemies alike" want American forces out of their country, and soon, a common goal that has united them for the first time in this war-stricken country as the scaling back of U.S. forces "will be the beginning of the end of the occupation" (Ghosh, 2008, November 26). During the presidential campaign Obama pledges to withdraw U.S. troops in 16 months, and put an end to this ruinous war.

BUSH AND LATIN AMERICA

The Bush administration's balance sheet in Latin America is negative: analysts point out the indifference of the U.S. leader toward the region, his meddling—through open as well as covert means—in its domestic politics, the diminished American presence in the region and the confrontational stances taken by local governments against the U.S. during his tenure in office. In April 2001, with Latin American support, the United States is voted off the UN Human Rights Commission in Geneva, a humiliating turn of events for a country that fancies itself a world leader in that field. The loss of its long-held seat can be seen as a rebuke of American abuses, the divisiveness of its stances, and its incessant condemnation of Cuba for human rights abuses while ignoring more egregious violations in other countries. The following year, however, the U.S. regained its seat.

In May 2003, the Bush administration seeks support in the UN Security Council for a resolution authorizing military intervention in Iraq. Chile and Mexico, both non-permanent members at the time, abstain. Typically a reliable ally, Colombia withholds its support when Washington seeks backing for diplomatic and military immunity agreements for Americans stationed abroad before the International Criminal Court. President Bush withdraws the U.S. from the Rome Statute, signed by President Clinton at the end of his second term, which entered into force in 2002. Human rights organizations fear this withdrawal may foster conditions conducive to impunity.

Another incident that seems to indicate a diminishing U.S influence in Latin America is the inability of Secretary of State Condoleezza Rice to muster sufficient support for the U.S.-backed candidate for secretary-general of the Organization of American States (OAS), the Mexican Secretary of Foreign Affairs Luis Ernesto Derbez of the right-leaning PAN. The majority supports Chilean Interior Minister José Miguel Insulza of the Socialist Party. It is the first time Washington is denied its preferred candidate. An even greater setback takes place later in the year, during the Fourth Summit of the Americas, when the FTAA—a pet political project of several U.S. administrations—which would establish a common regional market under U.S. leadership, dies from lack of support. This is its "burial," gloats Hugo Chávez. Lula da Silva characterizes the FTAA as an attempt at "annexation."

To assuage the anti-Castro Hispanic voting bloc in Florida—a traditional bastion of Republican support—upon taking office President Bush assigns hardliners to pivotal roles in hemispheric relations. He appoints the Mexican-American Roger Noriega—a former senior staff member of the right-wing Senator Jesse Helms—U.S. Ambassador to the OAS (during a congressional recess in order to bypass Democratic opposition). Another critical appointee is the Cuban-American Otto Reich for assistant secretary of state for western hemisphere affairs. Both figures are fervently anti-Castro. Reich previously served as an aid to congressional Republicans on Latin American issues.

The U.S. has a long track record of political and military—and often covert—intervention in Latin America, though Washington is either loath to acknowledge any inappropriate meddling (regardless of how flagrant an offense may be) or quick to justify it on national security grounds. Going back to the Reagan Era, many such interventions have been financed by the National Endowment for Democracy (NED), a non-profit organization founded in 1983 supposedly to "promote democracy" around the world—though its true objective is to destabilize governments deemed unfriendly to American interests. It presents itself as an NGO despite being funded primarily by the U.S. Congress. Allen Weinstein, one of the founders of the NED, in a 1991 interview to the Washington Post, claimed: "A lot of what we do was done 25 years ago covertly by the CIA."

Following the military-led 2002 coup in Venezuela against the democratically-elected Hugo Chávez, President Bush wastes no time recognizing Pedro Carmona, whom the coup leaders had designated "provisional president." He lasts three days in power. The coup fails, commanders loyal to Chávez reinstate him in Miraflores—the presidential palace—and he immediately accuses the U.S. of intervention. He has evidence of Carmona visiting Washington prior to the coup, as well as his interviews with President Bush and key members of his administration. The coup turns out to be financed by the International Republican Institute (IRI), which in turn is supported be the NED.

Hoping to undercut the 2002 presidential campaign of Evo Morales, the indigenous labor leader opposed to the U.S. policy of coca eradication, Reich, Noriega and Ambassador Manuel Rocha threaten economic sanctions and diminished relations between the U.S. and Bolivia should Morales emerge victorious. At the same time, they initiate a campaign to discredit him, accusing the cocalero candidate of having "a certain form of" relation with the drug trade and terrorism. In 2002, Morales falls short by less than 1% of the total vote, but three years later, in spite of intense opposition both internal and from Washington, Morales is elected Bolivia's president on December 20, 2005, gaining 54% of the popular vote.

The U.S. meddles time and again in Nicaragua frustrating the presidential aspirations of Daniel Ortega. The Sandinista leader falls short in the elections of 1990, 1996, and 2001, but comes out on top in 2006, and enters office on January 10, 2007.

In February 2004, Haiti is the scene of another U.S. intervention, a coup staged against President Jean-Bertrand Aristide. Aristide falls out of favor with Washington for opposing the privatization of state-run industries—as prescribed by the World Bank and Inter-American Development Bank (IDB)—and France in turn is threatened by his demand for a 21-billion USD compensation for the 90 million gold francs France obligated the island nation to divvy up, some 200 years earlier, in exchange for its independence. Amid the violence and internal opposition incited by Washington, Roger Noriega, the newly appointed Assistant Secretary of State for Western Hemisphere Affairs (replacing Otto Reich, now a White House consultant), carries out the coup in situ. He plots, finances, and arms a "rebel" force to overthrow the democratically elected leader. Flown in a U.S. Air Force plane to "exile" in South Africa, the ousted president denounces the operation, claiming he was kidnapped. When it comes to light that President Bush, along with French President Jacques Chirac, plotted his downfall, the world reacts with outrage.

For George W. Bush, the global war on terror is always first and foremost. The president concerns himself little with Latin America, and has his minions carry out intimidation on his behalf. Secretary of Defense Donald Rumsfeld invokes terror to subdue governments, conjuring a dangerous world of narco-terrorism, and radical Islamic groups infiltrating South America. During several visits to Latin America, the Secretary of Defense attempts to gain military advantages and access to new bases on the continent.

"RADICAL" POPULISM

There is a strong tendency towards militarism in many of Washington's policies in Latin America. President Bush attempts to enlist the region in his global war on terror, requesting troops on the ground, as well access to military bases. The Pentagon supports the deployment of national armies in the drug war and war on terror, and floats an unfounded theory that Islamic terrorist cells have infiltrated South America with the objective of carrying out violent plots and undermining democracy. The demands of conducting internal warfare against terrorist threats, however, are at odds with the constitutional mandates of national armies.

The principal spokesman for U.S. security policy towards Latin America is the Commander of the United States Southern Command (USSOUTHCOM), responsible for Central and South America, in addition to the Caribbean. In March 2004, General James T. Hill delivers a detailed report to the Senate Armed Services Committee on the geopolitical panorama of the region, which he describes as "unstable" and "explosive"; the general recapitulates the threat of narco-terrorism, by which he means renegade armed groups financed by drug money, while also emphasizing the threats posed by organized crime, pervasive corruption and the "radical populism" of left-wing governments, whom he accuses of subverting the democratic processes in their respective countries, exploiting the frustrations of their citizens, and nurturing anti-American sentiment with the goal of undermining U.S. interests. Cuba and Venezuela are singled out. He too floats the theory of Islamic terrorist cells operating in the tri-border region between Paraguay, Brazil and Argentina, and Margarita Island, in Venezuela. These groups, he claims, are financed by drug money. As Commander of USSOUTHCOM, General Hill describes his primary duty as maintaining and broadening relations with his military counterparts throughout the region. "We have worked very closely in recent decades," he reports. According to Hill, Latin America is the most violent region in the world.

The Pentagon continues directing attacks at the age-old enemy, Cuba, and now its strongest ally Hugo Chávez as well. Wary of his growing influence in the hemisphere, and tireless promotion of regional integration, it brands the Venezuelan president a threat to democracy. Looking to bolster continental solidarity, Chávez grants loans to his Latin American peers, and purchases government bonds so they can repay outstanding IMF and World Bank loans. Flush with petrodollars, Chávez is able to help his friends out: he signs agreements to sell petroleum below market value, and offers favorable conditions in barter exchanges. Washington looks askance on their rival's "checkbook diplomacy," and accuses him of undermining regional democracy, objecting to his support of Evo Morales's presidential campaign.

Three American human rights organizations issue a joint report calling attention to the "dramatic increase" in U.S. military aid to Latin America, the militarization of the drug war, and millions of dollars being siphoned into Plan Colombia. The Colombian and Mexican armies receive training assistance and arms in their fight against illicit drugs, organized crime and terrorism, despite charges of serious human rights violations leveled against them. American Special Forces provide training in those countries and, between 2003 and 2008, in Fort Benning, Georgia—where the notorious "School of the Americas" once groomed a generation of military strongmen—the Western Hemisphere Institute for Security Cooperation now trains more than 81,000 military personnel; of those, 40,000 are Colombian. Other bases in the U.S. serve as training centers (Cason and Brooks, 2004, October 6).

CHINA AND LATIN AMERICA

There are real consequences to the indifference and carelessness with which the Bush administration engages Latin America. A rising economic power, China begins to compete with the U.S. in its traditional sphere of influence. In the first decade of the 21st Century, commercial exchange between the U.S. and the region declines nearly 50%. Bolstering relations with China allows Latin American countries to expand trade, access new credit markets, pursue joint ventures, and reduce their dependence on exports to the United States. Gaining access to petroleum and nickel reserves is of particular importance to China. In Cuba, the emerging Asian super power signs trade, investment and exploration (nickel and petroleum) agreements; in Venezuela, oil is the key concern. China imports 300,000 barrels of oil a day from Venezuela. By broadening ties with China, President Chávez hopes to reduce his country's economic dependence on the United States. In February 2009, China reaches an agreement with Brazil to finance the exploration of its rich offshore oil deposits in exchange for a long-term supply guarantee. Chinese investment in Venezuelan petroleum rises to 10 billion USD. President Chávez invites the China National Petroleum Corporation (CNPC) to participate in the exploration of the oil-rich Orinoco belt.

Chinese officials travel to several countries in Latin America and sign cooperation agreements in a wide range of areas. In April 2001, Chinese President Jiang Zemin embarks on a 12-day tour of the region, including visits to Argentina, Brazil, Uruguay, Cuba, and Venezuela. In November 2004, President Hu Jintao visits Argentina, Brazil, Chile and Cuba, signing 39 bilateral agreements totaling an investment of 100 billion USD over a ten-year period. In May 2005, the president of the Communist Party of China travels to Colombia, Mexico, Uruguay and Cuba. In 2002, in response to the Argentine economic crisis—which impacts the entire Southern Cone, as well as Brazil—China increases trade with the countries hit hardest.

Washington is by no means indifferent to China's commercial expansion into Latin America, and cannot ignore the cooperation agreements signed by Venezuela and Cuba with Russia and Iran, for those agreements contain military components. In March 2009, just a couple months after President Obama takes office, a Russian Air Force General makes public comments on the possibility of stationing Russian strategic bombers in Cuban or Venezuelan bases. Chávez offers temporary use of the military base on La Orchila Island. U.S. Navy Admiral Michael Mullen, Chairman of the Joint Chiefs of Staff, concedes that those countries have the right to collaborate "if they see fit."

BUSH BIDS GOODBYE

President Bush leaves behind as much resentment on the home front as confusion around the world. In December 2008, the outgoing president commences a farewell circuit of prominent media outlets, which provides him with an opportunity to defend the most controversial decisions of his presidency, of which the Iraq invasion continues to rank first and foremost. Like a scratched record, the president remains adamant that "his" decision to overthrow Saddam Hussein—the country knows that Vice President Cheney was the brain behind the war—was ultimately justified for liberating the world of a tyrant; regarding the nonexistent weapons of mass destruction, his stated reason for launching the invasion, he blames the intelligence services for furnishing faulty data. Many believe he has deceived the American public and world; other presidents have done so before, but this instance takes the cake for having plunged his country into a bloody war that the majority of its citizens deems unnecessary, and founded on false premises. On the other hand, oil magnates—including Bush and Cheney—considered that war necessary. Oil is the principal objective of this war whose human cost has been astronomical. By 2008, more than 4,000 American soldiers have died in the conflict, with more than 30,000 injured—many severely maimed—and more than 1.2 million Iraqis have died, the overwhelming majority civilians. That is the balance paid after five long years at war.

On December 15, 2008, President Bush travels to Baghdad to bid farewell to the troops, and celebrate an agreement reached with the Iraqi government to maintain American troops on the ground for another three years. In a joint press conference with the Iraqi Primer Minister, Nouri al-Maliki, an Iraqi journalist, Muntadhar al-Zaidi, hurls both his shoes at the American leader's face, shouting, "This is a farewell kiss from the Iraqi people, dog!" followed by, "This is for the widows and orphans and all those killed in Iraq." Striking another person with a shoe is a sign of deep contempt, a profound insult in Arab culture. Bush dodges both shoes, and later claims to be unaware of what might have caused such aggression.

The New York Times interviews ordinary people in the streets of Baghdad regarding the shoe-hurling episode. Some do express regret over the incident, characterizing it as at odds with Arab and Muslim traditions of respecting one's guests, but many others come to al-Zaidi defense. (*The New York Times*, 2008, December 15). These casual remarks reflect the deep hatred of the Iraqi people toward President Bush and the United States for having "destroyed" Iraq and created violence and sectarianism among the people: what al-Zaidi did is the true expression of the "hatreds planted in the hearts of Iraqis," one affirms. Another says that al-Zaidi "will be marked in history as the first Arab who hit an American president with shoes. It seems that he assembled all the anger of the Iraqis and he expressed it this way even if it was not a democratic way" (*The New York Times*, 2008, December 15).

The Iraqi prime minister condemns the action, and the offending journalist is detained and tortured, according to reports from the international press. Intellectuals, scientists, politicians, journalists and Iraqi professionals support al-Zaidi and large street demonstrations demand his release: the protestors clap shoes in the air, and even hurl them at patrolling U.S. Marines. In Washington, peace activists leave shoes in front of the White House and others throw them at effigies of the American President in prisoner garb. Though the general reaction in Washington is of amusement, many analysts suggest that President-elect Obama and Congress, rather than dwelling on the offense, should reflect on the anger underpinning these street demonstrations, and the words of Iraqis professing a profound hatred of their country, and rejection of the military occupation, which instead of the "liberation" promised by President Bush has delivered them an endless stream of misfortune. (*The New York Times*, 2008, December 15) The invasion has set off a death battle between Sunnis and Shiites, who previously lived side by side in peace, in the same neighborhoods and provinces.

The tarnished legacy of the outgoing president is evident in films, hundreds of books, tens of thousands of articles by respected analysts, writers and commentators, not to mention countless blog posts and videos circulating the Internet daily, full of strident criticisms of presidential failures, and mocking assessments of the administration's all-encompassing incompetence. This widespread disgust manifests itself in the merciless ridicule of the man supposed to be the most powerful in the world.

OBAMA AND LATIN AMERICA

The sweeping electoral victory of Barack Obama on November 4, 2008, gives birth to high hopes both within the country and around the world. The ascendance of a black man to the highest office of the global super power, considering its long history of racial discrimination, is a transcendent event. Many hope that the incoming president will rectify all the mismanagement of his predecessor, and act as a lifeline to ailing economies both at home and abroad.

In Latin America, there is hope as well as skepticism concerning the policy implications of an Obama administration. Political observers scrutinize the one event during his campaign—in May 2008—dedicated entirely to the region. In Miami, Obama addresses the Cuban American National Foundation (CANF), an influential anti-Castro Cuban exile organization, where he delivers much lofty rhetoric on "his firm commitment to hemispheric freedom," through regional cooperation to bring about political and religious freedom, and advance democracy. He speaks of the social inequality plaguing the region, and the imperative of equal opportunity for all. He offers to reinstate the special envoy for the Americas, a position created by President Clinton, and form new regional alliances, without delving into specifics. He criticizes Hugo Chávez, characterizing his rhetoric as dangerous, comprised of anti-American demagoguery and false promises, and cites "checkbook diplomacy" as the means by which the Venezuelan leader has made political inroads in Bolivia and Nicaragua; he also criticizes Chávez for not governing democratically, despite being elected to office by popular vote. Though there is virtually no distinction between this position and that of the current administration with respect to Venezuela, Obama describes President Bush's attempts to undermine Chavez as "clumsy," having served only to "strengthen his hand."

After Israel and Egypt, Colombia—the largest cocaine-producing country in the world—is the largest recipient of military aid from the U.S., and President Álvaro Uribe the only staunch Bush ally in South America. Obama pledges to continue the failed Andean Counterdrug Initiative, by which President Bush sought to regionalize the war: coca cultivation continues to increase and tons of cocaine continue to enter the U.S. market. Obama may not be aware of the deleterious effects of spraying aerial herbicides over coca crops—advocated by Washington—on the health of peasants, livestock, subsistence crops, and the rural ecology. People and animals can become sick; land can remain sterile for months. Obama pledges full support in the war against the FARC, and an end to the paramilitary "reign of terror"; and, like President Bush, the candidate defends Colombia's "right" to hunt terrorists (guerrillas) beyond its borders—likely referring to the Colombian military strike in Ecuadorian territory, in March 2008, an incursion censured around the continent, and "rejected" by the OAS and the Rio Group Summit as an egregious violation of Ecuadorian sovereignty. (*Miami Herald*, 2008, May 23). Colombia, however, manages to avoid an OAS "condemnation" of the assault. The only support President Uribe receives is from the Bush administration and U.S. Congress.

Regarding Cuba, a topic of particular interest to those in attendance, Obama speaks at length on freedoms of expression, press, assembly, and the importance of democratic elections, and essentially rehashes the same criticisms of the Cuban government articulated by ten previous administrations. However, he goes on to state his intention to open dialogue with the Cuban government and lift restrictions on travel and remittances for those with family on the island, but announces he will maintain the embargo for leverage, despite the failure of this tactic for over half a century. Obama receives a warm ovation from the predominantly Hispanic, anti-Castro audience, since many had opposed those restrictions on travel and remittances imposed by President Bush. In fact, Obama will lift them his first days in office. The criticisms leveled against Chávez, demands made of Cuba, and drug policies in Colombia and Mexico strongly suggest continuity with previous administrations. Many observers wonder if, despite the slogan of change, Obama's plans for Latin America amount to more of the same.

By the end of the Bush administration, a shift can be discerned in some political as well as business circles favoring an opening toward Cuba, and President-elect Obama comes under increased pressure to pay greater attention to Latin America, formulate a new drug policy, implement wholesale reform of immigration laws, recalibrate relations with the Cuban government, and rethink the decades-long embargo. Many Hispanic business and political leaders hope for renewed relations based on mutual respect and understanding with the incoming government.

STANDING BY PALESTINE

In contrast to the great powers' silence in the face of the tragedy of the Palestinian people—subjected for five decades to a brutal occupation—Latin America for once makes its voice heard in protest of the December 2008 Israeli assault on the blockaded Gaza Strip. Known as Operation Cast Lead, the incursion targets Hamas, the Islamist organization in control of the territory. Hamas emerges during the first Intifada, in 1987, against the illegal occupation of Palestinian lands. When Hamas, designated a terrorist organization by the U.S. and its allies, wins parliamentary elections in January 2006, and takes over the government of the Palestinian territories, Washington and Tel Aviv are unnerved. Israel proceeds to jail numerous elected Hamas officials without raising any objections from the West. Tel Aviv invokes the right to defend itself against repeated rocket attacks launched by Hamas's military wing into Northern Israel. International news and human rights agencies report large-scale destruction of buildings, homes, mosques, civic institutions, and thousands of civilian deaths caused by the Israel bombardment. The Israeli offensive unleashes a wave of protests around the world, in cities such as Paris, Madrid, London, and Caracas. Middle Eastern demonstrators burn Israeli and American flags, and governments around the world petition Washington to condemn the operation; for their part, Latin American leaders urge Washington to use its influence to end the carnage. Since its creation, U.S. support of the Jewish state has been immeasurable: Israel is the largest recipient of American military aid. Equipped with nuclear capabilities, the Israeli Defense Forces (IDF) is undeniably one of the most powerful armies in the world. It is this carte blanche U.S. support that has allowed Israel for decades to disregard UN Security Council decisions.

Despite more than 300 resolutions, as well as another 70 vetoed by the U.S., condemn the illegal occupation of Palestinian territories—the West Bank, Gaza Strip, and East Jerusalem—demanding immediate Israeli withdrawal. Without unwavering U.S. support, Israel would have been expelled from the UN years ago.

Even for an American president, George W. Bush has been Israel's friend par excellence. He strengthens its military, and supports the expansion of illegal Jewish settlements into Palestinian land, which is condemned by the UN and most of the international community. Throughout his two terms in office, President Bush shows little interest in the peace process, yet one year before leaving office, concerned by widespread accusations of inaction, he calls a conference for "peace in the Middle East." The meeting convenes in Annapolis, Maryland, in December 2007, with the objective of moving closer to a bilateral peace agreement through direct negotiations between Israeli Prime Minister Ehud Olmert and Mahmoud Abbas, the president of the Palestinian Authority. The talks, however, amount to little more than a publicity stunt. By the end of the year, they have been stalled by a whole range of obstacles, including Israeli military operations and Washington's silence.

The Western powers respond to the latest IDF campaign in Gaza with their standard-issue justification—"Israel has the right to defend itself"—without taking into account the staggering imbalance in military capability between the adversaries. Ban Ki-moon, Secretary General of the UN, protests the attacks in which a UN official and eight employees are killed, and many others injured in a shelling of a UN field office and storage facility housing 700 Palestinian refugees. The Secretary General declares that the suffering of the Palestinian people in Gaza has reached an "intolerable" level. (*BBC Mundo*, 2009, January 15). In Geneva, the UN High Commissioner for Human Rights convenes an emergency session, and declares that the attacks have "all the elements of war crimes." (*Associated Press*, 2009, January 9). Israel bans foreign journalists from entering its theater of operations, but the Arab news agency Al Jazeera, having already established a presence inside the territory, broadcasts macabre scenes of death and destruction to the entire world.

Despite worldwide protest against the Israeli operation, the European Union goes only so far as to lament the casualties on "both sides," while calling on "both parties" to cease hostilities—as if the clash were between symmetrical forces. The UN Security Council ultimately approves a tepid resolution, introduced by Lebanon, asking for both parties to immediately cease operations, after the U.S. ambassador to the UN, Zalmay Khalilzad, blocks a stronger resolution calling for a cease fire (*Agence France-Presse, Reuters, Deutsche Presse-Agentur*, 2008, December 29). Brazilian President Lula da Silva declares: "What is being proven here is that the UN is incapable of making a decision and bringing peace to Gaza, because the United States has veto power and prevents things from happening." He characterizes U.S. mediation efforts as inadequate and announces that his foreign minister is coordinating with the French and other governments to call a global conference to bring an end to hostilities. (DPA et al, 2008, December 31). The conference is never held.

Some of the harshest criticism leveled against the Israeli assault on Gaza comes from Latin American heads of state and human rights organizations. Tel Aviv dismisses such criticism as "anti-Semitism." Zionist organizations respond to the criticism of their government with propaganda in a similar vein. Responding to the request of 118 nations, Miguel d'Escoto, a priest and former Nicaraguan Foreign Minister, President of the UN General Assembly, calls an emergency session—which Israel tries to block. D'Escoto accuses Israel of violating international law, and questions the shelling of civilian targets—including mosques, universities, and schools—which have been described as "simple errors." *(AFP,* Reuters, and DPA, 2009, January 16).

During a meeting with foreign diplomats in La Paz, Evo Morales declares that he is willing to bring an international suit against Israeli officials for crimes against humanity committed by their forces in Gaza. Michelle Bachelet, President of Chile, and the governments of Peru, Nicaragua, Argentina and China, state their disapproval of the Israeli operation. Cuba, President of the Non-Aligned Movement, in a communiqué expresses its vigorous condemnation of Israel's "criminal" attacks and the "illegal" blockade of the Gaza Strip. Hugo Chávez calls Israel an "assassin" and suggests that Presidents George Bush and Shimon Peres should be brought before the ICC to answer for the barbarities committed in Gaza; the Venezuelan leader expels the Israeli ambassador in protest. The Palestinians applaud this "extraordinary" measure and proclaim Chávez the "only dissenting voice," and a hero (AFP, 2009, January 10).

On January 14, 2009, unknown assailants hurl rocks and metallic objects at the Venezuelan embassy in Paris; they break windows and paint the slogan "Israel will win" on the facade of the building (*El Observador*, 2009, January 15). This same month Bolivia and Mauritania sever diplomatic relations with Israel; in a speech Pope Benedict XVI censures "the renewal of violence, for causing immense damage and suffering among the civilian population." Cardinal Renato Martino, President of the Pontifical Council for Justice and Peace, compares the Gaza Strip to a "big concentration camp." Through its spokesman, Yigal Palmor, the Israeli foreign ministry protests. "It's shocking," Palmor says, "to hear the vocabulary of Hamas propaganda from a member of the church." A Vatican spokesman laments the cardinal's "inappropriate" word choice for creating more "irritation and confusion" than "illumination." (Dinadio, 2009, January 9). Facing widespread protest against their assault on Gaza, Israeli authorities see nothing but rampant anti-Semitism around the world.

While on vacation in Hawaii, President-elect Obama receives daily briefs from Secretary of State Condoleezza

Rice—who herself believes the Israeli operation to be justified—on developments in Gaza. When questioned about the conflict, however, Obama withholds comment, on the grounds that there can be only one president at a time. His principal adviser, David Axelrod, of Jewish descent, sets the tone for the incoming administration on CBS's "Face the Nation": he blames Hamas for instigating the conflict, which is the same line taken by the Bush administration. Later, on ABC's "This Week," the President-elect reiterates to George Stephanopoulos that Israel has the right to defend itself—in other words, it's business as usual.

The December offensive in Gaza coincides with the final days of the Bush administration, which from the outset has lavished Israel with steady, open-ended support. In December 2008, the Republican House majority and influential media outlets all support the Israeli offensive and the House of Representatives adopts a resolution, by a 390-to-5 margin, supporting Israel's "right to defend itself." Two days prior to Obama's inauguration, Israel begins a gradual withdrawal of its troops from Gaza. They do not have a good read yet on the incoming President.

Since the creation of the Jewish state in 1947, the intractable Israeli-Palestinian conflict has been a black hole in U.S. foreign policy. It will be difficult for the Obama administration to ignore the responsibility his country bears for the tragedy of Palestine, an innocent victim of aggressive Holocaust survivors. For many, the incoming president's worldview, coupled with the wave of popular support he rides in on, uniquely positions him to demand that Israel adhere to previous UN resolutions: the return to pre-1967 borders; removal of all illegal Jewish settlements in the West Bank and East Jerusalem; and the right to return of Palestinian refugees. This is the justice for which much of the world waits.

In January 2011, three years after Operation Cast Lead, an editorial in *The Guardian* sums up the sorry state of affairs: "It is hard to tell who appears worse: the Palestinian leaders, who are weak, craven and eager to shower their counterparts with compliments; the Israelis, who are polite in word but contemptuous in deed; or the Americans, whose neutrality consists of bullying the weak and holding the hand of the strong." The newspaper goes on to accuse Washington and Tel Aviv of conspiring to "create a puppet state in Palestine, at worst a surrogate for an occupying force."

THE STORY CONTINUES

As change in the White House approaches, the country remains hobbled by the economic crisis, the consequence of economic mismanagement and deregulation of the financial markets. Financial deregulation dates back to the Clinton administration, and culminates in the catastrophic events of 2008. The financial tsunami makes salient a startling hypocrisy in U.S. economic policy, according Nobel Laureate Joseph Stiglitz. "The American government gave lectures on the rules to developing countries," he claims, "while its own policies were a total failure" (Castro, 2009, March 12).

In the international arena, President Bush leaves behind strained relations with key European allies, as well as Russia and the Muslim World, while Latin America is increasingly distant, no longer the subservient sphere of influence. For the first time, the majority of Latin American nations have elected left-leaning proponents of regional integration through newly formed bodies that exclude the United States. The Banco del Sur, a Chávez initiative, is created to take the place of credit institutions like the Washington-dominated World Bank and IMF. Some leaders of the left advocate a 21st century socialism to revitalize their countries, and express solidarity with Fidel Castro and the Cuban Revolution. A broad coalition of Hispanic business and political leaders asks Obama to change the course in U.S. relations with Latin America and Cuba, and lift the embargo. Nevertheless, President Obama continues the Bush administration's hard line towards both Cuba and Hugo Chávez; his rhetoric is nearly identical to that of his predecessor. And yet, many in Latin America hold out hope that the new president will not repeat with Venezuela the same mistakes made with Cuba over the previous 50 years. For his allies in the region, that would be a difficult pill to swallow. The future of hemispheric relations, as such, is full of question marks, but also hope. Many trust in the change promised during the 2008 presidential campaign.

2

The Rise of the New Left

WHO ARE THEY?

In the first decade of the 21st century, Latin America undergoes a profound transformation. For the first time, the majority of its countries—including Argentina, Brazil, Chile, Bolivia, Ecuador, Paraguay, Uruguay, Venezuela—are led by left-leaning democratically elected heads of state, opposed to the neoliberal development model endorsed by the Washington Consensus, and free trade agreements with the United States, from whose political and economic domination they seek to break free. This new generation of leaders comes to power supported by popular movements and indigenous groups disillusioned with the traditional democratic process that for centuries has excluded them while failing to deliver their most basic needs. These historically marginalized groups displace traditional political parties, largely discredited by their own venal and ineffective governance; they are the driving force behind the profound geopolitical shift sweeping the continent. In Ecuador, over a ten-year period, indigenous and popular movements remove three incompetent, corrupt neoliberal presidents from office. In Bolivia, they bring down two.

The leaders of this new progressive wave fall at varying points along the ideological spectrum: there are populist firebrands as well as more conventional politicians, dogmatists who reject neoliberalism outright as well as those more ideologically flexible and pragmatic; all of them, however, support regional integration, a gradual process aiming to diminish the American role in the economic and political life of the continent. Presidents Lula da Silva and Hugo Chávez, the most vocal proponents of the integration movement, guide the creation of regional bodies such as Union of South American Nations (UNASUR) and the Council for South American Defense.

This "New Left" emerges out of decades of regional violence, hard-fought battles for social justice, countless dreams unfulfilled; it emerges out of guerrilla warfare against neo-fascist dictatorships in the Southern Cone and genocides in Central America. In 1973, the first socialist president elected by popular vote, Salvador Allende, is brought down by a brutal military coup, led by General Augusto Pinochet and supported by Richard Nixon and his Secretary of State, Henry Kissinger. In 1983, in Grenada, the leftist Prime Minister Maurice Bishop, leader of the Marxist-Leninist New Jewel Movement (NJM), is executed in a shadowy conspiracy. From the outset, the Reagan administration sought to undermine his government, and following his death U.S. forces invade and occupy the island. In Nicaragua, after eleven years of Sandinista revolution, President Daniel Ortega, the FSLN candidate, is defeated in the 1990 election by Violeta Barrios de Chamorro, a candidate openly supported by the first President Bush.

Following decades of armed conflict, by the end of the 1980's many Central American governments and guerrilla movements have signed peace treaties. The Esquipulas Peace Agreements I and II provide the framework for the governments of Guatemala and El Salvador to end hostilities with the Farabundo Martí National Liberation Front (FMLN) and Guatemalan National Revolutionary Unity (URNG), respectively. After agreeing to demobilize, these guerrilla movements form political parties and integrate themselves into the democratic process. In Nicaragua, after a ten-year war against paramilitary groups—armed, trained, financed and directed by the CIA during the Reagan administration—the Sandinistas sign a peace treaty with the "contra." Driven by the United States, the war decimated what already was one of the poorest countries in the region. By the end of the 1980's, neo-fascist dictatorships in Argentina and Uruguay have collapsed, and citizens once again elect civilian presidents. In Uruguay, the Tupamaro guerrilla movement forms a political party, Movement of Popular Participation (MPP), and enters the leftist Broad Front coalition. In 2004, Tabaré Vázquez, a candidate of that coalition wins the presidency, the first time a leftist has been elected to that office in Uruguay. In 2010, the ex-Tupamaro José Mujica succeeds him. His wife, president of the General Assembly, was also a guerrilla. In South America, only the Colombian guerrilla armies the FARC and ELN, and Sendero Luminoso in Peru, remain active.

The fall of the Berlin Wall in 1989, followed by the disintegration of the Soviet Union and Eastern Bloc, brings an end to the Cold War and marks the beginning of a decade in which the U.S. reigns as the sole global super power. Conservative voices proclaim the triumph of the United States over the USSR, and by extension of capitalism over socialism, forecasting the disappearance of the Latin American left without a pole star to guide it. Though the end of the Cold War does draw to a close a particular era of international socialism—characterized as "real" socialism by some—it by no means represents the final chapter of the progressive movement in Latin America.

THE ELECTED ONES

The most radical South American leaders, Hugo Chávez of Venezuela, Rafael Correa of Ecuador, and Evo Morales of Bolivia, are the standard bearers of anti-imperialism, exponents of a 21st Century Socialism opposed to neoliberalism and its institutional pillars. They are allies of Cuba, personal friends of Fidel Castro, admirers of his revolution. They form the political axis of the regional integration movement.

Drafting new constitutions invested with socialist principles, they strive to "re-found" their countries, bringing to bear profound changes to the political, economic and social order.

Other leftist heads of state, such as Néstor and Cristina Kirchner of Argentina, Ricardo Lagos and Michelle Bachelet of Chile, and Tabaré Vázquez from Uruguay, are more akin to social democrats in the European style. Following similar economic models to their predecessors, they are less fixated on extricating their countries from the neoliberal system (Lanzaro, 2008, September–October). Lula da Silva emerges out the Brazilian labor movement, and helps found the Worker's Party (PT), the largest leftist movement on the continent; though his political ideology is progressive, upon taking office he tacks toward the center in search pragmatic solutions that in many instances are not so distinct from the neoliberal policies of his predecessor. Under his stewardship, Brazil's booming economy is the toast of the developing world.

In this multifarious political panorama, Hugo Chávez is elected to the presidency in 1998 with the support of the party he founded, the Fifth Republic Movement (PVR), and then re-elected in 2001 and 2006; in Chile, Ricardo Lagos (1998) and Michelle Bachelet (2006) of the Concert of Parties for Democracy and the Socialist Party, respectively, win consecutive elections; Lula da Silva, the former union organizer, is elected to consecutive terms in 2002 and 2006 (with 60% of the vote, the highest percentage in Brazil's history); in

Argentina, Néstor Kirchner of the left-wing Peronist Justicialist Party, takes office in 2003 after the resignation of Eduardo Duhalde; in 2004, Tabaré Vásquez of the Broad Front becomes the first candidate of a left-wing party to win the Uruguayan presidency; in 2005, the indigenous labor leader Evo Morales, of the Movement for Socialism (MAS), is voted into office with the highest vote tally ever registered in Bolivia, and then ratified, in August 2008, by referendum with 63% of the total vote. In Ecuador, Rafael Correa is elected in 2005 with the support of the party he founded, the PAIS Alliance, and in Nicaragua Daniel Ortega, of the Frente Sandinista de Liberación Nacional (FSLN), finally triumphs in 2007 after coming up short in three previous elections (1990, 1996, and 2001) owing to shameless U.S. intervention. In 2007, Néstor Kirchner is succeeded in office by his wife Cristina Fernández, from the same political party; in Paraguay, the former catholic bishop Fernando Lugo (2008), a former champion of Liberation Theology, puts an end to the 61-year domination of the corrupt right-wing Colorado Party (PC), which for 35 years helped buttress the brutal dictatorship of General Alfredo Stroessner. In El Salvador, Mauricio Funes, ex-guerrilla of the FMLN, which converted into a political party after a 20-year civil war fought against genocidal military dictators, wins the presidency after a ten-year political struggle against civilian governments led by Arena, a right-wing party with paramilitary roots. According to analysts, the Funes victory constitutes a slap in the face of imperialism. In Mexico, another left-wing candidate, Andrés Lópes Obrador, of the Party of the Democratic Revolution

(PRD), makes it to the doorstep of the presidency, but is ultimately defeated by Felipe Calderón, of the right-wing PAN, by .56% of the total vote. López cries foul, alleging that electoral fraud was committed, and demands a recount. After two months of noisy public protests throughout Mexico City, the Federal Electoral Tribunal, in a unanimous decision, declares Calderón president-elect, despite acknowledging "irregularities" in the election.

MARCHING TOWARDS INTEGRATION

That the U.S. has been relegated to the sidelines of the Latin American integration movement reflects a radical shift in hemispheric relations. The movement's chief architects—Presidents Chávez and Lula—push for the creation of Union of South American Nations (UNASUR) and the South American Defense Council, and the Bank of the South, forums for economic, political and defense matters. During an April 2004 energy summit in Venezuela, Hugo Chávez proposes integrating two existing customs unions, Mercosur and the Andean Community of Nations (CAN), to form UNASUR—a political, economic, security, and energy alliance. In May 2008, the proposal is made official at a summit convening ten South American heads of state, in Santiago, Chile. In March 2008, during a Mercosur summit, Lula had called for the first extraordinary summit of UNASUR in Brasilia to mediate the escalating crisis between Colombia, Ecuador and Venezuela following the Colombian strike against a group of FARC guerrillas, including a high-ranking commander, camped inside Ecuadorian territory. Quito was not consulted in advance. The FARC commander, known by the alias "Raúl Reyes," is killed in the attack, along with 25 others, the majority guerrillas. President Correa calls the Colombian strike an act of aggression, a violation of national sovereignty, and declares that a "massacre" has been committed. The operation is censured by the OAS and Rio Group (convened at the time in the Dominican Republic) as a territorial violation. Colombia successfully lobbies, however, for the joint statement to fall short of an official "condemnation."

According to its constitutive treaty, UNASUR is dedicated to defending national sovereignty, territorial integrity and inviolability, self-determination of the people, solidarity, cooperation, peace and democracy, and the promotion of citizenship and pluralism and unconditional respect for individual and universal human rights; to the reduction of economic and social inequality and maintaining harmony between human societies and the natural world that sustains them. Quito is selected as the permanent site of the Secretariat headquarters. The alliance will enter into force in 2011 upon ratification by the parliaments of its member countries.

Michelle Bachelet is named the first pro tempore president of UNASUR when Álvaro Uribe abstains following continental censure of his 2008 military incursion in Ecuadorian territory. The ensuing diplomatic crisis, the most acrimonious in decades between South American nations, provides the impetus for President Lula's proposed Council of South American Defense, which he envisions as a forum for dialogue between the region's defense ministers on matters pertaining to hemispheric security; the creation of this council, however, is not finalized owing to Uribe's insistence on members issuing a joint condemnation of "terrorist" organizations (which is how he classifies the FARC).

In September 2008, UNASUR convenes in response to the crisis Evo Morales faces in the Media Luna provinces, where 21 peasants have been killed amid violence incited by separatist leaders who oppose his government. The summit, which is called by Michelle Bachelet, takes place in Chile, and concludes with a vote of support for Evo Morales and the creation of a commission to investigate these acts of violence. Analysts note that the UNASUR summit has rendered the U.S.-dominated OAS irrelevant, and as such represents an act of regional independence. Raúl Roa García, the former foreign minister of Cuba, once called the OAS a "the Empire's Ministry of Colonies."

President Lula continues organizing forums to advance regional integration, calling a Latin American and Caribbean Summit on Integration and Development in December 2008 that brings together 33 nations—including Cuba—with the United States and Canada once again left out. Washington is concerned by this recent pattern of exclusion—an impediment to carrying out its regional agenda—and by the hemispheric rejection of its Cuba policy, which has subjected the island to a half century of isolation. The attendance of all the Latin American and Caribbean heads of state—with the exception of Colombia's Álvaro Uribe and Peru's Alan García, both of whom send representatives—presents an opportunity for other regional bodies, such as Mercosur, the Rio Group and UNASUR, to convene as well. The Council of South American Defense is finally made official, its first meeting scheduled for March 2009, in Santiago, Chile. In that meeting, the ministers of defense of Argentina, Brazil, Bolivia, Chile, Ecuador, Uruguay, and Venezuela formally petition the United States to suspend the Cuban embargo in order to promote stronger relations in the region. A coordinated action to combat drug-trafficking—excluding the U.S.—is also agreed upon (Gutiérrez, 2009, March 11).

The Bank of the South, a Chávez initiative, is established in December 2007 in a meeting of finance ministers of seven South American nations, as an alternative to the IMF, World Bank, and Inter-American Development Bank (IDB). Like many critics of those institutions, Chávez rejects their practice of attaching policy-related conditionality to loans, such as calling for the privatization of government-owned industries and natural resources. The World Bank, for instance, might require a country to sell off a vital industry for a low price to a multinational corporation in exchange for a credit line. This imposed conditionality coupled with high interest rates means countries may repay millions in outstanding loans without reducing their debt burden. The Bank of the South will attach no such conditionality to its loans.

Along with Venezuela, its members are Argentina, Brazil, Bolivia, Ecuador, Paraguay, and Uruguay. Colombia will join later. The initial capital of the Bank of the South, established through contributions from its members, is twenty billion dollars. Venezuela, Brazil and other countries remove the IMF and World Bank shackles by repaying their outstanding debts, and suspending agreements with those institutions. As a result, Washington loses an important lever of influence. The financial sector views the shifting panorama with concern. In October 2007, an IDB employee reveals to the *Financial Times* that with Venezuela's money, and Brazil and Argentina's good will reserves, it is a bank that could have a lot of money and a distinct political focus. Though nobody will say so in public, the U.S. financial sector is concerned. In March 2009, however, facing a worldwide credit crunch caused by the financial crisis, some countries resort to requesting loans from the international banks.

Despite receiving minimal coverage in the U.S. media, and being met with silence by Washington, American experts in hemispheric relations view Latin American political, economic and military integration with concern. The United States no longer is, and never again will be, the principal interlocutor in the region," according to Riordan Roett, Director of Latin American Studies at Johns Hopkins University. Peter Hakim, director of the Washington-based Inter-American Dialogue think tank, affirms that there is no doubt that South American integration has to do with the exclusion of the United States. Other commentators point out that holding the Latin American and Caribbean Summit on Integration and Development just four months before the Summit of the Americas—which excludes Cuba—called by the United States in Trinidad and Tobago, in April 2009, is significant in and of itself (Barrionuevo, 2008, December 17). By the time that summit convenes, Barack Obama has already entered the White House.

On February 22-23, 2010, President Felipe Calderón hosts the Rio Group in Cancún, Mexico. Thirty-two Latin American and Caribbean countries attend, while the U.S. once again is excluded. The "Unity Summit," as it is christened, gives birth to the Community of Latin American and Caribbean States. The U.S. and Canada are excluded. In the wake of a military coup against its constitutional president, Manuel Zelaya—condemned by the majority of the region's countries, most of which do not recognize Porfirio Lobo, the victor of fraudulent presidential elections—Honduras is also not invited. As a gesture of support to the U.S., Peruvian President Alan García declines his country's invitation, maintaining that the necessary unity is lacking. Without mentioning the United States by name, his foreign minister suggests that one country is missing. A firm majority, however, believe the establishment of this new community is necessary step toward hemispheric unity. Antonio Simões, Under-Secretary for South America at the Brazilian Ministry of Foreign Relations, who has worked for several years on the project, contends that the time has come to take a step forward. Hugo Chávez enthusiastically offers to host the next summit in Caracas, in July 2011, to make the alliance official. "It should be a select organization, our own space, America," says Chávez.

On the table are several topics of critical importance: the Cuban embargo; the reconstruction of Haiti after its devastating earthquake; the ominous security situation arising from the expanding U.S. presence in Colombian military bases; Colombia's internal conflict, its diplomatic crisis with Ecuador, and Venezuela, and the question of UNASUR involvement in its stalled peace process; support of Argentina in its diplomatic conflict with the United Kingdom over the Falkland Islands; the restoration of Manuel Zelaya to the Honduran presidency. These topics will not be approached as they were in years past by the OAS. U.S. domination of that organization is no longer acceptable to the majority. Mark Weisbrot, co-director of the Center for Political and Economic Investigations in Washington, emphasizes that the creation of this new community represents a historic, unprecedented step forward, and Latin America's growing independence should be viewed as the most significant geopolitical change of the past decade, affecting "not only the region," he asserts, "but the rest of the world as well." He calls attention to the diplomatic independence demonstrated by Brazil in response to the controversy surrounding Iranian nuclear development: President Lula supports Iran's right to enrich uranium for peaceful means, and opposes the economic sanctions imposed by the U.S. on that country. Venezuela and Bolivia also support Iran. Weisbrot claims,

"An organization without the US and Canada will be more capable of defending democracy, as well as economic and social progress in the region when it is under attack. It will also have a positive influence in helping to create a more multipolar world internationally" (Weisbrot, 2010, February 25).

Hugo Chávez proves himself to be a tireless promoter of continental cooperation and unity. He offers economic assistance to several countries, purchases government bonds to help them service their World Bank and IMF debt, and pledges to "share the energy potential" of his country with the entire region. The leading exporter of crude oil in Latin America—and fifth largest in the world—Venezuela has vast petroleum wealth at its disposal. Of its total production Venezuela exports 60% to the United States. In June 2004, President Chávez hosts the First Energy Summit of Caribbean Heads of State and Government, in Puerto La Cruz, a port city located 380 kilometers from Caracas. Fifteen heads of state from Central America and the Caribbean—including Fidel Castro and Leonel Fernández of the Dominican Republic—attend. They establish Petrocaribe, the first regional energy alliance, whose members can purchase Venezuelan crude on conditions of preferential payment. In October 2004, Chávez signs a similar agreement with Néstor Kirchner, establishing Petrosur for Southern Cone countries, and in August 2001 in Entre Ríos, Bolivia, the Venezuelan leader signs the PetroAndina treaty, which he hopes other countries in the region will join. The primary objective of these treaties is to buffer member nations from the economic shocks resulting from price fluctuations in the world market by guaranteeing them, through barter exchanges, access to Venezuelan crude at discounted rates. Venezuela furthermore will assist in the construction of refineries, based on the theory that their scarcity contributes to high petroleum prices. Chávez points out that the U.S. has not invested in refineries in 25 years, while Venezuela has eight in that country. "We are ready to be free, and need to be free," he writes, "self-determined, self-defined, self-leading, and let us not follow like little sheep a path that someone else lays out for us" (Chávez, 2005: 367, 374).

INDIGENOUS MOVEMENTS AND THE NEW LEFT

After enduring five centuries of servitude and violence, the plunder of their ancestral lands and endless humiliations dating back to the European conquest of the New World, in the 1990's indigenous communities become a decisive force in defining the new democracies and profound social and political change overtaking Latin America. Their assertiveness analysts describe as a significant geopolitical development: they play a central role in the reconfiguration of hemispheric relations that leaves U.S. dominance over the region diminished.

In 2008, people identified as indigenous account for 11% of the region's 569 million inhabitants. They represent majorities in Bolivia (71%) and Guatemala (63%); in Peru they make up 47% of the total population, in Ecuador 43%, in Mexico 16%, in Colombia 3.1%, and in Venezuela 2% (van

Cott, 2008: 39). In Bolivia and Ecuador indigenous activists manifest in defense of Mother Earth, the habitat of their communities. They take control of their own destinies, in defense of their culture, customs and beliefs. While affirming their participatory, collective, democratic, and autonomous way of life, they fight to regain control of their ancestral lands. Grassroots indigenous movements forge ties of solidarity with local, regional and international groups—"unity in diversity" (Cockcroft, 2008, November 28-30). In Ecuador, after a historic uprising, they force President Rodrigo Borja to recognize their ancestral lands.

In the past decade some indigenous movements form political parties. This is the case in Bolivia, Colombia, Ecuador, and Venezuela, whose governments for the most part recognize their ethnic, political, and cultural rights. Ecuador and Peru lift voting restrictions, and under the new constitution of Colombia (1991), drafted with indigenous participation, their communities register considerable gains: a high level of political and legal autonomy, and two additional seats in the senate, to which they can elect their own candidates. To be allowed to participate in drafting the new constitution, a year earlier the Regional Indigenous Council of Cauca (CRIC) had to demobilize its guerrilla group, Quintín Lame (van Cott. 2008: 38-40).

The meteoric ascension of indigenous movements and political parties should be understood in the context of the collapse of the political left at the end 1980's, and its reconfiguration and resurgence in the last decade, according to Donna Lee van Cott, professor at the University of Connecticut in a study on indigenous Latin Americans (van Cott, 2008:33). These activist groups comprise the base of the New Left. They question the legitimacy of the democratic model that has traditionally excluded them, and oppose neoliberalism, including free trade agreements with the U.S., and the privatization of natural resources and state industries.

The advance of the indigenous movement in Colombia serves as an example to other countries. In Ecuador and Venezuela indigenous communities send their own delegates to the constituent assemblies. Hugo Chávez dedicates one of his Bolivarian Missions to protecting indigenous rights, and guaranteeing the survival of their cultures and religious beliefs; in 2005, he recognizes their inalienable right to ancestral lands and the government draws up property titles for their communities totaling over 6,600 square kilometers, which can never be bought or sold (van Cott, 2008: 38-40).

INDIGENOUS ACTION

On January 1, 1994—the same day NAFTA enters into force—a violent rebellion breaks out in San Cristóbol de las Casas, a town in the Mexican state of Chiapas, against the federal government. EZLN insurgents burn property deeds, ransack and set fire to ten government offices, and a town hall, attack a military garrison, shoot down an army helicopter, free 179 prisoners and hide out in the jungle. The federal government responds with troops and tanks, bombarding ten settlements, resulting in the deaths of four hundred indigenous people. Mexican as well as international human rights organizations condemn the attacks.

The Zapatistas enter the world stage declaring war on NAFTA and the neoliberal development model. In contrast to many armed guerrilla movements of the Cold War era, the EZLN has no interest in seizing power. In 1995, the organization renounces armed struggle to pursue a peaceful resolution to its grievances, and through drawn-out negotiations with the government of President Ernesto Zedillo makes advances with the San Andrés accords. However, talks stall when congress passes a bill all but refusing to recognize the EZLN. In response to the uprising, the federal government, collaborating with paramilitary groups, wages a low-intensity war against the indigenous population of Chiapas. Indigenous groups denounce the repression, disappearances, rapes, assassinations, massacres and widespread destruction caused by the ongoing bombardment of their towns and countryside. In the absence of federal legislation protecting indigenous communities, the states of Chiapas and Oaxaca approve laws recognizing their collective rights

Indigenous groups, in coalitions with popular movements and leftist political parties, begin to put forth their own presidential candidates, and when they enter face off against the traditional political elite they defeat them. In Ecuador, over a 10-year period, they play a role in the downfall of three corrupt, incompetent neoliberal presidents. The first, Abdalá Bucaram, lasts a mere six months in office; plagued by allegations of corruption, he resigns in 1997 in the midst of an economic crisis. The second, Jamil Mahuad, oversees the dollarization of the Ecuadorian economy as part of a package of IMF prescriptions that only serve to accentuate poverty, and trigger the country's worst economic crisis in 70 years; following a drop in the price of crude oil, the Ecuadorian financial system collapses; two banks go under, foreign debt obligations become unmanageable. In January 2000, amid indigenous protests and growing opposition of political elite and leftist parties, Mahuad is forced to resign after only 16 months; the Vice President Gustavo Noboa assumes the presidency. The third president to fall, Lucio Gutiérrez (2003-2005), is elected with broad support from indigenous communities and the working class after pledging to adopt a progressive agenda, including agrarian reform, and expanding health and education services. These groups eventually turn on him, however, for failing to fulfill his campaign promises: for kowtowing to the IMF, privatizing state-run energy, telecommunication and water utilities, and social security and imposing public-sector salary adjustments, measures that are harmful to the average person, while submitting to the militaristic demands of the Colombian President Álvaro Uribe. The removal of the majority of judges from the Supreme Court of Justice, paving the way for former-President Bucaram's return from exile, provokes a massive uprising led by the Confederation of Indigenous Nationalities of Ecuador (CONAIE) and the Pachakutik Plurinational Unity

Movement and forces Congress to remove Gutiérrez from office. In his place, Vice President Alfredo Palacio is nominated. Gutiérrez goes into exile.

Indigenous Bolivians represent 71% of their country's population, and are generally recognized as the most organized and assertive in the continent. Beginning in the 1980's, Bolivia's adherence to the Washington Consensus results in the deepening of poverty and corresponding increase in social and economic inequality, exacerbating indigenous groups who finally rise up, in 2002, when the former military dictator—now democratically elected president—Hugo Banzer decides to privatize water in Cochabamba, the fourth largest city in the country, with a population exceeding one million, half of whom are indigenous. His plan is to turn the public utility over to Aguas del Tunari, a consortium of which Bechtel is a principle shareholder. Indigenous and other activist groups respond with massive protests; they block highways and other transit routes, disrupt daily life for four days forcing the government to reverse the privatization and expel the multinational from the country. Aguas del Tunari files a lawsuit against Bolivian for revoking its contract, but years later backs off.

Gonzalo Sánchez de Lozada wins the presidency for the second time in 2002 after defeating Evo Morales by 1.41% of the popular vote. In response to an untenable economic and social situation, indigenous groups lead by Evo Morales form the "The People's High Command" to coordinate various popular movements in opposition to coca eradication, privatization of the hydrocarbon sector, the exploitation of natural resources by multinational corporations, among other causes. The final straw comes when Sánchez de Lozada unveils a plan to export natural gas (of which Bolivia is the second largest producer in South America) to Mexico and the U.S. through a Chilean port. This plan offends many Bolivians as their government is engaged in an ongoing litigation against Chile over access to the sea, which the landlocked nation lost in the War of the Pacific (1879-1884). Indigenous and popular revolts against the government proliferate throughout the nation; protestors blockade highways and roads, leaving many cities, including La Paz, paralyzed. Sánchez de Lozada responds to the protests with military force, with the death toll reaching 70, according to official figures. In the wake of this massacre the masses call for the president's resignation. He goes into exile in the United States. In 2007, the Bolivian government formally serves the U.S. with a request to extradite the former head of state for corruption and the deaths of 63 people during the "Gas War." In 2008, they resubmit their request, compelling the exiled leader's American lawyer to respond that his client's actions were "constitutional, legal and appropriate" and the call for his extradition "politically motivated" (*Associated Press*, 2008, November 12). Washington does not respond until September 2012, when it denies the request.

Sánchez de Lozada is succeeded in power by his vice president, Carlos Mesa. Popular protests against the exportation of natural gas through Chile rage on and demonstrators demand a new law nationalizing the hydrocarbon industry. Led by Evo Morales, they persuade President Mesa to repeal the law and push an alternative bill through congress. Weary of ongoing popular and indigenous protest, Mesa himself resigns in 2005.

In 2005, Evo Morales, leader the Bolivian cocalero movement, once again aspires to the presidency, but must confront the racist, violent opposition of the separatist elite from the prosperous Media Luna provinces, as well as Washington. In the 2002 election, Otto Reich, Assistant Secretary of State for Western Hemisphere Affairs, and Roger Noriega, U.S. Ambassador to the OAS, threaten sanctions if Morales is elected. Issuing public warnings while also applying pressure behind the scenes, they mount a slanderous campaign to discredit the indigenous leader.

Three years later, however, on August 28, 2005, Evo Morales is elected president after garnering 54% of the popular vote. His electoral triumph is unprecedented. Morales becomes the first indigenous leader on the continent to reach the highest office of his country through a democratic election. The Bush administration immediately maneuvers to undermine him. The nonstop interventions against his government ultimately lead to the expulsion, in 2008, of the U.S. ambassador, Philip Goldberg, for conspiring with the separatist opposition, not only to overthrow his government but also to divide the country. The DEA is expelled for similar reasons.

In Colombia, members of indigenous communities comprise 3.1% of the population; 64 languages are spoken by 80 distinct ethnic groups across the Andean nation's 32 provinces, a rich cultural diversity represented by several umbrella organizations: The National Indigenous Organization of Colombia (ONIC), which represents 90 communities; Indigenous Authorities of Colombia (AICO), a progressive political party with a senator in the national congress; the Regional Indigenous Council of Cauca (CRIC) and the Association of Indigenous Councils North of the Cauca (ACIN). In November 2008, there is a march of the Gathering ("Minga") of Indigenous Resistance—an ancestral association of native communities comprised of fifty thousand men and women; after traveling 500 kilometers, and receiving enthusiastic support in towns and cities along the way, they arrive in Bogota to engage in dialogue with the national government. Their goal is to increase awareness about unresolved problems affecting their communities, and unfulfilled promises, constitutional mandates that live only on paper. According to a 1999 report issued by the Inter-American Court of Human Rights, though the government has recognized approximately thirty million hectors as indigenous territory, those claims are often threatened by landowners, settlers and paramilitary as well as government forces. The marchers demand the return of lands that have been taken from them, and respect for their ethnic and cultural identities. They also denounce violations of their human rights by government, paramilitary and guerrilla forces: assassinations, massacres, disappearances. Throughout the several decades of armed conflict, indigenous communities have been caught in the crossfire between guerrillas, paramilitaries and government forces, constantly threatened by irregular armed groups attempting to co-opt them.

President Álvaro Uribe's tendency is to confront social conflicts as military problems, indiscriminately accusing demonstrators of being "terrorists." Critics of his government are also labeled "terrorists," including NGO and human rights activists, even newspaper columnists. Uribe denies that armed conflict exists in his country; for him guerrillas are nothing but "terrorists," "bandits" and "delinquents" with whom he refuses to negotiate; only by brute force can they be vanquished. When politically advantageous, however, the president may profess in public a desire for dialogue, but his preconditions for negotiation and demobilization are impossible to accept. Uribe refuses to receive the indigenous marchers, accuses them of being terrorists—infiltrated by the FARC—and of killing government soldiers. "When we take action and confront the violence you denounce us to the international community," he claims. He asks his minister of the interior and justice, Carlos Holguín Sardi to draft laws to criminalize this sort of popular protest. The indigenous marchers depart the city leaving behind a harsh letter, full of recriminations and complaints, for being denied the meetings with ministers they requested. In October, 2008, the magazine *Cambio* publishes a report on the march, and the overall indigenous situation in Colombia. It is titled: "Time Bomb."

ADVANCES AND CONFLICT

The new constitutions of Venezuela, Ecuador, and Bolivia represent a great advance for indigenous causes. For the first time, indigenous rights are codified in constitutions that incorporate socialist principles. They aim to "re-found" those countries, establishing more egalitarian societies. In Venezuela, indigenous people comprise 2% of the population and the new constitution of 1999 recognizes their languages and cultures, and commits the state to respecting and promoting them. It also guarantees their participation in elected bodies: in the National Assembly they are assigned three seats. A Bolivarian Mission is dedicated to indigenous rights.

Following drawn-out negotiations with the powerful, violent opposition in the Media Luna provinces, and three years of hard-fought political battles, in 2009 Evo Morales wins the referendum on a new constitution. For the first time, Bolivia recognizes and respects its own cultural diversity, and is officially decreed a plurinational society. After congress ratifies the new constitution, Morales exclaims: "Whatever they say, whatever they do, we are never going back to neoliberalism." And indigenous rights will remain consecrated in law (*Redacción Rosario*, 2008, October 21).

The Ecuadorian constitution, ratified in October 2008, is considered one of the most progressive in the world, as well as the "greenest" for defending Mother Earth—or "Pacha Mama, where life flourishes and reproduces itself through caring for the diversity of natural resources" (*BBC Mundo*, 2008, October 7). The new constitution requires the state to safeguard the environment, protect animal species, the ecosystem, the earth's natural cycles, and the rights of indigenous communities. Many progressive provisions are contributions made by the indigenous delegation at the constitutional assembly. Though development projects aiming to exploit energy and mineral resources in indigenous regions must consult the affected communities in advance, those communities do not hold veto power. Health and education services through secondary schooling are provided free of charge; indigenous languages are made official; obligatory military service is abolished; foreign military bases are prohibited; illegal immigrants are offered amnesty; same sex civil unions are permitted; abortion is legalized. No other constitution in the region embraces an agenda so progressive.

For consecrating in law so many liberal ideals, Ecuador's new constitution is admired by progressives around the world. Ecuador is the fifth largest producer of petroleum in the continent, and smallest member of OPEC. The country is rich in mineral reserves, including gold, silver and copper. In the 1990's, foreign companies began to exploit those resources, as the country lacked the necessary economic and technical capability. These mining concessions prove to be a source of constant friction between President Correa and indigenous groups. In 2009, the national legislature passes a bill re-authorizing large-scale mining projects, which would permit a handful of Canadian corporations, whose concessions had been cancelled under the new constitution, to resume activity. The indigenous organization CONAIE leads the opposition to the bill, alleging it does not comply with articles in the new constitution prohibiting the contamination of water sources and other forms of environmental degradation. The organization also protests that the multinational companies will make off with 90% of the wealth, without benefiting residents of the affected regions, or the Ecuadorian people as a whole. CONAIE also fears that the new law will result in land expropriations. Rattled by the furious protests, Correa accuses the organization of "infantilism" and declares, "They want to condemn us all to be beggars sitting atop a bundle of riches" (*Associated Press*, 2009, January 20). When congress approves the bill, on January 12, protests proliferate throughout the nation. More than four thousand indigenous people march through the streets of Quito, blocking vital roads and highways; dozens of protestors are arrested, accused of being "terrorists" by President Correa. Indigenous groups in turn accuse the president of continuing the same neoliberal policies that failed his predecessors. Though the government has ignored its constitutional mandate to consult indigenous leaders prior to carrying out development projects that will affect their communities, Correa authorizes the bill citing "national interest." Despite promising modifications, Correa signs the original version into law.

Despite considerable advances made by Latin American indigenous populations in the last decade, they continue to rank among the most vulnerable members of society. In accordance with a 1989 convention, the International Labour Organization requires member countries to consult indigenous groups prior to carrying out development projects that affect their communities. Yet governments routinely ignore this mandate, as well as prohibitions in their own constitutions against the exploitation of natural resources in indigenous territory. Their justification is invariably economic development, progress. They remove as many barriers as possible for foreign corporations seeking to extract petroleum, natural gas, and mineral wealth, activities that often contaminate water supplies and leave communities exposed to serious—sometimes fatal—health risks. Indigenous groups denounce these violations, and the laws and decrees that threaten their habitat and way of life; their protests at times end in mass arrests and even fatalities. Demonstrators blockade roads, highways and rivers, descend on cities causing mass disruptions.

In September 2009, indigenous communities of the Ecuadorian Amazon, the majority Quechuas and Aymaras, are stirred into action once again by a bill permitting multinational mining companies to take possession of water sources in areas close to their communities; they fear the government intends to privatize these supplies, despite a constitutional prohibition. Protestors march through the city, blocking roads and highways and causing massive disruptions. President Correa confronts the protests with force inciting clashes that leave injured people on both sides. Protests last for 55 days. The government revises the bill and the indigenous groups gradually lift their blockades. Correa complains of economic and environmental damages the protestors have caused.

The previous Ecuadorian government expelled Chevron and the Occidental Petroleum Corporation, large American multinationals for failing to fulfill the terms of their contracts and violating national laws. Upon taking office, President Correa looks to rectify the unfair terms on which Ecuador has in the past ceded control of its natural resources to foreign corporations; he revokes 587 concessions to mining companies, and promises recompense if they leave the country. Petrobras, Respol-YTF (from Spain) and Andes Petroleum, a Chinese consortium, accept revisions to their original contracts.

The documentary film "Crude" (2009) investigates the devastating environmental damage caused by Chevron in the rainforest of Ecuador's Sucumbíos Province. Toxic waste is discovered in the soil, water supplies are contaminated, humans and animals fall ill, harvests destroyed. A rise in cancer diagnoses, including among children, is reported in the contaminated area. Indigenous communities file a 27-billion-dollar lawsuit against Chevron. Democratic Congressman James McGovern visits the contaminated region and writes to President Obama of the monumental humanitarian and environmental crisis. Chevron defends itself, accusing the Ecuadorian government of violating a bilateral agreement. After losing in U.S. courts, the company asks for an arbitration hearing before the International Court of Justice in The Hague. Correa contends that an indigenous victory would serve as an example, and compel other multinational companies to operate in an environmentally responsible manner throughout the Third World (Correa, 2008, February 11).

Continuing disputes between Correa and indigenous groups, the president's one-time allies, have eroded popular support for his government. Indigenous communities are offended that the president turns a deaf ear to their complaints and characterizes them as infantile; disillusioned with his government, they accuse Correa of continuing neoliberal policies. On February 27, 2010, CONAIE orders a work stoppage to protest the continuation of neoliberal and other policies it believes reduces Ecuador to colonial state, and ending the dialogue they had previously maintained with the government. Though Correa laments the shutdown, he affirms the right of indigenous groups to protest so long as "they are peaceful and respect the law and constitution" (*Agencia EFE*, 2010, February 27).

The most cowardly treatment of indigenous communities by a head of state may belong to Peruvian President Alan García, whose complete capitulation to Washington dictates is a throwback to the sort of submission that the region has largely left behind. In February 2009, García signs a bilateral free trade agreement with the United States, and to meet its requirements issues a series of legislative decrees aimed at opening Peru to foreign investment, in effect turning over large portions of the Amazon (which comprises 60%

of the country) to Canadian multinational companies looking to exploit energy resources. As they will impact indigenous lands—which are protected by law—as well as the environment, the decrees are unconstitutional. García responds with the old Cold War toolkit: he decrees a national emergency, suspends constitutional rights, characterizes the protests as sedition, insurrection, and rebellion (crimes punishable with up to six years of imprisonment), and deploys force against peaceful demonstrators. García claims that international communism is conspiring against his country, and suggests that Hugo Chávez and Evo Morales are behind the protests. His brutal treatment of the indigenous population causes outrage around the world (Renique, 2009, June 8).

In the absence of constitutional protections, and facing a right-wing government, 65 ethnic groups from the Peruvian Amazon rise in protest against these legislative decrees, which are detrimental to the national interest as well as their communities. On a remote highway, in the Bagua province, police open fire on a crowd of indigenous demonstrators. The government claims that nine people died, but indigenous leaders maintain that the number exceeds 25; according to witnesses, however, the police disposed of bodies in the river, and the true death tally could be as high as 60. The operation also results in hundreds of injuries and arrests. For 55 days, indigenous protestors in several jungle regions blockade highways and rivers, impeding the passage of boats belonging to petroleum companies, which causes food and fuel shortages in Lima as well as Amazonian regions. On June

19, following the international outrage provoked by the violent disregard with which the government responded to the demonstrators, García repeals the controversial decrees (*AFP, DPA*, and *Reuters*, 2009, May 17). His worst misstep was neglecting to consult indigenous leaders, paying no mind to their complaints, and instead spreading propaganda, according to a Peruvian daily, attempting to discredit and blame them for the violence. García himself acknowledges that "there was no conversation with leaders of the native communities [...] Agitators and political intriguers convinced many natives of good faith that the bill was going to take away their water and land [...] all of which is untrue." His minister of internal affairs, Yehude Simon, the only progressive figure in his government, comments: "Being small in number, and distant, [indigenous communities] have always been ignored." One fact beyond dispute is that the crisis has exacted a political toll: García's disapproval rating soars to 84% (Pinedo García, 2009, June 28). The indigenous communities have unquestionably come out on top of this particular fight. However, the broader struggle against state power wedded to large corporate interests remains a daunting one. Indigenous leaders find themselves at a considerable disadvantage.

UNDESIRABLES: THE WORLD BANK, IMF AND FTAS

The World Bank and IMF stand as pillars of the neoliberal globalization strategy, a fundamentally imperialistic project.

In the 1980's, under pressure from Washington, the IMF converts itself into an agent for controlling the political economies of developing countries through the practice of conditional lending, by which a loan's approval might be predicated on a the implementation of a specific policy prescription, such as privatization of public services or natural resources. The IMF mandates cutbacks on health and education spending, the lifting of state subsidies, reduction of public salaries, free-market reforms (through modifications to existing laws), currency devaluations, as well as structural reforms to the public sector. These measures, however, prove harmful to the majority of people: they cause inequality and poverty to spike, hamper economic growth, and slow social progress, fermenting social unrest, including protests, strikes, and violence (Dillon, 2009, February 16).

After the Latin American debt crisis of 1980's, which saw several critical economies collapse under mounting external obligations, the IMF foists its kit of neoliberal fixes on the region. Take the case of Argentina, for example. In the 1990's, the country is widely viewed as a model for responsible economic policy, but by the end of the decade the government is no longer able to service a foreign debt of 146 billion dollars, which leads to a mass government default and the most devastating economic meltdown in recent history. To prevent the collapse of its currency, the government submits to the IMF, which extends a "rescue package" of 48 billion dollars, provided the government curtails spending, cuts food subsidies to the poor, and privatizes state businesses among other free-market reforms. The Argentine government privatizes water services in Buenos Aires province, which Enron purchases at a discounted rate. It also sells off the oil pipeline between Argentina and Chile to American multinationals. Millions of Argentineans lose their jobs, banks freeze accounts. Amid this financial chaos protests and violence breaks out, mobs loot stores and warehouses. Economists blame the IMF's neoliberal interventions—once enthusiastically welcomed by the economic elite—financial institutions and national banks for the calamity (Engdahl, 2005, November 8).

The New Left rises to power atop a wave of popular discontent with the neoliberal interventions of the previous decade, acquiescence to the IMF and World Bank, and free trade agreements with the United States. Throughout the region these policies have proven immensely harmful to the average person. Between 2006 and 2007, Venezuela, Brazil, Argentina, Bolivia, Uruguay, and Ecuador settle IMF debts, and suspend agreements with both institutions. Bolivia, Ecuador, Nicaragua and Venezuela withdraw from the International Centre for Settlement of Investment Disputes, where grievances involving transnationals are resolved; as it receives funding from the World Bank, they question its impartiality (Dillon, 2009, February 16). Ecuador expels the World Bank representative, and forbids the organization from continuing to regulate its economy.

The final declaration of the November 2008 G20 summit,

convened by President Bush in response to the global economic crisis, calls for restructuring and strengthening the World Bank and IMF, despite their past support for the deregulation that caused the crisis. Over 25 years those institutions have ruined developing economies and hindered growth; since their establishment after the Second World War both organizations have strayed from their original missions: the World Bank has not aided, as it was supposed to, sustainable economic and social development; and the IMF, rather than provide assistance to developing countries, has bolstered the bottom line of multinational corporations (Dillon, 2009, February 16). Attaching policy-related conditionality to emergency loans can be seen as a form of extortion, according to some analysts. Most harmful to the public interest have been conditions involving the privatization of water. A worldwide movement has coalesced against this trend, and some governments have succeeded in preventing multinationals from taking control of their water supplies. The growing scarcity of fresh water around the world is one of the gravest crises threatening humankind, and the planet.

In Latin America, people are aware of the harm wrought by free trade agreements with the United States, whose asymmetrical terms favor the super power, transnationals, and the economic elite. NAFTA, which dissolved trade barriers between the United States, Canada, and Mexico, was the first such agreement. Upon entering into force, on January 1, 2004, the EZLN entered the public eye declaring itself opposed to the treaty. Indigenous groups characterize

NAFTA as "a death sentence" and a gift to the rich, which will only deepen division of wealth, already narrowly concentrated, and augment the misery of the masses, destroying what is left of indigenous society (Chomsky, 2009: 137). Mexican bishops, as well as the Latin American Episcopal Conference (CELAM), convened in Mexico at the time, criticize the free-market policy for generating greater inequality and poverty.

While large corporations celebrate the signing of NAFTA, small- and medium-sized businesses are less convinced of its benefits. The Excelsior, the most influential daily newspaper in the country, predicts that the agreement "will only benefit those Mexicans who already own almost the entire country," and views it as just the latest in a long history of "unfettered abuses and plunder" marking Mexican-American relations. Large labor unions also oppose the treaty on the grounds that Mexico will lose sovereignty while only investors and big business stand to profit. The largest environmental organization in the country denounces the agreement as the "third conquest" of Mexico (Chomsky, 2009: 139-140).

The implementation of NAFTA coincides with the economic collapse of Mexico. When the peso falls precipitously, the domestic market is inundated with subsidized food exports from the United States; the price of Mexican corn falls by half, while that of tortillas—a popular food staple—goes up 40%. In 2005, 1.3 million farmers abandon their lands, and 2.4 million are unemployed. According to World Bank estimates, inequality in Mexico is surpassed only by countries in Africa. The Mexican economy grows tepidly, creating 2.4 million jobs, the majority at the lower end of the pay scale. For workers and peasants who comprise the majority of the population, free trade falls short of fulfilling the grand promises made by President Salinas de Gortari when he signed the treaty. NAFTA has proven disastrous for agriculture; farms are no longer productive, unable to compete with subsidized imports from the United States. Increased rural poverty results in an exodus of migrant workers to the United States. President Bush, a proponent of NAFTA, claims that the treaty will generate greater wealth for all, and Mexicans will no longer need to migrate to the United States. "It's in our interest for wealth to spread across the continent through trade," he declares. Nevertheless, he orders the construction of a steel fence, taller than the Berlin Wall, spanning the length of the Mexican border to impede the crossing of illegal immigrants.

According to analysts, the Zapatista uprising against NAFTA in the 1990's spurred the regional movement against the neoliberal model, inspiring the Landless Workers' Movement in Brazil, the Piqueteros (unemployed workers) in Argentina, and the Bolivian coca leaf growers (cocaleros). All are left-wing anti-capitalist movements that oppose FTAs.

In 1994, during the First Summit of the Americas, Bill Clinton presents his vision for a free trade zone that would span from Alaska to Patagonia; a decade later, in the fourth summit, held in Mar del Plata, the proposed FTAA fails for lack of support. Undeterred, Washington pursues bilateral free trade agreements—following the FTAA model—with different countries in the region, but encounters resistance (Dillon, 2009, February 16). It begins with the most vulnerable countries in Central America. In 2007, Colombian President Álvaro Uribe makes a strong push to convince the U.S. Congress to enter a free trade agreement with his country. Many Democrats, however—including Senator Barack Obama—voice concern over Colombia's human rights record, specifically the systematic assassinations of labor leaders, carried out by paramilitaries in cahoots with Administrative Department of Security (DAS), often working on behalf of powerful industrialists.

IN DEFENSE OF WATER

Of all the natural resources providing sustenance to human populations potable water is unquestionably the most vital. It is also among the most vulnerable to capitalist thirst. The World Bank and IMF use all means at their disposal to persuade governments to privatize water supplies. The growing scarcity of fresh water around the world poses an existential threat not only to human beings, but to all living creatures, as well as the world's ecosystem. Water sources are drying up, and immense arid zones growing. The scientific community predicts a dire situation in the near future.

In 1999, Ismail Serageldin, then vice president of the World

Bank, warns: "If the wars of [the 20th century] were fought over oil, the wars of the next century will be fought over water." Its scarcity is already a source of conflict between countries that share rivers, lakes, and inland seas. Mexico and the United States share the Rio Grande (Rio Bravo in Mexico) and the Colorado River; Syria, Turkey, Iraq, and Kurd territories all border the Euphrates River; the Nile flows between Egypt, Ethiopia, and Sudan, and one of the Israeli motivations behind the Six-Day War is taking control of fresh water sources in the West Bank, Gaza Strip, and Golan Heights; Israel seizes full control of the Sea of Galilee, a freshwater lake, as well as the Dead Sea.

Fresh water is running out at an alarming rate, the result of wasteful and excessive human consumption; climate warming and deforestation; the contamination of supplies, accelerated industrialization, and unbridled urban expansion. UN Secretary General Kofi Annan, on World Environment Day, warns that if there is not a dramatic reversal of these trends, in 20 years 60% of human beings will suffer from a grave scarcity of water, and reserves in Mexico, the Middle East, Northern China, California, and 20 other African nations will run out. He calls attention to advancing desert-like zones that already occupy 20% of the Earth's land mass. Every six seconds a child dies from a water-related diseases; in the developing world, 80% of these diseases could be prevented (Barlow and Clarke, 2004, July–August).

Since 1977, when the first United Nations Water Conference

was held in Mar del Plata, countless other conferences, summits and international forums have been dedicated to the threats posed to fresh water supplies: goals have been set, standards agreed to, concepts defined, strategies put forth; dangers resulting from water contamination to food supplies, human settlements, and the poor have been studied, as well as related topics of sustainable development, desertification, and environmental degradation.

Although the UN defines water as a human "necessity," it is not classified as an inalienable "human right" or "common good" barred from commercialization—a conceptualization advocated by social, environmental and citizen movements around the world. Despite growing awareness, however, the cause has faced many challenges in forums dominated by multinational corporations with large water investments, and international credit and commerce institutions, such as the World Bank, IMF and WTO, themselves supported by some of the most powerful government and business interests in the world. Facing these pressures, governments of developing nations find themselves with little choice but to accept the terms of their emergency loans, including water privatization and commercialization conditions.

Around the world fresh water supplies are coveted by the great powers and international capitalist institutions. In free trade agreements with developing countries, the U.S. inserts clauses that commit governments to privatizing water services, imposing hefty sanctions for failure to comply with that demand. Three corporations control 70% of water services worldwide and rank among the hundred richest businesses in the world. Their profits, according to *Fortune* magazine, equal 40% of those from the U.S. petroleum industry, and exceed those of the U.S. pharmaceutical industry, which is approximately 5 billion dollars. The three companies are Suez Lyonnaise de Eaux, the largest, Vivendi Environment, which is also French, and the German RWE-Thames; all receive financing from the World Bank and private banks (Barlow and Clarke, 2002: v). Clauses are inserted into concessions that prohibit governments from setting rates, and enact exorbitant penalties if the contracts are nullified. Conflicts that arise between governments and these corporations are resolved in the International Centre for Settlement of Investment Disputes, a member of the World Bank Group.

Despite going up against powerful institutions determined to bring about its privatization, the worldwide movement to defend water rights gains momentum. The 1999 WTO protest in Seattle is a milestone in the history of anti-capitalist popular protest, bringing together thousands of activists from around the world. It inspires other protests in various capitals around the world. Activists flock by the thousands to increasingly far-flung locales where the economic powers congregate in heavily guarded halls to make decisions that impact the entire world. They protest globalization, neoliberalism, and privatization, including of water, and sometimes manage to disrupt meetings and influence their outcomes. The movement to protect water gains traction in rich and poor countries alike, and in some instances succeeds in impeding the privatization of public utilities; they put a stop to the mining of subterranean water sources by bottled water companies, preventing its exportation on large tankers. Yet the World Bank offers reassurance that "one way or another, water will soon be moved around the world as oil is now" (Barlow and Clark, 2002: vi; Barlow and Clark, 2002, August 15).

"Water is life and not for sale" is the passionate refrain heard throughout alternative forums attended by thousands of activists from NGOs, environmental and human rights groups, grassroots organizations as well as regional movements, representatives of populist and indigenous and other social causes around the developing world. They are the manifestation of the progressive backlash to the capitalist conferences whose goal is the commercialization of water.

Many activists ask the UN to declare water a "fundamental human right" and "common good," which would lay the moral foundation for banning its commercialization. They petition for these concepts to be added to the Universal Declaration of Human Rights (1948) as well as national constitutions. The ill-fated European Constitution (abandoned in 2007) denounced the World Bank, IMF and WTO, and World Economic Forum for supporting multinational companies dedicated to commercializing water supplies.

On March 22, 2009, Water World Day, the Fourth World Water Forum is held in Istanbul, Turkey, convening heads of state and government, municipal and ministry representatives, civic, labor and NGO leaders, elected officials from numerous countries, as well as water corporations. The World Water Forum, which is organized by the Water World Council, a think tank, convenes every three years with some 20,000 attendees from more than 70 countries, the majority from developing countries in Africa and Latin America. In Istanbul, several countries—including Bolivia, Cuba, Chile, Ecuador, Guatemala, Honduras, Panama, Paraguay, Uruguay, Venezuela, Switzerland, Germany and Holland—propose that access to potable water be declared a "human right" and "basic necessity" and its commercialization prohibited. Despite failing to garner consensus, 25 nations sign a joint statement declaring water to be a fundamental human right, and requested that the issue to be dealt with in the UN—not the Wold Water Forum, a private institution—while also calling for rigid compliance with the Kyoto Treaty. The environment minister of Bolivia expresses his discomfort in having his proposals consistently ignored from the preliminary sessions through the end of the conference. In Istanbul, the powerful current favoring privatization succeeds in bolstering the concept of water commercialization.

In the same city, an alternative forum—attended by environmental, human rights and labor activists—convenes simultaneously with the goal of raising awareness about the global scarcity of water, and the millions of people at risk of losing access to it. They are critical of the World Water Forum, a private institution, contending that an issue as vital as water rights should be addressed by the UN through a democratic, participatory process.

WATER IN LATIN AMERICA

Latin America abounds with natural resources. It contains more biodiversity than any other region in the world, including 31% of the planet's fresh water. Its main rivers—the Amazon, Orinoco, Paraná and Magdalena—rank among the 25 longest on Earth, and their volume nearly equals that of all the others combined. The continent is also covered by large lakes: Titicaca, between Bolivia and Peru; Poopó, a saline lake in Bolivia; Lake Maracaibo in Venezuela; the Buenos Aires between Chile and Argentina, and other smaller ones scattered throughout various countries in the region.

Industrialized nations have long coveted natural resources in the developing world: petroleum, gas, minerals, wood, and water. Subscribing to the doctrine that the private sector can deliver public services more efficiently, governments auction utilities to foreign corporations. Privatization is met with popular protest, which in some instances prevents the deals from being finalized. The public is wary of multinationals that in the past have too often extracted natural resources on unfavorable terms. Cognizant of this widespread distrust, multinationals sometimes set up subsidiaries under local names.

Two major victories for water rights merit particular attention. In January 2008, the World Bank announces it has denied a 25-million-dollar loan request by the Bolivian government to improve water services in Cochabamba, the country's fourth largest city, if it is not privatized. President Hugo Banzer ultimately acquiesces, granting a 40-year concession to the American multinational Bechtel, which the company transfers to a subsidiary, Aguas del Tunal. When the company raises rates by 25% and charges, door to door, for the rainwater households collect in cisterns, a popular protest erupts. Over the course of several weeks tens of thousands of indigenous and peasant protestors take to the streets, declaring a strike, blockading roads, pledging to paralyze the city until the concession is revoked. Banzer dispatches the military, yet the rancor of the demonstrators forces him to eventually rescind the contract and expel Bechtel. The company brings a grievance before the World Bank and files a law suit against Bolivia—for "expropriation"—for 40 billion dollars. Years later it backs down.

Uruguay is the scene of another significant victory for water rights. In October 2004, a coalition of activists garners the support necessary to call a national referendum on a constitutional amendment that would declare water a "public good" and "fundamental human right" barred from commercialization on the open market. The same day Tabaré Vázquez, the Broad Front candidate, is elected president with 50.45% of the popular vote. In his campaign he declared support for the constitutional amendment on water rights.

The history of popular mobilization in Peru demonstrates the close relationship between the struggle for water rights and mineral exploration. Peru and Chile are the largest mineral producers in the continent. Peruvian mines are operated by American, Spanish, and British companies. Located in remote reaches of the Andean Plateau, they are populated by impoverished indigenous communities whose relations with the multinational companies are extremely tense; their lands are occupied and often expropriated by the government. Mining activities can contaminate rivers with toxic chemicals, people become sick, the transport of heavy machinery destroys roads. Moreover, the presence of a multinational workforce raises the cost of living. In 2004, 97 conflicts are registered in Peru and the government responds with force to defend the foreign corporations, clashes that generally result in injuries and arrests.

One such conflict takes place in September 2004, when indigenous groups from the sierra protest against Yanacocha ("Black Lagoon" in the Quechua language), mine belonging to the Newmont Mining Corporation, an American gold mining company, to expand exploration to the Cerro Quilish mountain, a sacred site in the native culture and bountiful source of fresh water. More than ten thousand protestors blockade the mine and, despite a military operation, manage to take control of the mountain. They demand that the government revoke Newmont's concession, accusing the company of using up and contaminating water supplies. The company suspends its exploration, an unequivocal victory for the indigenous protestors.

In June 2005, labor, indigenous and peasant activists from 23 regions of Peru converge in Lima to protest the Ley General de Aguas, a bill allowing the privatization of water services—for an open-ended period of time—and authorizes foreign mining corporations to spill their waste in water sources in exchange for payments to the government. A number of indigenous, labor, environmental, and other grassroots organizations sign a statement in opposition to the bill, and warn of the dangers of water contamination, the harm to the environment, and the health risks posed to communities in mineral regions. A month earlier, social, inter-ethnic, labor, farmer, indigenous, peasant and miners organizations formed the National Commission in Defense of Water and Life, a vehicle for organizing protests against the proposed law. Nevertheless, powerful interests that support the Ley General de Aguas, including President Alejandro Toledo, congressional representatives of his "Peru Posible" party, right-wing elites opposed to any obstacle to foreign investment. Another strong source of support of the law is the World Bank, IMF, and IDB, and multinationals operating in Peru. And yet the forceful indigenous backlash succeeds in postponing passage of the bill. Four years later, in March 2009, congress approves the bill and it is signed into law by President Alan García. Water services in Peru can now be privatized.

In Brazil, President Lula resists World Bank pressure and

democratizes water services in his country. This is the work of a handful of experts and technicians, state agencies, NGOs, environmentalists, engineers and scientists who design a system drawing on popular participation. Water is declared a public good.

President Néstor Kirchner manages to keep Aguas Argentinas—a multinational consortium in which Suez, a French company, is the largest stakeholder—under control. He demands that the consortium fulfill the terms of the contract it signed with the government of Carlos Menem, and invest in improvements to the water system.

Steered by the "Chicago Boys"—a group of free-market economists who studied under Milton Friedman at the University of Chicago—during the Pinochet years Chile became the privatization pioneer in Latin America. Twenty years after that regime's defeat in a national plebiscite, it comes to light that the minister of the treasury, Hernán Büchi, sold off state companies below their market value, costing the country more than 6 billion dollars.

According to the Food and Agriculture Organization (FAO), among Latin American countries Colombia is second in average annual renewable fresh water sources, and seventh in the world. Despite this natural wealth, eleven million people in the country (out of a total population exceeding 45 million) lack secure access to potable water. The Ministry of the Environment files a suit in 1998 against the Occidental Petroleum Corporation for environmental damage and water contamination. In 2008, more than two million signatures are collected on a petition calling for a constitutional amendment declaring water a "fundamental right" and prohibiting its privatization. In February 2009, in a letter to the presidents of the Senate and House of Representatives—both controlled by right-wing Uribe loyalists—the organizers respectfully request that the referendum be called. Two months later, they become indignant upon learning that their proposals have been modified. The House approves a bill in which articles declaring access to water a fundamental right, and public good, and prohibiting its privatization, have been eliminated. Included in the bill is a paragraph declaring "waters that pass through and terminate on the same estate" to be the property of the estate's owner. (Caracol Radio, 2009, April 22). Land tenancy is a major issue in Colombia, where paramilitary groups, through torture, assassination, and massacres have driven more than 4.7 million peasants from their land, which they have then appropriated for themselves. The story of these displaced people is one of the great tragedies of the country, and continent, surpassed in scope only by the crisis in Sudan. Though previously opposed to the referendum, Uribe and his bench, which holds an absolute majority in congress, approve since the wording has been modified to their liking. Now Uribe feels at ease allowing the people to decide.

THE STORY CONTINUES

In February 2010, Latin America takes another historic step towards independence and integration when the Community of Latin American and Caribbean States is established. The new community is comprised of 33 Latin American countries, including Cuba, with the U.S. and Canada excluded. According to analysts, the message could not be clearer: the region is distancing itself from Washington, establishing itself as a as a regional block with its own independent agenda. The creation of this community is the largest step, according to analysts, toward its independence—and the marginalization of the U.S. in regional affairs.

In the first decade of the 21st Century, Latin America catapults itself into the vanguard of the democratic movement against the domination exerted by transnational corporations and militarism. Ecuador expels Occidental Petroleum Corporation and Chevron, and rescinds 587 contracts with foreign mining companies for violating the terms of those contracts and national laws. An indigenous community sues Chevron for ecological disasters caused in the Ecuadorian Amazon dating back to 1964. In February 2011, an Ecuadorian court orders the company to pay 19.5 billion dollars, the largest fine for environmental malfeasance ever divvied up—anywhere in the world. President Correa suspends foreign debt payments, likening them to a "million-dollar stick-up" (*AP* and *Agencia EFE*, 2008, November 17), plagued by bribery and fraud. He amends petroleum and mineral concessions detrimental to the national interest. Ecuador withdraws from the Centre for Settlement of Investment Disputes, and lets the agreement granting U.S. access to the Manta base expire. U.S. military personnel leave the country in September 2009.

For many Latin Americans, including U.S. allies, the 2008 financial collapse serves to discredit neoliberalism and the Washington Consensus. The crisis alerts people and governments to the potential dangers of free-market doctrines. Even moderate leaders, such as Michele Bachelet, express their wariness of the laissez-faire approach. In March 2009, in New Delhi, Bachelet publicly questions the Washington Consensus. "They sell it to us as the best remedy, but that is not exactly true," she says. The past failure of those policies, she claims, is the reason "many countries turn to more progressive leaders." Despite speaking of the "neoliberal excess" inherited by her government, she defends the "necessity" of the markets, while emphasizing the need for regulation to ensure they remain "strong and healthy." She describes her administration's reforms as combining "economic growth with social justice," and declares her support for restructuring the IMF and World Bank, in which "important countries like India and China are not represented as they should be." When questioned about South American integration she responds: "We face the same challenges and understand that only through integration can we resolve our problems." On the Council of South American Defense, which some observers view as competition to the OAS and UN, she comments that the creation of an institution such as this one would have been "unthinkable a few years ago" (Prensa Latina, 2009, March 19).

Indigenous communities, their rights now codified in the new constitutions of Colombia, Bolivia, Ecuador and Venezuela, grow more assertive, which reinforces the democratic values of their countries. Indigenous and popular movements have been fundamental to the change taking place on the continent. The IV Continental Summit of Indigenous People and Nationalities of Abya Yala, in Puno, Peru, in May 2009, brings together five thousand activists from around the continent during a moment of crisis in the global financial system. Indigenous groups oppose neoliberal policies, privatization of natural resources, petroleum and natural gas exploration, concessions to multinational companies; they fight against the criminalization of social movements, and the repression of their people. While the summit is convened Peruvian indigenous communities in the Amazon fight against President Alan García's attempts to seize their lands and deny them property rights (Becker, 2009, June 12).

In Latin America the progressive movement crests in the first decade of the 21st Century. Its gains, however, can be reversed with the election of right-wing presidents. In Chile, some view the conservative Sebastián Piñera as a natural heir to Pinochet, but thus far he has not sought to undo any advances made under Michele Bachelet; in Brazil, the election of Dilma Rouseff, of Lula's Worker's Party, all but ensures continuity with her predecessor's measured policies;

for eight years Colombia was governed by Álvaro Uribe, a right-wing militaristic thug, viewed around the continent as a Trojan horse against regional unity and integration. In May 2011, Juan Manuel Santos, supported by large segments of the population that believe Uribe's former defense minister will continue the policies of his administration, is elected to the presidency. A vote for Santos, they assume, is as good as a vote for a third Uribe term. Upon taking office, however, President Santos immediately returns to a more liberal, democratic style of governance, pursuing harmonious relations with neighboring countries, and rolling back some of the policies of his predecessor. This radical change of course is received with relief and approbation around the country and continent. It inspires renewed hope for peace.

3

The Cuban Revolution in the 21st Century

CUBA AND THE NEW LEFT

Latin America's transformation in the first decade of the 21st Century is ushered in by the New Left, which holds the Cuban Revolution—"the first free territory of the Americas," as the bearded revolutionaries once proclaimed—in the highest regard. Analysts see in the New Left the imprimatur of the Revolution, and argue that these recent political and social movements would have been unable to achieve the same results without the example of the small island that for half a century has stared down "The Empire." More than just a reference point, though, Cuba helps the New Left achieve its objectives (Milne, 2009, January 29). Ten years after taking office, Hugo Chávez acknowledges that without Cuban assistance his government would have been unable to meet its goals in health and education, such as the eradication of illiteracy. "The horizons, and magnitude of assistance the Cuban Revolution has given to the Bolivarian Revolution, could never be calculated," he declares (*Granma*, 2009, February 3).

The Cuban Revolution is a watershed event that transforms the geopolitical panorama of the entire hemisphere. Cuba becomes the first country in the Americas to free itself from U.S. hegemony; it likewise is the first to declare itself socialist and align with the Soviet bloc. With the proliferation throughout the region of armed groups determined to repeat the Cuban success, the alarm in Washington grows. Crushed under the burdens of poverty, endemic social and economic inequality, disillusioned by pervasive corruption and the democratic dysfunction that marginalizes them—but which a small elite will defend at all costs—the people turn for guidance to the Cuban model, with its free healthcare and education programs, its universal social security and promise of work for all. They see that change is possible.

The revolutionary airs blowing through Latin America instill fear in national governments. That a country in the region with more Catholic souls than any other has declared itself communist, and the people burn with revolutionary fervor, is also a source of concern for the Vatican. In communism, people see a clearer path toward social justice, an answer to their most vital needs. This great yearning for change sets both Washington and the Vatican on edge.

With John XXIII as pontiff, the Church has undergone a

profound transformation of its own. During his brief papacy, he lays out a radical new path: rather than defending church doctrine—the primary preoccupation, for centuries, of his predecessors—he instructs the clergy to work for the poor, attend to their earthly, as well as spiritual, needs. They must strive to be the "Church of the Poor." In light of the Vatican's long, reactionary history, this change of direction is nothing short of revolutionary, and galvanizes progressive sectors within the Church. Following the Second Vatican Council, Latin American Episcopal Council (CELAM), which was established in 1953 and Liberation Theology emerges. The Church adopts programs that will favor the dispossessed. Exponents of Liberation Theology create basic ecclesial communities (BEC) in the most indigent regions of Central and South America, where priests as well as laymen encourage the poor to defend and fight for their rights. When espoused by respected prelates, catholic teachings on social justice infuse the revolutionary fights with greater moral legitimacy. The revolutions in the Church and Cuba open new portals of hope. In Nicaragua, clergymen and revolutionaries fight side by side, guided by a shared vision of social justice. Priests occupy high positions in the Sandinista government, which aims to transform the country, one of the poorest in the hemisphere. The triumph of the Cuban Revolution radiates throughout the Sandinista movement, which is also socialist in character. Years later, Hugo Chávez and Rafael Correa adopt Christian and socialist teachings in their own political philosophies and plans for development. They proselytize a new socialism for the 21st Century that, by their own char-

acterization, is distinct from the Cuban Revolution: less dog-
matic, more respectful of property rights, and adaptable to the
particular history and culture of a given country; and it genuinely feeds off Christian currents. Chávez asks the Venezuelan clergy to sift through the gospels, including the Sermon
on the Mount, for socialist messages; but the church hierarchy
is opposed to his political agenda. Western media outlets are
far more concerned with denigrating the Cuban regime than
acknowledging any of its achievements. They dwell on its
shortcomings without even comparing those to the graver ills
plaguing the rest of the region; they maintain that Cuba, subjected to one-party rule, is not a democracy. They highlight
the harsh restrictions imposed by the Cuban government on
its citizens while ignoring more egregious human rights violations being committed in Central America and the Southern Cone. They consider Fidel a dictator. And with that same
animosity they criticize, and ridicule, the New Left; they refer
to its leaders as "populist," which carries a pejorative con-
notation; they falsely accuse them of being communist; they
accuse democratically elected heads of state of being dictators
bent on applying the Cuban model to their own countries,
and root for their failure or elimination.

In contrast to the armed revolutionary movements of the
1960's, the New Left governments enjoy high levels of popular support. The masses vote them into power, and manifest
their support in street rallies in Chile, Argentina, Venezuela
as well as indigenous uprisings in Bolivia, Peru, and Ecuador.
This explosion of popular protest historians identify as a new

cycle of civil resistance in Latin America, motivated in large part by opposition to the neoliberal policies advocated by Washington.

THE CUBAN REVOLUTION

On January 1, 2009, the 50th anniversary of the Cuban Revolution is commemorated with a modest ceremony in Santiago de Cuba, a city where the first revolutionary battle was fought. The austere spirit of the celebration stands out for its marked contrast to more boisterous festivities of years past. The Revolution's Maximum Leader, Fidel Castro, absent due to illness, sends a short, congratulatory message. High-ranking officials also attend a thanksgiving ritual celebrated by Christian churches in Havana.

Such a remarkable milestone draws considerable media attention. Analysts from around the world reflect on the half-century of the Cuban Revolution. In the West, critiques of its economic shortcomings and restrictions on civil society dominate the coverage; few bother to point out its achievements in health, education, and the sciences, not to mention the substantial advances made towards building an egalitarian society. This sort of negative coverage has been standard for the international media throughout the fifty years of revolutionary history.

An underdeveloped country, located just 90 miles off the coast of the global super power, Cuba has for half a century faced harassment, unyielding aggression, and economic hardship resulting from the embargo ordered by President Kennedy. In the intervening years, ten different administrations, driven by varying degrees of hostility, have attempted to snuff out revolution. During the Kennedy administration, the island's sugar regions—its principle economic engine—come under endless bombardment, including criminal sabotage and assassination attempts on its directors. The U.S. launches the ill-conceived Bay of Pigs invasion, organized, armed and financed by the Eisenhower administration, which Cuban forces repel within 72 hours. The first defeat suffered by the "Empire," the revolutionaries declare. They also succeed in foiling countless assassination attempts by the CIA against their leadership, more than three hundred against Fidel Castro alone.

After purging the government of Batista loyalists, the revolutionary government sets in motion a series of reforms to the political, social and economic structures of the country, while freeing itself from the shackles of American power. Expropriations and nationalizations begin, and within three years all American assets on the island have been liquidated, its military mission (which advised Batista's army) expelled, and relations with the USSR broadened. According to Diana Raby, a senior fellow at the Institute of Latin American Studies at the University of Liverpool, Cuba's transition to socialism "is one of the most rapid and thorough anywhere in the world" (Raby, 2009, January. It is a transition, of course, unacceptable to Washington, which wastes no time in responding through open as well as covert actions. Three months after the rebel seizure of Havana, President Eisenhower orders preparations for an invasion of the island by anti-Castro exiles residing in the United States. He is convinced that he can extinguish the revolution, like the CIA did five years earlier in Guatemala, when President Jacobo Arbenz had the nerve to expropriate unused lands owned by the United Fruit Company, which he intended to hand over to thousands of poor peasants. In the last week of his term, Eisenhower cuts diplomatic relations with Cuba.

Despite shortages of consumer goods, low wages and poverty, restrictions on freedoms of the press, assembly and movement—measures considered necessary in the face of relentless U.S. aggression—the Revolution spawns an egalitarian society, one in which health and education services are universally guaranteed, an advance praised by UNESCO and the WHO. The Revolution does away with abandoned housing and tenant eviction, and guarantees the right to shelter and work for all. Ration cards are introduced to ensure the equitable distribution of vital goods. Through agrarian reform, property deeds are transferred to landless peasants. The revolutionary government also launches a national literacy campaign: Cuba becomes the first country in the world to declare itself free of illiteracy. Cuba has the lowest birthrate in the hemisphere (1.6 children per woman) and the life expectancy on the island ranks alongside those of more developed countries: 77.3 years (Romero, 2009, January 1). And no resident of the island dies of hunger.

With Soviet assistance, the revolutionary government assembles one of the most effective security apparatuses in the world. When four bombs detonate during a speech he was giving in Plaza de la Revolución, Fidel Castro proposes right there on the spot the creation of Committees for the Defense of the Revolution (CDR), a network of neighborhood groups extending throughout the country. They will remain vigilant in every town, city and street, day and night.

Inspired by the Cuban Revolution, armed struggles proliferate throughout Latin America in the 1960's. Alarmed by the growing revolutionary fervor, President Kennedy devises a sophisticated counterinsurgency strategy aimed at smothering the spread of communism. He puts his plans into action in Guatemala, where revolutionary sentiment is percolating among the ranks of the armed services. The strategy is adopted by national armies, which commit grave human rights violations in what becomes known as the "dirty wars." Under the pretext of quelling communist insurgencies they persecute peaceful demonstrators and activists.

For once, the United States pays heed to the economic and social ills afflicting Latin America, launching the Alliance for Progress, an ambitious plan for collaboration between governments aimed at mitigating poverty and social inequality, conditions fueling the armed rebellions. During its brief existence the project fails due to protectionist measures adopted by the U.S. Congress and other obstacles imposed by obtuse Latin American leaders. Critics of Kennedy's aggressive counterinsurgency strategy characterize the Alliance for Progress as a development plan carried out by death squads.

President Kennedy inherits the plan for the Bay of Pigs invasion from the Eisenhower administration. Despite harboring doubts it will succeed, the president proceeds with the preparations. On April 15, 1961, CIA bombers painted to look like Revolutionary Air Force (FAR) attack Cuban airfields. A day later, the land invasion is launched; but 72 hours after disembarking in the Bay of Pigs the anti-Castro force is defeated. Following the failed assault, Fidel declares Cuba a socialist country, and moves closer to the USSR, signing economic, military, and technological cooperation agreements with countries in the Soviet Bloc. Kennedy takes responsibility for the debacle, and less than a year later strengthens U.S. economic sanctions to a near-total embargo. That November, he initiates the Cuban Project (also known as "Operation Mongoose"), the largest covert operation ever undertaken by the CIA. The plan revolves around sabotage, provocation and support—in the form of arms and funding—to counterrevolutionary groups. Washington hopes the Cuban people will rise against their government and the U.S. will be able to launch a military operation to end the Revolution. The Cuban people, however, do not rise up against Fidel. Having failed to achieve its desired results, the program is suspended after two years.

The most dangerous crisis in the U.S.-Cuban conflict is precipitated by the installation of Soviet rockets on the island in

October 1962. The world finds itself on the brink of a nuclear conflagration. Behind Fidel's back, President Kennedy negotiates with Nikita Khrushchev to remove the missiles. After a standoff lasting thirteen days, the world can finally exhale.

Jimmy Carter is the only American president to attempt to improve relations with Cuba. In September 1977, he establishes the United States Interests Section in the Swiss Embassy in Havana; Cuba, in turn, opens a Cuban Interests Section in the Czech Embassy in Washington. President Carter also authorizes travel by U.S. citizens to the island.

The deployment of Cuban troops to Africa, however, is unacceptable to the Carter administration. The Cuban force arrives at the request of local governments in response to South African aggression towards Angola, as well as Somali incursions into Ethiopian territory. Collaborating with the Soviet Union, which provides funding and arms, Cuban troops contribute toward victories in each of those conflicts. When President Carter declares that this military engagement makes it "impossible" to normalize U.S.-Cuban relations, Fidel responds, "With what moral authority can the United States complain about our troops in Africa when it has troops here in Guantanamo? It would be ridiculous for Cuba to ask the United States to withdraw its troops from the Philippines, Greece, South Korea, and the innumerable other countries in which it keeps them stationed in order for us to normalize relations" (Franklin, 1997: 137-138).

In 1991, the USSR—Cuba's principal military ally, trade partner, and political supporter—disintegrates. Analysts around the world predict that the days of the Cuban Revolution are numbered. In the absence of Soviet aid, and subjected to the continued U.S. embargo, a period of food shortages and economic hardship ensues. The Revolution, nonetheless, survives, in large part by introducing a rigorous savings and efficiency plan during what becomes known as the "Special Period in Times of Peace." The program proves to be a success. Transportation challenges are resolved in part through the importation of millions of Chinese bicycles, as well as ox and horse-driven wagons; to mitigate the energy crisis, the government introduces periodic rationing, and installs electric plants in key sites throughout the country; decentralized, they prove to be efficient and inexpensive. In response to food insecurity, the government provides stimulus to private farms and implements the "Urban Agriculture" program. Organopónicos, small urban gardens for cultivation of fruit and vegetables in small spaces, planted around the outskirts of Havana are now responsible for 60% of food consumption. With Cuban assistance, these urban gardens are later replicated in other parts of the world, as they are considered environmentally sustainable.

CUBA IN THE WORLD

In the 1970's the situation in Cuba improves. Countries that, under pressure from Washington, had severed ties with the Castro government in the previous decade, one by one reestablish relations. Costa Rica remains cut off, as well as El Salvador, which suspends relations after the Revolution and does not reestablish them until 2009. Despite having traded epithets in the past—the Costa Rican president, Óscar Arias, compared Castro to General Pinochet and Fidel referred to Arias as a "vulgar mercenary" and "imperial lackey"—in March 2009 Arias reestablishes diplomatic relations, a decision Cuba applauds. In this same year, President Álvaro Colom travels to Cuba, a first for a Guatemalan head of state, and shocks many by issuing an official apology for the role his country played in the Bay of Pigs operation. In 1961, the CIA established training camps for anti-Castro paramilitaries in Guatemala (Lacey, 2009, February 18).

Of Latin American countries, Cuba is the most interconnected with the rest of the world. It is a founding member of the Non-Aligned Movement (NAM) and maintains economic and diplomatic relations with the majority of its 114 members. In September 2006, following the XIV Non-Aligned Movement Summit, held in Havana, it is decided that Cuba will preside over the group for the next three years. Cuba extends assistance to 33 countries in Asia, Africa and Latin America in the form of education initiatives, illiteracy eradication campaigns, as well as health, sports and agriculture programs. It is a member of the Caribbean Community (CARICOM). Its relations with the European Union, which in 2003 imposes restrictions following perceived civil liberties abuses on the island, are unstable; by 2008, however, all sanction have been lifted. That same month, in the twenty-second year of its existence, the Rio Group finally accepts Cuba as a full member. The Rio Group succeeded the Contadora Group, which was created by the foreign ministers of Colombia, Mexico, Panama and Venezuela in the 1980's to mediate the armed conflicts roiling Central America, and advocate for a softening of President Reagan's militaristic counterinsurgency policy.

The U.S. will not succumb to worldwide pressure to end its sanctions on Cuba, despite the UN General Assembly voting against the embargo for twenty years. Only Israel, and a couple small states that would be difficult to locate on a map, vote alongside the United States. In December 2008, CARICOM calls for the embargo to be lifted, and the first Summit of Latin America and the Caribbean, convened that same month by Lula da Silva, issues a statement critical of the Helm-Burton Act, which strengthens the embargo, claiming certain provisions violate international law.

Its relationship with Russia is of enormous importance to Cuba. Before its collapse, the USSR was Cuba's most powerful ally—the Revolution's principal lifeline. Russia, however, continues to be the largest importer of Cuban sugar, and Cuba continues purchasing Russian oil, in smaller quantities, and spare parts for the Soviet vehicles and equipment that keep many sectors of its economy moving.

After Vladimir Putin's 2000 election as Russian president, relations and trade between his country and Cuba grow. Putin travels to Havana in December 2002, and other high-ranking Russian officials visit the island and sign various agreements. Following the 2008 Asia-Pacific Economic Cooperation (APEC) Summit in Peru, the new Russian President Dmitry Medvedev travels to Cuba, Brazil and Costa Rica. Western media outlets report on Russia's growing interest in Latin America. In January 2009, Raúl Castro visits Russia for a week and signs 34 agreements pertaining to petroleum exploration, nickel mining, loans and other aid, totaling 354 million dollars. According to Russian sources, the two countries finalize joint venture agreements, as well as a strategic alliance whose scope and details are not publicly disclosed. Cuba offers assistance in biotech ventures, and the pharmaceutical industry. Russia is its fourth largest trading partner, after Venezuela, China, and Brazil.

Hugo Chávez signs the Petrocaribe treaty with seventeen Caribbean and Central American nations, guaranteeing them access to Venezuelan petroleum at subsidized prices. Barter exchanges favorable to those countries are negotiated. Cuba receives a hundred thousand barrels of crude per day at half the market price, with a payment schedule extending twenty years at low interest rates. It is Venezuelan support that maintains the Cuban economy afloat. In return, Cuba dispatches specialized personnel—23,000 doctors, paramedics, sports trainers, and agriculture experts—to Venezuela. Chávez himself acknowledges that without Cuban assistance he would have been unable to carry out his full education and health agenda. Bolivia is another recipient of Cuban educators and, along with Venezuela, launches a literacy program: "Yes I

Can." With Cuban assistance, Bolivia and Venezuela ultimately declare themselves free of illiteracy. Cuba provides similar assistance to 33 countries in Latin America, Asia and Africa.

FIDEL PASSES THE TORCH

As his health declines, Fidel Castro distances himself from the public eye and, in June 2006, transfers executive power to his younger brother, Raúl, then serving as the vice president and defense minister. Two years later, Fidel officially announces his retirement from the presidency and the national assembly, in a unanimous decision, names Raúl his successor. The retirement of the Revolution's maximum leader is carried out in an orderly, exemplary fashion. There is no chaos, no uprisings as Florida's anti-Castro dissidents, and Washington, had hoped for.

The Cuban Revolution celebrates its 50th anniversary on January 1, 2009, and the ceremony takes place in Santiago de Cuba, a city of enormous historical importance, for it was there that on July 26, 1953 Fidel led an attack on the Moncada Barracks, a military stronghold of the dictator Fulgencio Batista. Many rebels died in the ensuing battle and others were imprisoned, among them Fidel and Raúl. Historians point to this event as marking the birth of the Revolution.

Fidel is absent from the ceremonies but sends a short congratulatory note. During the ceremony, Raúl repeats what

Fidel himself declared in December 2005: "The United States can no longer destroy the political system of this island, only Cubans themselves can." Both leaders express concern as the revolutionary generation, to which they belong, approaches the end of the road. They fear that subsequent generations will lack the legitimacy and moral authority of those who took up arms at Moncada (Arreola, 2009, January 2).

On February 24, 2008, upon assuming the presidency, Raúl Castro pledges "conceptual and structural" reform, including streamlining bureaucracy and the elimination of "absurd prohibitions." He acknowledges that salaries on the island do not cover the basic needs of the population, and that there is room for improvement in the quality of education. He calls on the Cuban people to investigate societal ills, denounce them and propose alternate paths (López de Guerrero, 2008, December 27). These comments unsettle some and surprise others. They compare Raúl's call for certain liberalizations to Gorbachev's glasnost. Daniel P. Erickson, of the Inter-American Dialogue, wonders: "Once [Raúl Castro's government] releases the genie of public opinion from the bottle, does it risk permanently reducing its control over Cuban society?" (Williams, 2008, April 29).

One of Raúl's first actions as president is lifting the prohibition on acquiring cellular phones and computers. "It's no longer a crime to buy a DVD, cellular phone or microwave, nor to rent a car or stay in a hotel, but for all that you need money," one Cuban comments. And a student points out that it's "absurd" for a doctor to have to commute to work on a bike or minibus while a person working in the food industry can own a car" (López de Guerrero, 2008, December 27). These concessions may come off as modest, but they carry political ramifications: cellular phones facilitate internal communication and the Internet connects Cuban citizens to the rest of the world.

Raúl has planted the seeds out of which it seems possible a certain glasnost may grow. Waldo Ramírez, of the Cuban Institute of Television and Radio, in an interview with the Juventud Rebelde, asserts: "Through television we need to promote dialogue that will replace the vertical model with a horizontal one" (Williams, 2008, April 29). Observers wonder how much longer the government will be able to maintain such strict controls over civil society when those sorts of restrictions no longer exist in the rest of the world. Some hope that improved relations with the newly elected Barack Obama may pave the way for a relaxation of state control.

The greatest challenge facing the Cuban government, however, is economic, and the outlook remains bleak. The robust annual growth of 10% from 2005 to 2007 slows to 4.5% in 2008, a decline that continues as the world financial crisis sets in, limiting prospects for foreign financing. In the summer of 2008 three hurricanes, whose total economic costs rises to ten billion dollars, also have a negative impact. Cuba now must import 80% of its food. The trade deficit swells to eleven billion dollars, an 80% increase, and the price of nickel, a major source of foreign currency, falls in the world market (*The Economist*, 2009, January 6). Cuba seeks to compensate for these losses by increasing trade with Venezuela, China, Russia, as well as the rest of Latin America and the European Union.

Amid this domestic unrest, Raúl announces an unprecedented upheaval: he merges several ministries and removes ten high-ranking officials from their positions in the government and Council of Ministers, the most prominent being Carlos Lage, a vice president and executive secretary of the Council, responsible for economic affairs, a figure widely recognized around the world, as well as the foreign minister, Felipe Pérez Roque, Fidel's former private secretary. Both officials boast distinguished resumes: Lage steered the country through the economic crisis of the Special Period, and Pérez Roque has played a critical role in building bridges toward the rest of Latin America, Cuba's admittance into the Rio Group and other bodies for region integration. He organizes Raúl Castro's foreign trips as well as visits by foreign heads of state to Cuba.

In letters to the President, published in *Granma* and *Juventud Rebelde*, Lage and Pérez Roque accept responsibility for having committed "errors." In those same periodicals, Fidel Castro accuses them—without mentioning names—of "having tasted the honey of power," of being ambitious and committing deeds "unworthy" of revolutionaries. The Western media portrays these removals as "purges" ordered by Raúl in order to consolidate control of the country, and remove figures loyal to his brother who could prove to be obstacles to reform. Raúl surrounds himself with military commanders and members of the communist party. Yet the most significant changes take place in the economic sphere: the press surmises that his primary motivation is coping with the precarious economic situation (Muñoz, 2009, March 8).

Three weeks later, Raúl Castro allegedly "removes" two vice presidents from the Council of Ministers: Pedro Miret and Osmany Cienfuegos. The *EFE* and *Reuters* news agencies present these as dismissals. In a statement published on March 6, an incensed Fidel goes on record asserting that the Council of State is in agreement with the officials "relieving themselves" of their duties: Miret for health reasons, and Cienfeugos (the brother of Camilo, a towering figure in the revolutionary pantheon) for little by little leaving his position as vice President of the Council of Ministers to manage a tourism complex in the provinces. He denies that his brother played any role in the retirement of these officials, and confirms that the process was constitutional. Miret is a revered figure in Cuba, a participant in the Moncada attack who later joined Fidel, Raúl and Che Guevara on the historic Granma expedition from Mexico. The men disembarked in Cuba in December 1956 and, after taking refuge in the Sierra Maestra, launched the revolutionary struggle, the 26th of July Movement. Three years later, the movement succeeded in toppling the Batista dictatorship.

Speculating on the internal dynamics of the Cuban government is a favorite pastime of the Western media, which never reports any changes as "necessary" or "important," and often times simply ignores them. In the Spanish daily *El País*, Carmen Muñoz speculates on the "mysterious" exits of Miret and Cienfuegos. She cites *The Economist*: "Deciphering the internal machinations of the Cuban regime is comparable to the Kremlinology en vogue before the fall of the USSR" (Muñoz, 2009, March 8). In an article titled "In Cuba, Change Means More of the Same, with control at the Top," Ian Urbina of *The New York Times* writes that under Raúl Castro "politics and decision-making are likely to remain as centralized and tightly controlled as they were under his brother" (*The New York Times*, 2009, April 5). The article further notes: "On the streets of Havana, the capital, people seem to care less about the politics of the shakeup than whether the changes will make any difference in their lives."

TOWARD A MORE RATIONAL POLICY

A November 28, 2008 editorial in *The New York Times* laments the diminished, "extremely sour" relations between the United States and Latin America during the Bush years. Barack Obama, the editorial suggests, should offer greater aid to the region, reconsider U.S. policy toward Cuba, and lift the embargo as well as restrictions on travel and remittances. The United States, moreover, should support internal reforms in Cuba, and "test the intentions" of Raúl Castro. The editorial advocates renewed dialogue with regional leaders on anti-drug, immigration and energy policy, as well economic integration and measures to protect the rights of immigrants. Days earlier, another editorial condemned the murder of an Ecuadorian youth in New York by a white gang whose pastime, they confessed, was "hunting Latinos." It's the latest manifestation of racism against immigrants, the article concludes (*The New York Times*, 2008, November 28).

Upon taking office, a wide range of individuals and groups, including the Council on Foreign Relations and Brookings Institution, the political scientist and economist Francis Fukuyama, congressional leaders of both parties, high-ranking military officials and business associations, call on President Obama to rethink U.S. foreign policy, and prioritize strengthening relations with Latin America, opening dialogue with Cuba, and wholesale immigration reform.

Even within the ardently anti-Castro Cuban-American community, there appears to be a mood shift taking place. According to a poll conducted by the University of Florida, 55% support ending the embargo, and 65% would like to see Washington reestablish formal relations with Havana (Ballvé, 2008, December 30).

In January 2009, the Secretary General of the OAS, José Miguel Insulza, expresses hope that the new American president will work towards building a consensus on certain thorny issues, such as the reinstatement of Cuba; he declares obsolete the 1962 resolution asserting that the Cuban government's Marxist-Leninist orientation was "incompatible" with the "principles and objectives" of the inter-American system (*AFP*, *DPA*, & *Reuters*, 2009, January 22). Of course, the brutal dictatorships sprouting up throughout the region during those years were not only compatible with Washington's values, but worthy of its praise and assistance.

According to Wayne Smith, the chief of the U.S. Interests Section in Havana from 1979 to 1982, the economic embargo has failed and is counterproductive, and lacks coherence and international support (*AFP*, *DPA*, & *Reuters*, 2009, January 22). American institutions such as the Business Roundtable, National Retail Federation, U.S. Chamber of Commerce and agricultural interest groups advocate opening up to Cuba. The embargo, however, is sustained through a complex tangle of legislation, of which the most far-reaching and punitive is the Helms-Burton Act. Congressional action would be required to lift all the sanctions, and influential congressional Republicans as well as conservative and anti-Castro groups consistently lobby against any legislative reversal of the status quo. The Cuban government, moreover, fears Washington would attempt to impose unacceptable conditions in exchange for lifting the embargo.

In February 2009, Richard Lugar, the influential Republican senator and his party's leader in the Senate Foreign Relations Committee, adds his voice to the chorus of those calling for a thawing of relations with Cuba, and greater attention to Latin America as a whole. The senior senator suggests that the recent presidential changes in the U.S. and Cuba could present an opportunity to thaw relations between the countries. Despite acknowledging that the embargo has failed to "bring democracy to the island," and provided a scapegoat for the Cuban government to "mask its economic failures," and complicated relations with key Latin American and European countries, Lugar stops short of calling for the embargo to be lifted. The senator also calls attention to positive developments in Cuba, including its admittance into the Rio Group and Michelle Bachelet's recent state visit to the country (Lugar, 2009, February 23).

Bachelet is not the only foreign head of state to make an official visit to the island; other presidents from Latin America, Central America and the Caribbean have traveled to Cuba for tête-à-têtes with Fidel Castro. Despite belonging to the right-wing PAN, Felipe Calderón accepts Raúl Castro's invitation to visit, and Mauricio Funes, the former FMLN guerrilla announces he will reestablish relations with the island. In October 2008, the Cuban diplomat Pedro Pablo Prada Quintero presents his credentials in San Salvador. That same day Óscar Arias, the president of Costa Rica, announces that he too will reestablish relations between his country and Cuba, which were suspended in 1961, under pressure from the Kennedy administration.

Although the majority of the Cuban-American community in Florida favors improving relations with Cuba and lifting the embargo, Congressional representatives from both parties continue to woo anti-Castro groups to advance their own political fortunes. Despite failing to win the anti-Castro vote, Obama takes Florida in the 2008 election, which analysts believe could allow the incoming president some leeway in defining an independent Cuban policy.

President Obama's first meeting with Latin American heads of state occurs during The Fifth Summit of the Americas, held in Trinidad and Tobago in April 2009. Cuba is excluded from the summit; all present call for a lifting of the embargo. In his speech, Obama declares that he is willing to work toward a fresh start with Cuba, and open dialogue with the Cuban government on a host of topics, including democracy and the hemispheric defense of human rights. The road ahead, he concedes, is a long one, but cites steps already taken, such as the reversal of restrictions on remittances and travel to the island, both of which were enforced by the previous administration. Those measures, however, only benefit Cuban-Americans and their relatives on the island. Since embarking on his presidential campaign, Obama has consistently professed his intention to continue the embargo. His rhetoric regarding Cuba is essentially the same as his predecessor's. According to Fidel Castro, his pleas for "democratic reform" amount to opening the door to capitalism.

There are many calls during this period for policy reversals regarding Cuba. In his first encounter with Obama, in Trinidad and Tobago, Hugo Chávez lets the American leader know—though without any hint of confrontation—that he opposes Cuba's exclusion from the OAS, as well as the economic embargo. The OAS General Assembly, in May of this year, annuls the resolution that suspended Cuba nearly half a century earlier. Cuba, however, has no interest in rejoining the organization. Hillary Clinton, then the U.S. Secretary of State, attempts to impose conditions for Cuba's reinstatement, but fails to garner the support necessary.

In Trinidad and Tobago, Obama expresses his willingness to engage Washington's longstanding adversary; Raúl Castro has repeatedly articulated the same desire, to openly and respectfully, without any preconditions, dialogue on any topic. A year later, however, substantive talks are yet to materialize. The "historic conflict," as Raúl characterizes the embargo, lives on. In December, Obama extends the sanctions for another year, citing national security concerns.

Nevertheless, the Obama administration maintains contact with Havana. High-ranking U.S. officials travel to Havana to meet with members of the government as well as dissidents; still, "nothing's doing," according to Cuban officials (*DPA*, 2009, October 1). The United States Interests Section hosts grand receptions in the Swiss Embassy, inviting the most distinguished representatives of Cuban arts and culture (invitations are not extended to dissidents, as they had been during the Bush years) and all accept, whereas during the Bush years the same invitations were routinely declined. During the last Art Biennial in Havana, thirty American artists are given the opportunity to showcase their work, and Cuban artists and intellectuals, invited to the U.S. by universities and other institutions, once again receive entry visas into the country. This can be seen a polite gesture; it does not go beyond that.

THE STORY CONTINUES

Washington's tone towards Cuba once again sharpens. In grandiloquent rhetoric Secretary of State Clinton accuses the Cuban government of repressing the opposition and violating human rights, and announces that the U.S. will continue to apply pressure until all prisoners of conscience are released. Cuba also hardens. In December 2009, at an ALBA summit held in Havana, Raúl Castro denounces the bilateral agreement granting the U.S. access to seven Colombian bases for ten years (with the possibility of future renewals) as a hegemonic act of aggression against the entire region (Arreola, 2009, December 14).

As the Obama administration takes over in Washington, change is in the air. In business as well as political circles there is a desire for new directions, for the embargo to come to an end. One year later, however, the headiness and optimism have subsided, and relations return to the tense norm of the past half-century. President Obama has shown little interest in moving closer to Latin America. His promises of change appear to have been nothing more than pretty sound bites. No progress has been achieved; on the contrary, many have come to see the policies of this new administration as no different from those of the previous one.

Despite its obvious failure to alter Cuba's course, Obama continues to wield the economic embargo as leverage against the Castro regime, a policy that has proven to be as punitive as it is petty. American agents, like bloodhounds, crisscross the globe intent on sabotaging any agreements Cuba reaches with other countries. Over the years congress passes a bevy of legislation strengthening the embargo, of which the harshest and most controversial is the Cuban Liberty and Democratic Solidarity Act, known as the Helms-Burton Act. Bill Clinton imposes sanctions to punish Cuba for shooting down two Cessna aircrafts belonging to the anti-Castro Brothers to the Rescue organization. José Basulto, the head of the organization, commissions planes to drop counterrevolutionary leaflets over the island. Basulto claims that the incident occurred over international waters. The Cuban government, however, insists it took place over Cuban territory and warns the United States that it will shoot down any aircraft violating its airspace.

European allies of the U.S. question the Helms-Burton Act for its extraterritorial application of U.S. legislation over international trade, and its attempt to restrict bilateral trade between other countries. They threaten to bring the matter before the International Court of Justice. Though Washington refuses to repeal or modify the law, year after year it postpones implementation of the provisions that upset its European allies, and the status quo continues.

A favorable view of Barack Obama is present at all levels

of Cuban society. The tone of Washington's rhetoric has changed, spawning a renewed sense of hope. "We are in no rush," proclaims Raúl Castro, "we are not desperate." He warns, however, against burgeoning expectations around the world. Just like his White House predecessors, Obama calls for "democratic reforms" and the release of imprisoned "dissidents." In a fiery speech before the National Assembly of People's Power, Raúl denounces covert actions against his government. Days earlier, Alan Gross, a 62-year-old employee of Development Alternatives Inc., a contractor collaborating with the U.S. Agency for International Development (USAID), was arrested for distributing satellite phones and computer equipment on the island without the required permit—a "grave" infraction, in the eyes of the Cuban government, which contends Gross was carrying out the "subversive politics" of the United States (Arreola, 2009, December 21). Washington objects to the arrest and accuses Raúl's government of "continuing the hard line of Fidel, curbing fundamental liberties and suppressing opposition, just as before." To negotiate Gross's release, former U.S. Ambassador to the UN Bill Richardson travels to Havana, where authorities propose an exchange for five Cubans who have spent eleven years in U.S. federal prisons, accused of espionage. Richardson rejects the proposed swap, stating that they represent different cases (*AFP*, *DPA*, and *Reuters*, 2010, August 27).

In a December 2009 report titled "In Cuba, Hopeful Tenor Toward Obama Is Ebbing," Marc Lacey, *The New York Times* correspondent in Havana, highlights the growing tension between the two governments: the Cuban authorities, including Fidel, are once again firing criticism at the United States. Wayne Smith, the former chief of the U.S. Interests section in Havana, claims that these barbs "do not help" (*The New York Times*, 2009, December 31). Hillary Clinton is next to ratchet up the tension. In a speech at Georgetown University, she accuses the Cuban government of not wanting to make the changes that the people deserve. She announces that she will continue to apply pressure on the Cuban regime until it ends the repression, and will support whoever works for a "change within the society"—in other words, opponents of the Castro regime. Nevertheless, Raúl reiterates his willingness to "respectfully" dialogue with the United States (Arreola, 2009, December 21).

In July 2010, Cuba releases 52 political prisoners and announces more will follow. This gesture is the result of negotiations between Raúl Castro, the Catholic Church, and Spain's Ministry of Foreign Affairs. The Spanish foreign minister hails the development, stating that it could motivate the U.S. to lift the embargo. Cuba considers "dissidents" to be American agents, financed and supported by Washington to wage war through the media against the Castro government. During a hunger strike one dissident dies, unleashing the anti-Castro wrath of the Western media. According to human rights organizations, there are 167 political prisoners on the island.

In its campaign to stamp out the Revolution, under President

Obama the State Department continues the hostile treatment of Cuba, maintaining the country on its list of state sponsors of terrorism, while classifying the Castro government among the worst human rights violators in the world. The news that Fidel Castro admitted that "the Cuban model doesn't even work for us anymore," makes headlines in the Western media. Fidel retorts, "My answer meant exactly the opposite of how the American journalists interpreted it." Jeffrey Goldberg, who interviewed the former leader for The Atlantic, nonetheless insists, "That is what he said." Fidel's subsequent acknowledgement that he was accurately quoted (*AFP* and *Notimex*, 2010, September 12) sets off a flurry of commentary: Will Cuba abandon the communist model? Will capitalism be allowed to enter the island? Or was it just the lapsus linguae of the aging leader?

After two years in office, President Obama has not brought about any meaningful changes to U.S.-Cuba relations. He has carried on the same policies as his predecessors with the same disappointing results.

4

Leaders of the New Left

THEY ARE THE NEW LEFT

Elected to office with strong support from the middle and working classes, from popular and indigenous movements and leftist political parties, they set forth to free their countries from the shackles of American power. The leaders of the New Left declare their independence, create mechanisms for consolidating regional integration, diversify their roster of trade partners, and establish new political and economic alliances with countries from other regions, such as China, Russia, and Iran. They envision a unified Latin America that acts as a formidable bloc on the world stage. Their governments adopt measures that diminish American influence in the region: trade with the super power decreases 50%. The U.S. ceases to be the region's primary trade partner. Some governments repay their debts to the IMF, others renegotiate with the World Bank, ending loan agreements that saddle them with onerous conditions.

The new wave of Latin American leaders is not part of the economic, social and political elite that for centuries has monopolized power in their countries. For the most part, they are ordinary people of the middle class or even humbler origins who possess direct knowledge of the poverty, inequality and social exclusion holding the region down. Upon gaining power, their foremost commitment is to the most disadvantaged sectors of society. They look to reduce poverty, and gaping social and economic inequality. They dream of egalitarian societies that offer greater opportunities for all.

Western critics refer to these new heads of state, pejoratively, as "populist"; they are portrayed as charlatans posing as revolutionaries, demagogues dishing out lofty promises they could never keep. Among the leaders of the New Left are self-described Christians, such as Rafael Correa and Fernando Lugo, a former Catholic bishop and proponent of liberation theology who enters politics in spite of Vatican objections. Hugo Chávez asks the Venezuelan clergy to study the scriptures in search of socialist messages in Christ's own words, but the leading prelates object and brand him a Marxist.

In turbulent economic and political times, marked by broad disillusionment with the political establishment, the candidacies of leftist leaders gain traction. The people support leaders who, like themselves, come from humble origins. "He's one of ours," goes the campaign slogan of Lula da Silva, the Brazilian labor leader and founder of the Worker's Party.

The former colonel Hugo Chávez channels the growing disenchantment with President Carlos Andrés Pérez, whose administration is plagued by allegations of corruption, as well as public fatigue with the traditional Democratic Action and Copei parties and their unpopular neoliberal agendas. When Chávez is released from prison in 1994, following his failed coup attempt, he founds the Fifth Republic Movement (MVR) and enters the political fray. In 1998, he is elected president, and in subsequent electoral contests triumphs again and again. In Brazil, the sputtering economic situation brought on by President Fernando Henrique Cardoso's neoliberal programs—including the privatization of public utilities and state-run industries—breeds popular discontent. The candidacy of Lula da Silva, a leader of the metalworker's union, surges. Riding the support of the working class he is elected president in 2002.

The neoliberal disaster reaches its nadir in Argentina between 1999 and 2002. The IMF orders a devaluation; the peso plummets. To compensate for its fall, many retailers drastically increase prices of basic food staples, and the economy enters a tailspin. Banks freeze private accounts, dollar-denominated debts become unserviceable, bankruptcies in retail and manufacturing sectors are declared one after another, and millions lose their jobs. Angry mobs take to the streets, loot stores and warehouses, smash windows. Chaos grips the nation. President Fernando de la Rúa resigns; desperation, violence and anarchy ensue. In the years leading up this financial melt-down, the IMF had held Argentina up as a model of neoliber-alism's virtues. Now, unable to service its mounting external obligations, the national government defaults. After de la Rúa's resignation, the Legislative Assembly appoints Eduardo Duhalde interim president until order can be restored and new elections held. A year later, Néstor Kirchner, a center-left governor from the Justicialist Party, succeeds him.

In Bolivia and Ecuador, dramatic measures imposed by the World Bank and IMF deepen poverty and lead to massive protests. The indigenous leader Evo Morales and the left-wing economist Rafael Correa ride a wave of popular disgust to the presidencies of their respective countries. In Uruguay, a precarious socioeconomic situation brought about by struc-tural reforms pushed by the IMF and World Bank contribute to the victory of the leftist Tabaré Vázquez, as well as ref-erendums on the privatization of state enterprises and water resources (Barrett, Chávez, Rodríguez-Garavito, 2008: 9-10, 239).

The goals of the Bolivarian Revolution in Venezuela, Cor-rea's Citizens' Revolution in Ecuador, and Morales's Social Revolution in Bolivia—and the new constitutions they draft—is nothing less ambitious than the rebirth of nation-hood on more equitable and just foundations, responding to the needs of the people, and defending national sovereignty and natural resources, especially petroleum and natural gas, from foreign corporations. These leaders believe a 21st century socialism offers the best path forward. The new constitutions recognize both indigenous rights and those of the working class; they codify equality irrespective of class, race, sex or religion, and recognize the political rights of groups that were previously excluded; they grant the state greater control over the national economy, confer enhanced powers to the executive branch and permit reelection to consecutive terms. The new governments are plebiscitary: the will of the people becomes the law of the land through national referendums that bypass legislative bodies. In the disarray left behind by discredited political parties, parliaments and supreme courts, the masses grow disillusioned with liberal democracy, and its failure to improve the socioeconomic lot of the marginalized classes. They turn to national leaders with heightened powers: modern-day caudillos.

"Few times in Latin America has there been such ideological convergence among the presidents of the so-called 'New Left,' who herald a socialism for the 21st century," declares Pablo Dávalos, of the Latin American Council of Social Sciences (CLACSO) (Dávalos, 2007, February 9). In 2008, Lula da Silva applauds the ascent of an African-American to the White House, which he sees as evidence of the profound change sweeping the world. "Latin America is in the midst of an extraordinary period that we of the left never had before, with movements committed to the poorest segments of society coming to power in so many countries" (*AP*, 2008, November 1). Mark Weisbrot, co-director of the Center for

Economic and Policy Research, argues that the trend is not merely coincidental, as this entire new generation of leaders is critical of the United States. These leaders, Weisbrot points out, concur when Lula speaks of the "abject failure" of the economic and political agenda of Washington—and its supplicant institutions—in Latin America, and nod their heads at the strident criticisms leveled by Hugo Chávez against President Bush and U.S. foreign policy in the region (Weisbrot, 2007, October 31).

WITH AND WITHOUT OBAMA

When Obama takes power in January 2009, leftist leaders govern the majority of Latin American countries. A few months earlier, Evo Morales expelled U.S. Ambassador Philip Goldberg for meddling in the internal affairs of Bolivia, supporting the separatist opposition and conspiring against his government. In a show of solidarity, Hugo Chávez also expelled the American ambassador from Caracas. For the same reasons, both leaders expel the DEA and its agents from their respective countries. In Ecuador, Rafael Correa allows the agreement granting the U.S. access to the Manta military base to expire, and accuses American petroleum companies of environmental damage, contractual breaches, and violating national laws.

Despite their political differences, Lula maintains a healthy but distant relationship with the Bush administration. Though he holds Barack Obama in higher regard, they too differ on certain policy issues; Lula is critical of the 2009 military agreement granting the U.S. access to Colombian military bases, citing its potential to destabilize the region; he also laments the American president's unfortunate handling of the military coup in Honduras, breaking the regional consensus to support the new regime. He also questions his Cuban policy, and opposes the embargo. Lula, Chávez and Morales all defend Iran's right to develop nuclear capabilities for peaceful ends and maintain good relations with the Iranian President Mahmoud Ahmadinejad, and oppose the economic sanctions the United States seeks to impose if the country refuses to halt its nuclear program. Several Latin American leaders clash with Washington over this heated issue.

LULA SUPERSTAR

Spanning some 8.5 million km2, its population approaching 200 million, Brazil is the continental giant, the region's largest economy—the first Latin American power. Though it does not aspire to be a military power, Brazil's armed forces rank among the fifteen largest in the world. The size of its military is comparable to that of Germany (Gratius, 2008, October 21); it is the primary exporter of combat planes and weapons to the rest of the region.

Lula transforms the Brazilian economy, elevating it among the ten largest in the world. The European Union acknowledges Brazil's advances; in 2007, the Ministerial Council of the Organisation for Economic Co-operation and Development (OECD) decides to increase cooperation with the Latin American giant. Brazil takes part in the economic conclaves of the great powers, which value its input as a representative of the agricultural economies of the developing world. With French support, Brazil seeks permanent membership on the UN Security Council (Perez, 2007, December 29); President Sarkozy argues for the necessity of admitting Brazil to this council (*BBC Mundo*, 2008, September 23).

Lula is admired within Brazil and around the world for his strong but compassionate leadership, and the soundness of his ideological convictions. He is the New Left's most universally appealing figure. Under his leadership, Brazil's influence around the world grows. One of Lula's priorities is integrating Latin America into a unified bloc. He promotes trade between countries in the region: his first year in office registers a 250% increase. He works to strengthen continental unity via the creation of regional bodies such as UNASUR and the Council of South American Defense, while simultaneously broadening Brazil's relations with Russia, China, and Arab nations, among others; he visits and signs cooperation agreements with 17 African countries; he makes official state visits to sixty countries and hosts dozens of foreign heads of state in Brasilia. He promotes the creation of the G3, along with India and South Africa, which increases the availability of generic drugs to disadvantaged community; together with Russia, India and China, Brazil forms a group of emerging economic powers known as BRIC. Along with Hugo Chávez and Cristina Kirchner, Lula agrees to eliminate the dollar from bilateral trade between their countries, a first step toward regional monetary integration. During his first term in office Brazilian exports double.

Brazil hosts the first Summit of South American-Arab Countries, which results in numerous agreements between Mercosur and Persian Gulf countries, including for the exportation of petroleum and its derivatives. After a condemnation of the Palestinian occupation in the summit's final declaration rankles the Israeli government, Lula dispatches his skillful foreign minister, Celso Amorim, to smooth things over in Tel Aviv, and also work out some cooperation agreements (*BBC Mundo*, 2008, September 23).

Despite the undeniable socioeconomic progress made under Lula, throughout his terms in office the president finds himself a frequent target of the Brazilian left. The Worker's Party is criticized for supporting neoliberal initiatives in congress, abandoning its socialist roots, and for the far-reaching bribery scandal involving many members of the party and government. Critics also pounce on the governing party's inability to deliver the agrarian reform it promised, and criticize the pension scheme passed by congress reducing public sector wages. The President's "Zero Hunger" program is also attacked for being too limited in scope, dismissed by some as charity of the cynical variety.

Nonetheless, 80% of the country approves of his administration's performance, one of the highest and steadiest such rates in the world. Despite the devastating worldwide consequences of the 2008 financial crisis, the majority of Brazilians believe they are in a stronger economic position with Lula as president. Lula adopts measures to mitigate the impact of the crisis: he stimulates growth and consumption, broadens access to credit from state banks, and requires private banks to do their part as well. Yet demand for Brazilian products, one of the driving forces behind Brazil's superb pre-crisis growth, is affected, and the national euphoria set off by the discovery of vast offshore petroleum reserves dampens as the price of crude oil drops. In December, at a roundtable sponsored by the British Chamber of Commerce in São Paulo, panelists express a "cautious optimism" regarding the Brazilian economy, citing its track record of navigating through past crises with aplomb (Fitzpatrick, 2008, December 22).

Despite his progressive views, and frequent criticisms of their policies, the Bush administration views Lula as a friend and, in January 2009, Barack Obama, invites him to Washington; the recently inaugurated president wants his opinion on the financial crisis prior to the G20 Summit in London. Brazil is a member of the G20. Lula speaks at length about the region and broaches the subject of Venezuela, and the hostility the Bush administration directed toward Hugo Chávez. When the Venezuelan president threatens to boycott the Fifth Summit of the Americas in protest of Cuba's exclusion, and the economic embargo, Obama calls Lula to enlist his help; the summit, to be held in Trinidad and Tobago, will be his first encounter with Latin America's heads of state, and he hopes to get off on the right foot.

LULA IN THE WORLD

Lula da Silva is the seventh child born to a poor family. As a boy shining shoes in the street, he becomes acquainted with the twin evils of poverty and social injustice. He drops out of school in the fourth grade to help his family out financially, and at fourteen lands his first job in a copper-processing plant as a lathe operator. At 19, he becomes involved with the Worker's Union. In 1964, President João Goulart is overthrown by a military coup. The ensuing dictatorship, which would last twenty years, suppresses union activity; as a labor leader Lula is radicalized. In 1975, he is elected president of a steel worker's union, which is very active in cities where the automobile industry—including Ford, Volkswagen, Mercedes Benz, and Toyota—operates. Throughout the 1970's Lula organizes union activities, including massive strikes, and is even imprisoned for a month (Ceccato, 2005, December 31).

Along with other labor leaders, left-wing intellectuals and academics, Trotskyites, and theorists of liberation theology, in 1970 Lula helps found the Worker's Party (PT), which becomes the first socialist party to qualify as a true political force in Brazil. Lula is also a founder of Unified Workers' Central (1983), a national trade union center, and for several years serves as its president. In 1984, Lula and the PT join the movement calling for direct presidential elections, which at the time are carried out by the Electoral Council, an institution created by the military that operates in conjunction with the Senate, Chamber of Deputies and representatives of state congresses. Under the 1967 constitution, drafted by the military command, this council "elects" the president, who always comes from the ranks of retired officers.

Throughout the dictatorship years, as Lula repeatedly clashes with the military authorities, his political aspirations grow. In 1982, he declares his candidacy for the São Paulo governorship, but falls short in the election. In 1986, he is voted into congress on the PT ticket and, following the end of military rule, collaborates in drafting the new constitution. Though he helps secure protections of workers rights, Lula fails to gain enough support for land redistribution, and ultimately refuses to sign the constitution. In 1989, he launches an unsuccessful bid for the presidency. In 1990, he opts against seeking congressional reelection in order to dedicate himself to building up the PT around the country. In 1994 and 1998 he again runs for the presidency, falling short both times.

Like the Southern Cone countries (Argentina, Chile, and Uruguay), by the 1980's the Brazilian military regime—enmeshed in corruption and embezzlement scandals, while the country sputters through an economic downturn—has been discredited beyond repair in the public's eye. The 1985 presidential elections are controlled, as usual, by the Electoral Council, but for the first time a civilian and opposition candidate, Tancredo Neves, emerges victorious.

Though democracy has returned to Brazil, its standard bearer dies from illness before he can take the oath of office, and in his place José Sarney assumes the presidency. Following widespread protest, the beleaguered military leaders agree to hold direct democratic elections in 1989. Fernando Collor de Melo, a promising young conservative, comes out on top, but after serving just two years is brought down by accusations, leveled by his own brother, of corruption, illicit enrichment, and matrimonial infidelity committed in the presidential palace. Despite these ups and downs, Brazil continues along the path of democratization.

Lula enjoys strong support among workers, labor leaders and the middle class, but his leftist leanings, defense of socialism and critiques of the capitalist system and globalization, cause the country's elite to distrust him. During the 2002 presidential campaign, the IMF warns all the candidates, including Lula, that it will change its policy towards Brazil should the new president break with Cardoso's economic program. Influential media organizations demonize the PT candidate and, facing the likely prospect of his election, the stock market fluctuates wildly. An effective advertising campaign, however, softens the PT candidate's leftist image. Meanwhile, widespread disenchantment with centrist and conservative parties catapults Lula, a true champion of the working class, to the front of the pack. On October 27, 2002, in the second round of voting, Lula defeats the conservative social democrat José Serra. He is sworn into office on January 1, 2003.

HIS GOVERNMENT

Millions of working-class citizens enthusiastically welcome Lula in Brasilia. "He is one of ours," after all, was his campaign slogan. They admire his progressive ideals; tens of thousands celebrate his anti-globalization stance at the 2003 World Social Forum, and delegates from the developing world applaud his role in shaping the outcome of the 2003 WTO summit in Cancún, where Lula rails against the subsidies wealthy governments grant to their agricultural sectors, which make it difficult for products from the Third World to compete; he assembles a group of twenty developing countries to defeat the agreement at the WTO. But despite his impeccable leftist credentials, as president Lula's economic policies are not as progressive as many of his supporters had hoped. Lula continues his predecessor's neoliberal programs, and hands over the reigns of macroeconomic institutions, such as the Central Bank, to business leaders connected to Wall Street. Upon learning that Brazil's economy and monetary policy will be steered by friendly figures, the IMF president lavishes Lula with praise (Chossudovsky, 2003, April 25). The Landless Workers' Movement, the largest and most radical social movement formed by the rural poor, and other progressive groups, express their disappointment with the president's political evolution.

The priority of Lula's domestic agenda is lifting up the most disadvantaged sectors of society and yet, despite a considerable decline in poverty, many former supporters reproach the president and his party for abandoning socialism. Lula responds: "I am no longer of the age to be of the Left. White hair and responsibility call for balance, and to evolve means moving from the Left toward social democracy. A person who is of the Left has problems, just as a young man has problems." They accuse him of being ashamed of his Marxist past after he declares: "I am not a Marxist, I am a metalworker." When posed a question about Lula and the left, José Saramago, the 1998 Nobel Laureate in Literature, laments the emergence of "Lula mutants." "It's time to shout," he says, "the Left has ceased to be the Left. We used to say that the Right was stupid, but these days I know nothing stupider than the Left" (Villavicencio, 2008, October 8).

Lula's approach to domestic policy is both measured and pragmatic. Rather than radical upheaval he pursues a more moderate path toward reform. His highest priorities are social welfare programs and raising the minimum wage, which will benefit tens of millions of impoverished Brazilians who constitute around 30% of the total population. Lula launches the "Zero Hunger" campaign to combat malnutrition, the greatest ill his country faces. He strengthens Cardoso's social programs, works to improve public health, ensures underprivileged populations have access to potable water, bans child labor, and implements Bolsa Familia, a program that rewards poor families with direct cash transfers provided they maintain children under fifteen in school, and comply with a set of vaccination requirements.

Lula pledges to repay the foreign debt, but only after conducting rigorous audits. Realizing the potential for conflict with the United States, World Bank and IMF—the country's principle foreign creditors—the financial sector grows anxious. Lula promotes joint ventures between the public and private sectors to start up new businesses and improve services to the most vulnerable members of society. During his first term in office, trade grows in spectacular fashion, flipping previous deficits into surpluses. In 2004, the surplus reaches 29 billion dollars, a result of growing demand for Brazilian goods. Lula turns speculative into investment capital. Despite having risen to 15 billion dollars by December 2005, Lula repays Brazil's entire IMF debt two years ahead of schedule, freeing the country from that institution's onerous demands.

Throughout his first term in office Lula's government is dogged by allegations that his party orchestrated a monthly payoff scheme to members of the congressional opposition for their support of its political agenda. The illicit funds are said to originate from both state enterprises and private financial institutions. Forty members of the government are implicated, including high-ranking PT officials and many legislators are removed from their congressional seats or forced to resign. Several aids to Lula also resign (Evenas, 2005, August 1). Additional accusations of illegal campaign contributions from Cuba and the FARC surface. Cuba denies the charges. In response to the scandal, Lula dismisses his three highest-ranking campaign officials. Despite evidence that the wrongdoing took place behind his back, Lula's public image takes a beating.

Brazil is the world's largest producer and exporter of ethanol, a petroleum substitute derived from sugar cane and other agricultural products. Ethanol production dates back to the 1970's, and by 2008 more than two-thirds of the vehicles in the country run on ethanol. There is, however, considerable opposition to this alternative source of fuel; an international campaign alleges that ethanol production leads to food shortages, the prices of sugar, corn and wheat to increase, and uses up land that could otherwise be allocated for food cultivation. The campaign's slogan is: "Corn for food not fuel." Lula considers the opposition unfounded: sugar cane production has risen 50%, its prices remain low in the world market, and no deforestation has occurred to clear the way for its cultivation. Environmentalists, however, point out that some cattle raisers sell their lands [to whom?] and relocate their livestock to the Amazon, where land is inexpensive, and it is easy to fell trees. To Lula, the anti-ethanol movement appears totally submissive to the interests of sugar exporters: "Just when Brazil steps onto the world stage, and not as a minor player but as a leader in agricultural production, people began to feel uncomfortable, very uncomfortable," he laments (Downie, 2008, May 5). The governments of Cuba and Venezuela oppose the production of ethanol on the same grounds, and on occasion clash with Brazil.

While the 2002 election is held during a period of economic stagnation, the next presidential contest, in 2006, takes place at the height of an economic bonanza. Garnering widespread support across the political and socioeconomic spectrum, Lula is reelected with 60% of the popular vote, the highest percentage ever attained in Brazil. Poverty has decreased 19%, the minimum wage raised, and millions of new jobs created. In his inaugural address, Lula pledges to continue combating poverty. After decades amassing foreign debt, Brazil has become a creditor; hard-currency reserves rise to 20 billion dollars, and inflation is the lowest among developing countries (*Newsweek* 2008, December 20). Within the party establishment there is talk of calling a constituent assembly, or plebiscite, to enable a third presidential term (Sola, 2008: 137). Lula claims to have no interest in another term, but admits he would like a say in selecting the party's candidate to succeed him.

BENEDICT IN BRAZIL

Home to more Catholics than any country in the world, Brazil has received the most papal visits in Latin America. Pope John Paul II alone makes four trips (in 1980, 1982, 1991, and 1997) and each time is greeted by enthusiastic throngs. In the 1960's, under the repressive dictatorship of Humberto Castelo Branco, Liberation Theology, a movement led by liberal prelates with the encouragement of Pope John XXIII, thrives. During the Second Vatican Council, the pontiff urges the clergy to work on behalf of the poor and oppressed. Theorists of liberation theology assimilate Marxist views on poverty and social justice, and their teachings spread throughout many of the poorest countries in the region, some of which are ruled by repressive military regimes.

Pope John Paul II disdains liberation theology's debt to Marxism, and views the movement as a threat to the faith; he charges Cardinal Joseph Ratzinger—the future Pope Benedict XVI—then Prefect of the Sacred Congregation for the Doctrine of the Faith (formerly the Supreme Sacred Congregation of the Roman and Universal Inquisition) with the task of turning back the tide. Ratzinger goes on the offensive against the movement's leading exponents, whom he claims represent a "fundamental threat" to the Church. He summons many prominent figures to Rome, and imposes orders of penitential silence on several, effectively barring them from the ministry.

On May 9, 2007, Benedict XVI arrives in São Paulo for a five-day pastoral visit. It marks his first visit to Latin America as pope. Perhaps the pontiff is surprised, *The New York Times* suggests, that despite the decades-long crackdown liberation theology is still alive in Brazil, and embraced not only be the people, but even by the current government, with which it shares a common goal of aiding the poor and ameliorating socioeconomic distress. In Brazil there are some 80,000 basic ecclesial communities ("base communities") and more than a million study groups meet to read the bible through the prism of liberation theology (*The New York Times*, 2007, May 7).

The papal visit is scheduled to coincide with the Fifth General Conference of the Latin American Episcopal Council

(CELAM) in Aparecida, 160 miles from São Paulo. It is the first CELAM conference in fifteen years. At previous editions, held in Medellín (1968) and Puebla (1979), the bishops defended progressive ideals censored by the Vatican. The central theme of the fifth conference is the future of the Church, which is threatened by the growth of other Christian faiths in historically Catholic strongholds, as well as the decline in seminarians entering the ministry. Other topics include the perennial problems of hunger, poverty and social inequality. Analysts predict conflicts will arise between the 162 bishops in attendance, who hold a wide range of views on the role, and future, of the Church. Some believe the practice of celibacy in the priesthood should be done away with, a notion the majority refuse to even consider. In his opening address, Pope Benedict criticizes the Marxism system: "When Marxism finds a path into government, it leaves behind a sad legacy not only of economic, social and environmental destruction, but also of the agonizing destruction of the human spirit." He is also critical of capitalism's negative byproducts (*The New York Times*, 2007, May 7).

On May 11, Lula meets with the Pope in São Paulo, an encounter the Brazilian press describes as replete with smiles and head nods but also subtle differences of opinion. According to official sources, when the Pope asks President Lula to sign a concordat mandating the inclusion of Catholic teachings in the core public school curriculum, Lula politely informs him that the constitution of Brazil, a secular country, guarantees freedom of all religions. The Pope also asks for assurances that Catholic priests will granted access to indigenous reserves and national parks. The president, however, is not so keen on the idea. A government official remarks that the presence of clergymen in remote regions of the Amazon is not particularly appealing; on the contrary, it could prove a nuisance.

Though Brazilians give a warm welcome to the new pontiff, his greeting is not as exuberant as those lavished upon Pope John Paul II, despite the Church's undeniable decline in influence over the course of his papacy. The crowds turning out are less voluminous than in years past. They are not fully sold on the German pope; many disapprove of his campaigns against liberation theology, a movement so empowering to the poor, and deplore the punitive measures that were imposed upon its leaders.

The number of Catholics in Brazil has declined by two-thirds. About half the country is of African descent, the largest black population outside of Africa, many of whom preserve their traditional belief systems and practice syncretized Afro-American religions, in which Catholic saints are sometimes represented as African deities. For instance, Saint Barbara corresponds to Shango, the Virgin Mary to Yemanja and the Holy Child of Atocha to Elegua, the Road Opener. Catholicism in Brazil, as in other Latin American countries, is often practiced "informally." Many people, even those who seldom attend mass, believe in God and devote themselves to a particular saint. Pope Benedict's journey to Brazil is not exactly a smashing success.

LULA'S FOREIGN POLICY

Lula sets out to solidify Brazilian leadership in the region and play a larger role on the world stage. Along with Hugo Chávez, he is a leading proponent of South American integration, a movement aiming to reduce American influence. Even so, President Bush considers Lula friend and ally. A few days before the 2008 presidential election, Lula declares, "In the same way that Brazil elected a metalworker, Bolivia an indigenous man, Venezuela Chávez, and Paraguay a bishop, it would be remarkable if in the world's largest economy a black man is elected president" (*AP*, 2008, November 1).

In 1985, Brazil and Argentina agree to a bilateral program for a free trade area, which Uruguay and Paraguay subsequently join; in 1991, the pact is christened Mercosur. The Mercosur countries enter an association with the Andean Community of Nations (CAN); in 2006, Venezuela joins Mercosur. Some economists view the agreement as a counterweight to the proposed FTAA, which crumbles during the Fourth Summit of the Americas. In January 2008, Hugo Chávez signs the Petrosur treaty with Lula and Néstor Kirchner, with the goal of integrating the national petroleum corporations of the Southern Cone—something akin to a Latin American OPEC.

The Brazilian government is critical of the March 2008 military strike Colombia carries out across the Ecuadorian border without consulting Quito in advance. At the OAS, Lula's foreign minister, Celso Amorim, denounces the operation's potential to "destabalize the region that has enjoyed peace for many decades." Hoping to avert a full-blown regional crisis, he calls on Colombia to come forward with a more "explicit" defense of its conduct (Colitt, March 3, 2008). A couple months later, in May 2008, Lula hosts a summit of twelve South American presidents in Brasilia to address the conflict. He proposes a regional mechanism through which countries can air out their differences. He also argues for finalizing UNASUR, a Chávez proposal intended to facilitate regional dialogue on economic matters, as well as social and cultural development. Furthermore, Lula proposes the creation of the Council of South American Defense, a forum for defense ministers to resolve geopolitical conflicts and work toward a shared vision on regional security. The alliance is not finalized, however, due to resistance put forth by Álvaro Uribe, who calls for a condemnation of all terrorist and guerilla organizations.

Lula continues to push ahead. In December 2008, he brings together 33 nations, with the United States and Canada left out, for the First Latin American and Caribbean Summit in Suaipe, Brazil. It is the final piece of the integration puzzle, and a resounding rejection of Washington's longstanding isolation of Cuba. To ensure their attendance, Lula sends military planes to pick up the presidents of the poorest countries. Raul Castro, though, is the center of attention. Following a half century of isolation, Cuba's participation is welcome to all. In its final declaration the collective commitment to defending national sovereignty is renewed; the right to self-determination free of external threats, aggression or coercive unilateral acts; a more just and equitable world order is called for; reform to the UN that will ensure the democratization of its various bodies, in particular the Security Council; faced with a worldwide economic slowdown, countries are encouraged to strengthen their own regional organizations; and an immediate end to the U.S. embargo of Cuba is called for. Once again, Lula has demonstrated his ability to bring people together, his determination to play an influential role on the world stage, and the indisputable leadership his country exerts in regional affairs. "In the midst of an unprecedented global crisis, our countries have discovered that they are not part of the problem. They are and should be decisive actors in the solution," he declares (*AFP*, 2008, December 18).

The attendance of so many heads of state—with the exception of Colombia and Peru, whose presidents send emissaries in their stead—allows Mercosur, the Rio Group, and UNASUR to convene as well. In a brief session, UNASUR finalizes the creation of the Council of South American Defense. Unlike the obsolete Inter-American Treaty of Reciprocal Assistance (TIAR) of 1947—to which the United States and several Latin American and Caribbean nations are signatories—this agreement contains no clause calling for reciprocal assistance in the event of outside aggression. In the past Washington has paid no mind to the TIAR when its call for reciprocal assistance seemed inconvenient. For instance, that clause is ignored in 1982 when the U.S. supports Margaret Thatcher after Argentina invades the Falkland Islands. In 2002, President Vincente Fox withdraws Mexico from the TIAR, which he considers obsolete. Mexico is the first country to abandon the treaty.

According to Lula, the Council of South American Defense should not be seen as an attempt to substitute the UN Security Council. Its objective is limited to addressing security issues within the region. Many Latin American governments, however, are critical of the veto power held by the five permanent members of the Security Council, which they consider a violation of the principle of equal legal rights among nations. Brazil presses for the democratization of the council, calling for an expansion of the permanent membership, whose ranks it aspires to join. Lula argues that the veto "distorts representation and is an obstacle to the multilateral world we all desire" (Padgett and Downie, 2008, September 25).

In the first decade of the 21st Century, Latin America, for the first time, voices its disapproval of Israel's occupation of Palestinian territories. Lula is critical of the country's UN violations, and the illegal nature of the occupation. In December 2008, when Israel launches an assault on the Gaza Strip, which remains under siege for over a year without an army to defend a population on the brink of collapse, Lula questions why the United States is the only country involved in negotiating a resolution to the conflict when it has been repeatedly shown that American mediation "does not work." He announces that his foreign minister is engaged in discussions with the French and other governments to call an emergency meeting on the conflict. (DPA et al, 2008, December 30). The discussions, however, go nowhere.

THE DWARF GROWS UP

Widely viewed as Latin America's primary interlocutor with the world, Lula is the first head of state from the region Barack Obama invites to the White House. The visit takes place in March 2009. According to media reports, one topic receiving special attention is Brazil's recently discovered offshore oil reserves, which Washington sees as a potential alternative to relying on Venezuelan imports. Lula also addresses Latin American concerns, including tensions between Washington and Caracas, which he offers to mediate. Obama, however, seems determined to continue his predecessor's hard-line.

Lula is treated like a rock star by the American media. In interviews he emphasizes the importance of developing countries contributing to world debates, including the one swirling around the current economic crisis. A G20 member, Brazil is invited to the economic conclaves of the great capitalist powers, where Lula calls for the democratization of the United Nations, and conveys Brazil's desire to become a permanent member of the Security Council. He advocates one or two African nations gaining permanent status as well. When asked by *Newsweek* why he has "remained silent while Chávez destroys democracy" in Venezuela, Lula responds: "Maybe we cannot agree with Venezuelan democracy, but no one can say there is no democracy in Venezuela. [Chávez] has been through five, six elections. I've only had two." When questioned about the exclusion of the United States from the First Latin American and Caribbean Summit, held in December 2008, Brazil's president responds: "We have never had a meeting of just Latin American and Caribbean countries, and it's important to have it without the presence of superpowers. It is a meeting of countries that have the same problems" (Zakaria, 2009, March 21). Obama refers to Lula as the most popular head of state in the world.

In preparation for the Fifth Summit of the Americas, Obama calls Lula to ask for his help. At the summit, to be held in Trinidad and Tobago, Obama will meet Latin America's heads of state for the first time. The encounter is expected to present a number of challenges for the new president, among those a boycott threatened by Hugo Chávez over Cuba's exclusion. Nonetheless, The American president's simplicity, intelligence and cordiality, the underlying warmth in his words and promises prove to be disarming. The Latin American leaders are won over and depart hopeful about what the future holds.

The relationship between Lula and Obama is respectful,

though the Brazilian president is not fully sold on the White House's latest occupant. He maintains an independent foreign policy, often at odds with Washington. For instance, Lula supports Iran's right to develop nuclear programs for peaceful ends. Brazil itself has maintained a nuclear program, dating back to the days of the military regime, approved by the International Atomic Energy Agency (IAEA). The Brazilian constitution bars the use of nuclear energy for military purposes. Lula also opposes the economic sanctions the U.S. threatens to impose on Tehran for not abandoning its nuclear ambitions.

In September 2009, in the wake of revelations that the United States has, through secret negotiations, gained access to seven Colombian bases, Lula expresses concern. The agreement, he claims, represents a destabilizing threat, an obstacle not only to harmonious relations within the region but to the integration movement as a whole. Around the continent alarm and protest are widespread. Although Lula put forth the most vigorous objections to the agreement, in April 2010 the Brazilian leader stuns observers when he too signs a military pact with the United States, to "strengthen"—according to both governments—bilateral relations. The agreement includes technical and educational cooperation, but unlike Colombia Brazil does not cede access to its bases or allow American military personnel to enter the country. Regardless, many experts believe this agreement will prove even more damaging to the region. Among Lula's admirers there is a general feeling of bitterness, anger, and betrayal. A beacon of regional independence, and leader of the integration movement, Brazil, for no apparent reason, has struck a blow to continental unity.

Making Brazil bend to its will is a diplomatic victory for Washington, a power play that serves warning to the rest of the region that the super power will continue to be "master" of its own backyard—and this is only the beginning. Upon signing the military agreement with Colombia, U.S. Ambassador William Brownfield announces that additional regional pacts will soon follow. Most Latin American countries, however, are uncomfortable with American military presence in the region, and reluctant to enter into this sphere of cooperation. Bolivia and Ecuador's new constitutions go so far as prohibiting foreign military bases on their soil.

In May 2010, the American military begins to operate "legally" in Colombia, amid concern about where the collaboration will lead. Throughout its history the United States has disregarded the terms of international agreements and breached borders when its national interests were deemed at stake. After violating international agreements Washington has typically resorted to denial, excuses or self-serving justifications. Many regional leaders, most of all Hugo Chávez, fear that President Uribe's acquiescence to Washington will facilitate American interventions beyond Colombia's borders. Lula wastes little time in requesting a dialogue with Obama, and asks that both countries put forth clarifications concerning the scope of their agreement, and issue written pledges respecting the sovereignty of neighboring countries. None of these requests are—or will be—granted.

THE IRANIAN CONTROVERSY

President Obama continues to woo Lula in an attempt to align him more closely with American regional interests. In November 2009, he writes a letter to the Brazilian leader, delivered one day prior to Iranian President Mahmoud Ahmadinejad's scheduled arrival in Brasilia. Lula's friendship with Ahmadinejad, support for the Iranian nuclear program, and opposition to sanctions against Tehran, rankle Washington. The American president's letter also addresses the climate summit to be held the following month, and upcoming DOHA development negotiations scheduled for December. In Latin America, there is frustration over the paucity of trade agreements outside of farming and livestock, discomfort with the pressure applied by the economic powers on developing nations—including Brazil—to open their markets. Another topic broached is the de facto government in Honduras, and the upcoming elections in that country. Lula is adamant that the deposed president, Manuel Zelaya, should be reinstated. He refuses to recognize the elections that will be carried out by the de facto government as legitimate, and criticizes Obama for breaking the regional consensus in recognizing them. The consequences, he believes, will be grave. Obama unsuccessfully lobbies Lula to change his position on Iran's nuclear program and the Honduran elections.

From Brasilia, Lula chastises the nuclear powers for demonizing Iran: "No head of state, among those pressing to impose sanctions on Iran, has spoken directly with its president. Why doesn't Obama call? Or Sarkozy? Or Angela Merkel?" In a last ditch effort to avoid sanctions, Lula flies to Tehran, where Turkish Prime Minister Tayyip Erdoğan joins him. Secretary of State Hillary Clinton is skeptical that their mediation will bear any fruit, but concedes that it could represent the last opportunity to avoid sanctions (Barrionuevo and Thompson, 2010, May 15). Brazil and Turkey are both non-permanent members of the UN Security Council. After 18 hours of negotiation they reach an agreement: Iran will send half its low-enriched uranium stockpile to Turkey and receive in exchange fuel for a medical research reactor. It's a victory for Lula, "his greatest diplomatic achievement, sealing Brazil's status as a global power," writes Samantha Eyler Reid for the NACLA Report. The Brazilian media and analysts around the world shower Lula with praise. President Obama, however, will not be swayed (Eyler Reid, 2010, June 4).

On June 9, 2010 the UN Security Council approves sanctions against Iran, with 12 votes in favor, including Russia and China. Brazil and Turkey vote against, while Lebanon abstains. The media praises President Obama for shoring up the support of Russia and China, both of whom expressed initial reluctance. Lula, on the other hand, refers to Obama's victory as "pyrrhic." The Brazilian Ambassador to the UN, Maria Luiza Ribero Viotti, expresses concern that the sanctions will exact a toll similar to those in Iraq prior to the

American invasion, which led to children starving among other humanitarian disasters.

LULA'S LEGACY

Lula's legacy is substantial. He reduces poverty by 30%, raises the minimum wage, and oversees a period of social progress in his country. Under his leadership Brazil boasts one of the most buoyant economies in the world.

Already the largest economy in the region, Brazil surpasses Spain to become the eighth largest in the world, according to the IMF. Lula solidifies the image of his country as a rising power. During his time in office, Brazil is admitted to the principal economic institutions of the great industrial powers. His administration pursues an ambitious, multipolar foreign policy, prioritizing economic and political cooperation among Latin American countries with the goal of forming a regional bloc, while simultaneously broadening relations with countries in other parts of the world. Lula is the first Latin American leader to promote South-South cooperation. At the First Africa-South America Summit, the participating nations agree to meet annually thereafter. Lula's diplomatic approach could not be further from the Bush administration's unilateralism (Eyles Reid, 2010, June 4). Lula broadens relations with more than 40 African and Asian nations, including some that openly defy the Western powers: North Korea and Iran. He establishes the Summit of South American-Arab Countries. Despite condemning the 2008 Israeli assault on

Gaza, Lula makes an official visit to Tel Aviv with more than 80 Brazilian businessmen and industrialists; he also meets with Palestinian officials, and supports the creation of a Palestinian state and restarting conversations between the Palestinian Authority and Hamas (Davies, 2010, May 18).

So what will happen after Lula leaves office? With two years remaining on his second term (which goes through 2010) the political climate is already heated: more than ten presidential hopefuls have thrown their hats in the ring. In February 2009, the Superior Electoral Court accuses Lula of favoring the PT candidate, his chief of staff Dilma Rousseff. Many left-wing parties, who have voiced strong opposition to the PT government, accuse Lula of presidential campaigning before it was legally permitted, citing his meeting with four thousand mayors to promote Rousseff's candidacy. Should he lose this suit in the Electoral Court, Lula would be required to pay a fine exceeding 22 thousand dollars (*AP*, 2009, February 26). Other left-wing parties bandy about names of potential challengers, determined to place one of their own in the presidency.

Despite polls showing Lula with an 84% approval rating, Rousseff has a hard fight on her hands. Her most formidable opponent is the governor of São Paulo, José Serra, of the centrist Social Democracy Party, the same candidate Lula vanquished in the 2002 election. By January 2010, the distance separating Rousseff from Serra has dwindled. Conservatives try to demonize Rousseff, suggesting she will be more liberal than her former boss. Similar propaganda was deployed against Lula in 2002, including threats to paralyze the country should the PT candidate come out victorious [unclear].

In the middle of 2010, when Lula officially throws his support behind her candidacy, Rousseff's poll numbers start to rise. Lula's prestige and popularity weigh heavily in favor of continuity. Under her mentor's leadership, 30 million Brazilians rose out of poverty, and Brazil managed to emerge from the global economic crisis relatively unscathed. Brazil has raised its stature among the most powerful nations in the world. For those reasons the majority turns out to support the candidate representing continuity.

DILMA TRIUMPHS

On October 31, 2010, Dilma Rousseff is elected president in a second-round runoff with 56% of the popular vote. Lula's support proves to be a decisive. Despite the election of his handpicked successor, who has pledged to stay the course laid out by his administration, Lula will be missed, not only in his own country, around the continent too. He has been a steadfast champion of Latin American unity, and tireless leader of regional integration. Despite proving himself to be a moderate statesman, he leaves a void in the Left.

After Rousseff's victory is announced the people take to the streets and celebrate with songs and cheers. The emotional president-elect thanks Lula for his support, and promises to "honor his legacy" and continue pushing forward his administration's economic and foreign policies. Having pledged to continue her predecessor's work toward regional unity, Dilma's victory is hailed around the continent as well.

CHAVEZ AND THE LIBERATOR

Venezuela's territory covers 912,050 km2, and its population exceeds 22 million. It is the hemisphere's largest petroleum exporter and sixth largest producer in the world. Some 60% of its production supplies the U.S. market. Not even the political acrimony arising from Washington's support of the 2002 coup can undo this symbiotic relationship. Both countries, however, look to diminish their economic dependence on the other. Chávez travels to China to promote trade and open new petroleum markets; Barack Obama, meanwhile, puts his faith in the large reserves discovered off the Brazilian coast, hoping to wean his country off Venezuelan production.

For decades, the left-leaning Democratic Action party and the Christian democratic Copei alternate turns in power, and Washington has no problem working with either. Complications arise with the election of Carlos Andrés Pérez, of Democratic Action, who in the 1970's nationalizes Venezuela's petroleum industry, an act that is popular around the country, but which requires alternative arrangements with American corporations. Moreover, Pérez reestablishes relations with Cuba, which were suspended under pressure from the Kennedy administration. Along with Presidents Alfonso López and Daniel Odúber of Colombia and Costa Rica, respectively, he supports the Panamanian general Omar Trujillo in his quest to regain full sovereignty of his territory by wresting control of the canal from the United States. Many analysts view this as a declaration of regional independence in defiance of American hegemony.

Seeking to resurrect the Liberator's continental vision, Hugo Chávez calls for Latin American unity outside the reach of American power; on repeated occasions, Simón Bolívar declared his opposition to American overreach in the region. In 1826, Bolívar organized the Congress of Panama, without inviting the United States, to "resist its expansionist designs." In 1829, in a prescient letter to Colonel Patrick Campbell, the British diplomatic representative in the Republic of Colombia, Bolívar writes: "The United States appears to be destined by Providence to plague Latin America with misery in the name of liberty."

In December 1998, Chávez is elected to the presidency despite fierce opposition from Venezuela's oligarchy, who organize large demonstrations against the incoming president, and waste no time turning their machinery against him. In April 2002 they carry out a coup d'état: military officers kidnap the president and imprison him on a military base off the coast, where they announce he has resigned from office. Three days later commanders loyal to Chávez rescue and reinstate him in Miraflores Palace. Chávez denounces

American involvement in the coup, alleging President Bush provided financing. The Venezuelan's verbal attacks against the American leader reach a fever pitch. He becomes Bush's chief antagonist in the region. The Washington and influential American news organizations wage a relentless campaign against Chávez: he is labeled a dictator, lambasted for subverting democracy in his own and other Latin American countries. Like President Bush, throughout his campaign Barack Obama characterizes the Venezuelan leader's rhetoric as "dangerous," a toxic blend of false promises and vitriol directed at the United States. Candidate Obama is also critical of his "checkbook" diplomacy, and loans granted to friendly nations with the goal of co-opting their governments. He mentions Bolivia and Nicaragua by name.

Declassified documents reveal an anti-Chávez bias in USAID programs in Venezuela, and the same with regards to Evo Morales in Bolivia. The documents also suggest a clear policy on the part of the Obama administration to sink both presidencies. A couple months after the 2002 coup, USAID establishes an Office of Transition Initiatives (OTI) in Caracas to funnel millions of dollars into parties, organizations and campaigns against the Venezuelan leader, including some 450 anti-Chávez NGOs (Golinger, 2009, May 20).

IN THE POLITICAL ARENA

In the early 1990's Hugo Chávez seeks to capitalize on widespread discontent during an economic downturn, a situation aggravated by the implementation of an IMF reform package by President Carlos Andrés Pérez, which eliminates social security, suspends indirect subsidies that benefit the affluent and reduces public wages, measures that predominantly affect the middle and lower classes. Protests break out when the government announces a 100% increase in fuel prices; the cost of transportation rises 30%. For several days, anarchy reigns in Caracas. Pérez responds with force; clashes with demonstrators result in 396 fatalities, according to official sources, or as many as 3,000 according to some observers, who claim thousands of bodies were buried in mass graves. This violent episode becomes known as "Caracazo." According to analysts, the turmoil stems from widespread disenchantment with neoliberalism and globalization. Victims' relatives bring a suit before the OAS Inter-American Court of Human Rights, and Venezuela's Supreme Court condemns the government for human rights violations.

It is in this climate of civil unrest and disillusionment that Hugo Chávez leads a coup d'état against Pérez in 1992. The operation fails and Chávez turns himself in. Two years later he is released from prison and applies himself to democratic politics: he founds the leftist Fifth Republic Movement (MVR), which unites groups of military officers and other political parties. In 1996, he travels to Havana in hope of gaining an audience with Fidel Castro. To his amazement, the revolutionary legend greets him on the tarmac. The two leaders forge a close friendship. The Cuban trip, however, brings Chávez onto the CIA's radar (Kozloff, 2007: 43-46);

the organization will follow his every step, and do its best to frustrate his political aspirations. Years later, a Venezuelan intelligence officer gives testimony about this espionage to a Cuban journalist (Elizalde y Báez, 2005, February 3).

Chávez runs his presidential campaign on a platform of combating poverty and corruption, themes that resonate with the poor and working classes, and within progressive circles as well. Chávez preaches the Bolivarian ideal of unity against the "Empire," and the need to found a new republic that will replace *puntofijismo* (a bipartite power arrangement dominated by the traditional political parties) with constitutional reforms that genuinely respond to the needs of the poor and working class. He emphasizes petroleum's potential as a "geopolitical weapon" and derides political leaders who "have not realized the power that a petroleum-producing country wields." The price of crude oil is at a low; many countries in OPEC (of which Venezuela is a founding member) disregard the quota regime adopted to regulate the market, a development Chávez believes is damaging to all. He accuses the state petroleum company, PDVSA, of operating as a "state within the state," criticizes the unfavorable terms of its agreements with foreign petroleum companies, and declares his opposition to the privatization of energy resources. His nationalist speeches raise awareness about what petroleum wealth can mean to a country, and the current government's waste and mismanagement of that abundant natural resource (Kozloff, 2007: 7).

THE CHAVEZ GOVERNMENT

In December 1998 Chávez is elected president with 56.4% of the popular vote. In February of the following year he is sworn into office, and declares his government's project to be the Bolivarian Revolution, "re-founding" the nation with the support of the masses. He announces forthcoming political, economic and social reforms leading toward a 21st century socialism. His government, he declares, will follow the teachings of the Liberator (Simón Bolívar is his hero), and work for continental unity and independence from the "Empire." In 2000, Chávez is reelected with 59.76% of the vote, once again drawing strong support from the middle and working classes. The oligarchic opposition, meanwhile, continues to plot his demise.

His first order of business is ratifying a new constitution that will bring to bear structural reform—political, economic, and judicial—a socialism reconfigured for the 21st century, "based on solidarity, fraternity, and love of liberty and equality [...] a New Socialism that should be built every day, and nourished by the most authentic Christian currents, within the framework of participatory democracy and equality for all." Chávez warns that the transition to socialism, in a globalized world, will be a "fairly prolonged" process. He urges the hierarchy of Venezuelan Church to read Marx and Lenin, and cull socialist messages from the Holy Scriptures. In a press release the Venezuelan Episcopal Conference warns: "The socialism promoted by the President for the country is based on the Marxist doctrine that sustained the regimes of Eastern Europe" (*DPA*, 2007, January 15). According to analysts, this ideological divergence represents a renewal of tension between Church and government.

Chávez refuses to stand by as the National Assembly blocks his political projects, and the constitutional change he seeks; he proposes holding two elections, and a referendum on calling a constituent assembly. The referendum is approved in July 1999 with 73% of the vote, and the Chavista coalition wins 120 of the 131 seats in the National Assembly; 6 months later, in December 1999, a new constitution is ratified. The most noteworthy changes are the extension of the presidential term from five to six years (with the possibility of reelection to consecutive terms), the nomination of judges based on merit, the creation of the office of the Defender of the People, whose duties include monitoring the executive and legislative branches. Furthermore, the national assembly will be unicameral; the senate is abolished. The privatization of PDVSA, the national petroleum company, is prohibited. The new constitution also establishes that property should serve social and general interest, and failing to do so is subject to expropriation with compensation (Kozloff, 2007: 34 35).

The first general elections under the new constitution are held with international monitoring on July 30, 2000; Chávez is reelected with 59.76% of the vote. Chavista candidates, moreover, win two-thirds of the seats in the National Assembly. The Carter Center, a non-profit founded by the former U.S. president, which serves in the role of election observer and conflict mediator, finds that there was no transparency in these elections and therefore cannot validate them, yet concludes that they were a "legitimate expression of democracy" (ACE Project, 2001). Chávez is sworn in on August 19, 2000 and embarks on a new six-year term.

Controlled by a Chavista majority, the National Assembly approves an "organic law" allowing the president to govern by decree for a period of one year—a power that will further enable the Venezuelan leader's authoritarian tendencies, critics warn. During this period Chávez approves new laws on land and hydrocarbons. National and International labor organizations, as well as the Venezuelan Workers Confederation and Venezuelan Federation of Chambers of Commerce, oppose the referendum of December 3, 2000, which seeks to establish state control over trade unions. The opposition calls for a general strike. Chávez wins the referendum anyway with 59% of votes cast.

On April 11, 2002 the military stages a coup against Chávez. The coup's leaders anoint Pedro Carmona—the president of the Venezuelan Federation of Chambers of Commerce, and a powerful business mogul—his replacement. During his three days in office Carmona issues decrees aimed at undoing the Bolivarian Missions; he dissolves the National Assembly and Supreme Court and changes the official name of the country back to the Republic of Venezuela. Military officers loyal to

Chávez call for a popular rebellion against the coup and the ousted president's supporters take to the streets in the largest demonstrations the country has ever seen. Ultimately, military officers loyal to Chávez rescue him from captivity and restore him to the presidency. Chávez resumes his term.

More combative than ever, Chávez denounces American involvement in the failed coup, of which he claims to have irrefutable proof, including that the International Republican Institute financed the plot. Claiming that several attempts on his life have been made, Chávez warns that if one should ever succeed, "the United States will never again receive another barrel of oil in a thousand years." In Washington, the Democratic Senator Christopher Dodd calls for an investigation into the role the government played in the coup, but no concrete evidence of American involvement is ascertained. Yet CIA documents dated April 6, 2002, which had been tightly guarded prior to their release under the Freedom of Information Act, reveal that the Bush administration was "at least" aware of the coup weeks in advance (*Democracy Now*, 2004, November 29).

The opposition continues to battle. In December, PDVSA calls for an industry-wide strike. Petroleum production and exports cease. Government security forces monitor, but do not clash with the protestors. The work stoppage lasts two months, a devastating blow to the economy. The gas scarcity is felt around the country. Chávez ultimately orders the military to occupy PDVSA, and dismisses its management along with workers who participated in the strike. Eight thousand employees, half the company's total, are let go without rights to lost wages or severance packages.

Carlos Andrés Pérez first nationalizes the petroleum industry in 1976, but a couple decades later, in the 1990's, President Rafael Caldera (1994-1999) authorizes foreign investment in the sector to prop up the price of crude oil. In 2007, Chávez mandates that all exploration and drilling should be undertaken through joint ventures with PDVSA to guarantee state control over the industry. Some companies agree to the new conditions, others pack up and leave.

An anti-Chávez civic association, professing its goal to be the protection of voting rights, *Súmate* gathers millions of signatures on a petition calling for a national referendum to revoke the president's mandate. This recall mechanism is elaborated in two articles of the 1999 constitution, provided a petition collects signatures corresponding to 20% of the electorate. The recall referendum is held on August 15, 2004, under international supervision. The "No" vote receives 58.4%. The opposition contends that "massive fraud" has been committed. Yet the OAS, the United Nations Development Program (UNDP), and the Carter Center certify the results (The Carter Center, 2004, September 5). A triumphant Chávez announces that he will redouble his efforts to combat poverty, and offers to engage the opposition in dialogue, despite accusing *Súmate's* members of conspiracy and treason for receiving a grant from the National Endowment for Democracy for "election education."

New Bolivarian Missions in 2003 and 2004 shore up popular support for the government. In the 2004 local and regional elections Chavistas wipe out the competition, winning 20 of the 25 state governorships (*AFP* and *DPA*, 2004, November 1) and 90% of municipalities, which results in the appointment of 12 new judges loyal to the government.

In March 2005, Chávez decrees laws criminalizing the defamation of the president or members of the government under a penalty of 40 months imprisonment—a warning to the radio and television stations, the majority owned by anti-Chávez plutocrats who supported the 2002 coup, to proceed with caution when throwing their weight in the political arena. The decrees spark widespread criticism of the government. Prominent figures and media organizations both within the country and abroad, including the Inter-American Press Association, accuse Chávez of infringing upon freedom of the press and information, intimidating journalists and crippling the foundations of democracy.

Controlled by Chávez supporters, the National Assembly passes legislation in 2005 curtailing the Central Bank's autonomy, and establishing the Venezuelan National Development Fund (FODEN), which authorizes the transfer of six billion dollars from the Central Bank to be controlled by the Ministry of Planning and Finance, which will also gain access to hard-currency reserves without any constitutional oversight.

In February 2006, another transfer of four billion dollars is approved, and others of 100 billion from PDVSA and one billion weekly from the Central Bank are announced. The government does not divulge how these funds are being used, but some insiders claim they are distributed to a number of programs, mostly as patronage (Corrales and Penfold, 2008: 191).

In 2006 Chávez runs for reelection on a platform of defending Venezuela's sovereignty against American interventions aimed at destabilizing the government. Chávez is reelected on December 3 with 62.7% of the popular vote. The following year he merges the party whose ticket he led in previous elections, the PVR, with other pro-government parties and political movements to form the United Socialist Party of Venezuela (PSUV). He triumphantly trumpets the progress of the Bolivarian Revolution and construction of a 21st socialist model.

In January 2007, the National Assembly once again grants Chávez the power to govern by decree, this time for eighteen months. Chávez changes more than sixty laws over this period, and creates a presidential committee for bringing the elimination of term limits to referendum. He reigns in the power of governors and mayors while increasing those of the president; he announces the nationalization of the telecommunications and electricity sectors, and expands state control over agro-industry and the banking sector.

Chávez and his loyalists now control the lucrative petroleum industry, the National Assembly, the Supreme Court, and the National Electoral Council. Chávez boasts of freeing the country from the bipartite stranglehold of the traditional party system. In 2005, the opposition declines to participate in congressional elections. The boycott diminishes its minority representation even further; its options are now fewer than ever. Morale is low among the rank and file. Anti-government rallies lack their previous verve. The opposition appears on the verge of capitulation.

In May 2007, Chávez declines to renew the broadcasting license of Radio Caracas Televisión Internacional (RCTV), a media network owned by business moguls that boasts the largest national audience. A response to the network's open support of the 2002 coup and petroleum strike the following year, the sanction is met with furious protest; media outlets and prominent individuals both within Venezuela and around the world voice their indignation. The outrage lasts several weeks. Chávez receives some support from the presidents of Nicaragua and Ecuador, and Brazil withholds condemnation. When questioned about the action, Lula responds that the matter is one of Venezuela's government and national laws and declines to comment further (*AFP*, 2007, June 8). Chávez meanwhile renews the broadcasting licenses of other television networks. His speeches and declarations about the Bolivarian Revolution, and 21st century socialism, are more impassioned than ever.

Along with his closest allies—Fidel Castro, Evo Morales,

Daniel Ortega, and Nicholas Liverpool, the president of Dominica—Chávez establishes, in December 2004, the Bolivarian Alliance for Peoples of Our Americas (ALBA), a free trade agreement to "confront imperialism" and the continuing legacy of the Monroe Doctrine, an 1823 declaration by the United States claiming North and South America as its sphere of influence (*La Prensa*, 2008, August 11). ALBA is founded as a counterweight to the proposed Free Trade Agreement of the Americas, which Chávez and his allies view as an American attempt to undermine the sovereignty of other countries in the region. The FTAA would support corporations and privatization without responding "to the social problems of education, housing, of pensioners, or even of hungry children," declares Chávez. Washington ultimately abandons the FTAA after the 2005 Summit of the Americas, but the U.S. Trade Representative, the neoconservative Robert Zoellick, proceeds to negotiate separate bilateral treaties (adopting a framework similar to the FTAA's) beginning in Central America, followed by the Dominican Republic and other countries in the region. Chávez warns those countries against signing bilateral treaties before the region's own commerce is solidified as a bloc (Kozloff, 2007: 72-73).

Chávez signs petroleum agreements throughout the region, including Petrocaribe with Cuba and Caribbean countries, and Petrosur with Argentina and other Southern Cone countries (centered on barters involving livestock). With oil prices high, he proposes the creation of the Bank of the South, the establishment of a regional currency, a Latin American university, regional health plans, and expanding economic opportunities to reverse "brain drain" to the United States. At the end of 2008, just a few months after the financial collapse, many of these projects are yet to be defined, or still in development, or find themselves stalled.

In Caracas, Chávez hosts the six members of ALBA, all of whom are critical of the G20 summit called by Bush in response to the financial crisis for failing to seek input from the developing world. Though some analysts contend Chávez is attempting to consolidate his regional leadership through ALBA, the reaction of big countries to the project is more blasé, due in part to the large wealth disparity among its members: though Venezuela carries economic clout, the other countries rank among the region's poorest. Rafael Correa acknowledges that the initiative is an important one, but declines to join before its objectives are clearly defined. Kurt Weyland, a Latin American specialist from the University of Texas, doubts that ALBA will pose a serious threat to the United States, or even expand trade much in Latin America, as Brazil, Argentina and Chile have maintained their distance. American officials, however, do not dissemble their concern over Venezuela's influence in the region. Though Brazil has taken a more moderate stance, they believe that the current ALBA members will struggle to attract other countries. Although the United States has some concern, according to Dan Erikson, of the Inter-American Dialogue, it realizes that ALBA does not have a lot to offer, as the countries that have joined are relatively small and poor. It views ALBA as more of a symbolic union" (Williams, 2008, May 29).

DOLLAR DIPLOMACY

Hugo Chávez views energy resources as a lever to influence political outcomes. Venezuela boasts the eighth largest hydrocarbon reserves in the world, and is the seventh largest producer of natural gas (and the largest on the continent). The Ministry of Energy and Mines, renamed the Ministry of Energy and Petroleum in 2005, controls Venezuela's hydrocarbon sector. Early in his presidency, to underscore Venezuela's stature within OPEC, Chávez calls a summit (in September 2000) to promote unity among the group's eleven members and ensure stricter compliance with the quota regime. Six years later, in June 2006, he convenes an extraordinary meeting and once again calls for greater unity in defending the quota system. On television Chávez announces that in addition to energy he will also address poverty, the foreign debt overwhelming developing countries, and trade pacts whose terms are unfavorable to them. At the summit OPEC recommits itself to defending oil prices in the world market.

A 2008 report by the Latin American Council of Social Sciences (CLACSO) highlights Venezuela's increased engagement with other continents, in particular the oil-producing Arab countries, but also European countries that have fallen out with the Bush administration. Through this diplomatic and commercial expansion Chávez hopes to bring Latin America into the worldwide energy debate, and position Caracas at its center. Chávez signs agreements with OPEC's largest producers. He travels to China, Russia, Iran and Libya, and invites Mahmoud Ahmadinejad and Dmitry Medvedev to Caracas. Medvedev arrives in November 2008, at the same time a Russian nuclear-powered missile cruiser, "Peter the Great," and three other ships undertake joint exercises with the Venezuelan navy. Chávez signs energy and military cooperation agreements with President Medvedev, including one for Russian assistance constructing a nuclear reactor in Venezuela.

Chávez purchases government bonds of several countries to help free them from the onerous terms of IMF and World Bank loans. Between 2005 and 2007 he purchases 4.5 billion dollars of Argentine bonds, 25 million dollars from Ecuador, and 100 million from Paraguay (*El Universal*, 2006, July 5; *Vdebate*, 2007, November 10). The purchase of half those Ecuadorian bonds his government negotiates with Rafael Correa, then serving as his country's finance minister. In November 2008, as president-elect, Correa describes Ecuador's foreign debt as illegal and immoral, having unfavorable terms negotiated by military dictators in the 1970's. His government, he announces, will cease foreign debt payments. If Ecuador follows through with that course of action, Venezuela stands to absorb a loss of 800 million dollars (the vast majority negotiated by previous governments).

With the price of crude oil sky high, Chávez signs petroleum agreements throughout the region, hoping that state-run enterprises, such as Petrobras from Brazil, Yacimientos Petrolíferos Fiscales Bolivianos (YPFB) and Venezuela's own PDVSA, can take over the role multinational corporations previously occupied. In June 2005, he signs Petrocaribe with Caribbean and Central American countries, and offers assistance in building refineries. In October [2005?], he signs Petrosur with Lula and Néstor Kirchner and, in August 2007, establishes YPFB-Petroandina, a bilateral gas and petroleum exploration agreement with Evo Morales. "Energy resources, previously in American hands, are now in Venezuelan hands. And we should share them with the people of Cuba and the Caribbean, Nicaragua and Central America, Brazil and South America, for at least a hundred years," Chávez declares (Bradley, 2007, April 10).

The regional integration movement expands into the realm of media when Chávez launches Telesur, a pan–Latin American television network headquartered in Caracas. Sponsor countries become shareholders in the company. Chávez then founds Radiosur, with the intention of creating a network of national broadcasting stations to counter the distorted image of Latin America disseminated through foreign media outlets. Telesur begins broadcasting in October 2005. Alarmed by this new media offensive, Connie Mack, a Republican member of the House of Representatives with a long track record of hard-line stances against Cuba, calls on Congress to authorize "special" radio and television transmissions to expose

Venezuelans to the ideas of liberty, security and prosperity, in spite of their government's socialist propaganda. What the congressman proposes is similar to Radio and TV Martí, deployed against the Cuban government. The Venezuelan Ambassador to the United States offers the following clarification: his country has 48 channels that can be accessed for free, as anyone who owns a TV with a small antenna can verify; he further points out that Venezuela receives transmissions from 120 channels from four continents (Chirinos, 2005, July 22)

A Chávez proposal intended to replace the World Bank and IMF, the Bank of the South represents another declaration of continental independence. Its loans come with no conditions attached. Along with Venezuela, the bank's founding members are Brazil, Argentina, Bolivia, Ecuador, Paraguay, and Colombia. Its initial capital, contributed by member countries, is twenty billion dollars. An IDB employee confides to the Financial Times the banking sector's concern over the impact a successful launch of the Bank of the South could have on the continent (Weisbrot, 2007, October 31). Washington stands to lose an important lever for applying pressure on countries that do no acquiesce to its agenda.

WITH AND AGAINST THE UNITED STATES

In the economic realm the United States and Venezuela maintain a steady, mutually dependent and beneficial relationship. Petroleum exports are Venezuela's primary source of foreign currency: about 60% of those head to the United States. At the end of 2008, 1.1 million barrels are exported daily. When relations between the two governments sour, Chávez threatens to suspend petroleum exports. Anxious to reduce his country's dependence on the U.S. market, he travels to China in September 2008 and agrees to increase crude exports to 364,000 barrels per day, and half a million by the end of 2009. Though with the distance costs increase, China becomes Venezuela's second largest energy partner (*AFP* et al, 2008, September 25). "In six and a half years in power," the Venezuelan president declares, "we have demonstrated that Third World governments can defend their national sovereignty against countries like the United States." His bold nationalism serves as inspiration to other developing countries (Kozloff, 2007: 70).

The Venezuelan leader's popularity at home, growing influence in the region, and relentless anti-imperialist rhetoric drives the opposition to carry out the 2002 coup. Washington and the American media lash out against the Venezuelan leader. Secretary of State Condoleezza Rice calls him a threat to regional stability, and criticizes his arms purchases (exceeding 120 million dollars) from Russia and Spain. In addressing the political situation in Venezuela, Secretary Rice repeatedly invokes the Inter-American Democratic Charter (2001), which authorizes collective action among OAS members in defense of democracy, in an attempt to galvanize continental opposition to the Venezuelan government. In April 2005, Rice embarks on a tour of friendly countries in the region—Brazil, Colombia, Chile and El Salvador—with the purpose of drumming up support for an OAS action; the majority, however, refuse to go along. Not even Colombia's staunchly conservative government comes onboard. Relations within the region are too vital to risk damaging them with an unnecessary confrontation.

In May 2005, the Bush administration throws its support behind the candidacy of Luis Ernesto Derbez, the Mexican minister of foreign affairs, of the conservative PAN government, for secretary-general of the OAS. The majority backs José Miguel Insulza, of Chile's Socialist Party. Rice agrees to support Insulza only after a compromise is reached in which the Chilean would support the creation of a "mechanism to continually evaluate democracy in Latin America" and other "tools" to prevent political crises. She proposes a new commission to "monitor" democracy. Insulza does his best to comply. "It's critical," he says, "to effectively apply the Inter-American Democratic Charter in defense of democracy." He points to the fact that the organization is yet to issue an official opinion on the coups against Chávez, Jean-Bertrand Aristide, and the removal of the Ecuadorian President Lucio Gutiérrez. The general feeling is that Washington has a collective action against Hugo Chávez in mind, but finds itself unable to garner the necessary support (*AFP*, *DPA* and *Notimex*, 2005, May 27).

In November 2005, at a routine congressional hearing, Tom Shannon, assistant secretary of state for western hemisphere affairs, presents a long and exhaustive report to the House Committee on Foreign Relations on the situation in Venezuela, arguing that Chávez is undermining democracy in that country, and that the "only" solution is for the OAS and international community to initiate collective action under the Inter-American Democratic Charter. Shannon claims to be addressing the situation on a multilateral level. His goal is to support Venezuelan civil society so it can speak out against the abuses endangering democracy and force the government to accept responsibility (Shannon, 2005, November 17).

Despite inheriting a very strained relationship, President Obama's first encounter with the Venezuelan leader in Trinidad and Tobago, in April 2009, is a polite one. The international media focuses on the warm handshake and smiles exchanged between the presidents. Two months later the countries reopen embassies. It is not long, however, before the media crossfire resumes. Obama revives the line of attack used by the previous administration, criticizing Venezuela's "checkbook" diplomacy, and reiterating the charge that Chávez is undermining democracy in his own country and the region. All Chávez really undermines, however, is American hegemony. Along with Lula, he is creating mechanisms for regional integration that marginalize the United States. He is establishing new institutions that undercut those controlled by Washington. He creates ALBA to replace the FTAA, the Bank of the South to isolate the World Bank and IMF and, above all else, works to unite Latin America into a political, economic and military bloc capable of standing up to American power. Many view Washington's conflict with Caracas as utterly intractable, on par with its conflict with Havana. Washington only tolerates submissive capitalist "democracies" and, under Hugo Chávez, Venezuela is a long ways from that.

ON THE BIG SCREEN

His ebullient, unbuttoned personality make Hugo Chávez a frequent headliner in the international media. When he attends the UN General Assembly, the great hall fills up. His attacks on President Bush and the United States are legendary—and, for many people, gratifying too. In addition to denouncing neoliberalism as the principal cause of poverty in the developing world, in November 2006 he ridicules President Bush from the same podium at which the American leader stood a day earlier. He claims to smell sulfur, referring to Bush as the "devil." He remarks that the American president "has come to the Assembly to defend the current model of domination, exploitation and pillage of the world's people" (Chávez, 2006, September 20). The delegates in attendance enthusiastically applaud. The "devil" remark, however, does not sit well in conservative circles; it is disrespectful of the Republican leader. Influential media organizations also disapprove. Appearing on CNN's "Larry King Live," the senior George Bush calls Chávez an "ass."

Another memorable incident, involving King Juan Carlos I

of Spain, occurs during the XVII Ibero-American Summit in Chile in November 2007. Ignoring the 10-minute time slot allotted for each speech, Chávez embarks on a 25-minute diatribe and then, in complete disregard of protocol and etiquette, repeatedly interrupts the Spanish Prime Minister José Luis Rodríguez Zapatero, even referring to his predecessor, José María Aznar, as a fascist, claiming he supported the 2002 coup in Venezuela. Zapatero retorts: "Aznar was elected through democratic channels and should be respected even if he does not share your ideas." Unrepentant, Chávez continues to interrupt the prime minister until, visibly disturbed, the king cries out: "Why don't you shut up?" Those in attendance applaud. The king withdraws himself from the meeting after Daniel Ortega accuses Spain of intervening in Nicaraguan elections. The feud spills over into the media with Chávez hurling accusations and insults at the king and threatening reprisals against Spain. According to *The New York Times*, the row brings to light "the complicated relations" between Spain and its former colonies (Romero, 2007, November 25). The king's outburst receives mixed reviews. Lula supports Chávez; Alan García and Salvadorian President Antonio Saca defend the king. The following July, Chávez makes an official visit to Spain and meets with Zapatero. The leaders exchange declarations of friendship. The Venezuelan president also pays a visit to the king, who presents Chávez with a t-shirt stamped with the sentence: "Why don't you shut up?" Chávez is amused by the gesture. Amid smiles and laughter both parties put the episode behind them.

THE NEW CONSTITUTION

The modifications Chávez seeks, including increased state control over the economy and an extension of presidential terms, are codified in the new constitution. He immediately begins implementing his Bolivarian Missions, which bring the plight of the poor and working class to the fore. Chávez improves the quality of life and protects the rights of these disadvantaged segments of society. He improves education and healthcare services and guarantees access to food at low prices. Through national referendums the people take part in the nation's most important decisions. After a decade in office the president is an idol to the masses.

In the 2008 elections, Chavistas win 17 of 22 governorships and 265 of 327 municipalities. Among opposition victories, however, are the five most important governorships, including the capital. In the same year the National Assembly approves a constitutional amendment that would abolish presidential term limits pending the outcome of a referendum. The opposition is caught off guard: the topic had not been listed on the agenda for that day. A year earlier, by a slim margin, the people, voted against the referendum. In February 2009, however, the amendment is passed. With a large congressional majority, Chávez and his followers are all but assured victory. Inside the country and abroad Chávez is accused of subverting the foundations of democracy, and plotting to hold power indefinitely as a quasi civilian "dictator."

While acknowledging his political and economic control over the country, international observers are not certain of a Chávez victory in the upcoming elections. An editorial in *The Washington Post* raises doubts about his political fortunes. The opposition has grown: in the November elections it took control of the country's three largest states, including the capital district. Oil prices have fallen. The economic slowdown will preclude additional nationalizations, arms purchases from Russia, or subsidies to allies such as Cuba and Nicaragua (*The Washington Post*, 2008, December 19). The editorial also predicts that Chávez will fail to corral enough support for the constitutional amendment lifting presidential term limits. In October 2008, the European Parliament criticizes his government for creating "impediments" to opposition candidates participating in regional elections. The Venezuelan representative to the EU counters that the candidates in question were declared ineligible under legislation from 1975 designed to curtail corruption, which has received broad support across the political spectrum. Others criticize the Venezuelan president's intolerance of opposition, authoritarian tendencies, and ubiquity in both public and private media.

Many critics latch on to the problems of bloated bureaucracy, public sector inefficiency, and pervasive corruption that Chávez had promised to ameliorate; they object to the president's domination of the National Assembly, and courts, attorney general's office, ombudsman and decry the growing insecurity on the streets, which has become a major public concern. Over the course of the decade more than 100,000 people have been murdered. The opposition also criticizes the Bolivarian Missions, which despite having contributed to poverty declining 30%, have failed to resolve unemployment, failing public health and other fundamental problems.

That Chávez is the only Latin American head of state firing nonstop diatribes at Washington endears him in many circles, including among U.S. allies. In this regard he has seized the torch from Fidel. The Venezuelan enjoys a level of popularity similar to Castro's, but petroleum wealth enables him to exert broader influence. In its 2008 survey, Latinobarómetro Corporation finds that Latin Americans are describing themselves as happier, and more hopeful about the future. It reports that 66% of Venezuelans are optimistic about the coming year (trailing Brazil, Panama and Colombia); a mere 41% of Venezuelans hold a positive view of the United States (only Argentina and Uruguay are lower) and 57% of the population singles out street crime as the most critical challenge the country faces (Forero, 2005, June 1). In 2006, *Time* includes Chávez of the 100 most influential figures in the world, underscoring his heightened prestige following the coup attempt. Chávez controls the largest petroleum reserves in the hemisphere, showers neighboring countries with his largess, and grants billions of dollars in loans to friendly governments (Padgett, 2006, April 30).

In 2008, however, Venezuela's situation deteriorates. The price of oil has fallen. Only two-thirds of Venezuelans support Chávez; even loyalists are critical of his authoritarian tendencies and eagerness to perpetuate his presidency. His uninhibited leadership style and interventions in other nation's affairs is another source of consternation, even in friendly countries. Nonetheless, Chávez wins the referendum on term limits, held in February 2009, handily. The next presidential election is scheduled for 2012.

ON THE OTHER SIDE OF THE FENCE

Colombia and Venezuela are neighboring countries, siblings in a sense, but in the first decade of the 21st century their electorates vote for governments at opposite ends of the political spectrum, which find themselves at odds over regional policy and the United States' role on the continent. An avowed socialist, Hugo Chávez is Washington's most vocal critic; Álvaro Uribe, a hard-line conservative, is its most loyal regional ally. Venezuela is of strategic importance to the U.S. for its energy resources and the influence Chávez exerts in the region. Though a trusted U.S. ally, Colombia—the world's largest cocaine producer and epicenter of the drug trade—is also a problem child of sorts. Under Plan Colombia, conceived by Presidents Clinton and Pastrana between 1998 and 1999, the South American nation receives seven billion dollars in aid over an eight-year period, of which 80% is allocated for military assistance. Under Uribe, Colombia becomes the principal American military enclave (similar to South Korea and Panama) on the continent, which President Obama confirms in his first State of the Union address.

Despite occupying opposite ends of the ideological spectrum, Chávez and Uribe share one thing in common: both seek constitutional amendments to extend their presidencies, and both fill their national legislatures and courts with loyalists. And yet the treatment the leaders receive from the two most influential American newspapers, *The New York Times* and *The Washington Post*, could not be more contrasting: while Chávez is routinely demonized, Uribe gets handled with kid gloves. Chávez is George W. Bush's greatest gainsayer in the region and Uribe his closest ally, a fellow warmonger and the only Latin American head of state to publicly support the Iraq War. Bush invites Uribe to his ranch in Crawford, Texas, an indication of his regard for the Colombian leader, and both agree to broaden the scope of Plan Colombia, originally conceived as a drug-combating initiative, into counterterrorism. Uribe puts Colombian air and naval bases at the disposal of American military personnel and private contractors.

In a study of *The New York Times* and *Washington Post's* treatment of the parallel ambitions of the Colombian and Venezuelan presidents, Kevin Young, an analyst for Media Accuracy on Latin America (MALA), finds that both dailies project a negative image of Chávez, highlighting his "authoritarianism" and desire to extend his time in power; Uribe, meanwhile, is treated as a "democrat" and his "immense popularity" in Colombia repeatedly emphasized, despite Chávez enjoying similar levels of popular support (Young, 2008, December 19). In reporting on the political scandals plaguing Uribe's government, the newspapers do not attribute blame directly to the president, and in some instances fail to cover them at all. "We can reasonably conclude that the propaganda model—which predicts systematic media bias in favor of official friends and against official enemies—holds in the case of Colombia and Venezuela," Young writes, confirming a theory elaborated by Noam Chomsky and Edward Herman in *Manufacturing Consent: The Political Economy of the Mass Media.*

In 2007, Hugo Chávez pushes for a constitutional amendment, to be decided by referendum, which would strike down presidential term limits. Despite losing the referendum, he tries again and in February 2009 prevails. Uribe, on the other hand, turns to congress for the constitutional amendment permitting his reelection and is likewise successful. A couple years later he is keen to repeat the trick—for a third term—but no longer certain of securing a congressional majority he advances the referendum option. Juan Forero, *The Washington Post* correspondent, pens a total of eight articles critical of Chávez's efforts to abolish term limits, which include interviews with opposition figures. "With the proposed referendum," Forero writes, "he could extend his presidency for life." The Post runs two editorials, and five op-eds critical the Venezuelan leader (Young, 2008, December 19);

in contrast, Uribe's attempts to prolong his time in office at times are never criticized.

Uribe is only able to run for a second term in 2006 after bribing two congressional representatives, Teodolindo Avendaño and Yidis Medina, to vote in favor of a constitutional amendment, a revelation that should have cost him the office. Seemingly oblivious to the toxic political climate, *The New York Times* correspondent, Simon Romero, interviews Uribe for an article titled "Colombian Chief Hails Democratic and Economic Gains," in which the president's own declarations of the "progress" achieved by his government, his defense of "democracy" and "immense popularity" are all prominently included. The Yidis scandal is broached only briefly in the twelfth paragraph, without mentioning Uribe by name, or directing any criticism at his government (Romero, 2008, April 23). In a similar vein, *The Post* editorializes that "Uribe stands out as a defender of liberal democracy" (Young, 2008, December 19).

In 2007, after Chávez opts not to renew RCTV's broadcasting license, *The Times* and *The Post* both accuse him of stymieing freedom of the press. They describe the protestors as "freedom fighters" who are battling "official repression," barely omitting any mention of the violent acts they commit. Nor do the newspapers report that RCTV openly supported a military coup that briefly ousted a democratically elected president (Young, 2008, December 19).

On September 18, 2008, Human Rights Watch (HRW)

releases a report titled "A Decade Under Chávez: Political Intolerance and Lost Opportunities for Advancing Human Rights in Venezuela," accusing Chávez of breaking his promise to adhere to the rule of law, undermining democracy and weakening its institutions, neutralizing and co-opting the judicial branch, intimidating the media and unions and showing scant regard for civil society, suppressing freedom of expression and taking punitive measures against critics, and failing to respect the separation of government powers. Intolerance of political dissent is singled out as a defining characteristic of his government. José Miguel Vivanco, director of the organization's Americas division, presents the report at a press conference in Caracas. The Venezuelan government responds by expelling Vivanco and Daniel Wilkinson, the Americas deputy director from the same organization, from Venezuela. Human rights organizations around the continent, as well as the Inter-American Court of Human Rights and Michelle Bachelet, express outrage. The Venezuelan government views the HRW report as "aggression against Venezuelan sovereignty," and accuses Vivanco of being "bought" and "an enemy of the [democratic] process and Venezuela" (Coronell, 2008, October 19).

In its Colombia report, released the following month and titled "Breaking the Grip? Obstacles to Justice for Paramilitary Mafias in Colombia," Human Rights Watch levels even graver allegations against Uribe, from his attempts to obstruct justice and undermine the Supreme Court to his shielding of administration allies—including political operators with ties to paramilitary chiefs ("*parapoliticos*")—from investigation. The report accuses Uribe of attempting to discredit the Supreme Court, of scuttling legislation that would curtail paramilitary influence in congress, and of pushing for a constitutional amendment that would strip the courts of their power to investigate and prosecute *parapolíticos* (Coronell, 2008, October 19). The report makes reference to the scandal involving sixty congressional representatives, the majority Uribe supporters, who vacated their seats to avoid being judged by the Supreme Court. Some are arrested for "conspiring to commit a crime" with paramilitary chiefs. HRW is also critical of Uribe's decision to extradite to the United States paramilitary leaders accused of drug trafficking and crimes against humanity. Under Colombian law, they should be tried first in Colombia; the president, many believe, wants them out of the way before their criminal activity can be linked to his administration. An infuriated Uribe dismisses the HRW report as "a compendium of falsehoods" contrived with "a bias and personal animosity" (*El Tiempo*, 2008, October 17). That same night, on *Noticias Uno*, the president accuses Human Rights Watch of being a FARC "defender" and "accomplice," and goes on to enumerate his government's accomplishments (*Noticias Uno*, 2008, October 27). HRW and Amnesty International describe Uribe's accusations as "false and dangerous" (Amnesty International and Human Rights Watch, 2008, November 19). Despite the gravity of its findings, neither *The Times* nor *The Post* gives any coverage to the HRW report.

Between them *The Times* and *The Post* run twenty articles and fifteen editorials critical of Hugo Chávez; on Uribe, a scant two uncritical pieces. Opining on his ambitions to run for a third term, a *The Times* editorializes that the Colombian president "should tell his friends that he does not want a third term" (*The New York Times*, 2008, August 22). Between them, the two papers run nineteen articles and two editorials criticizing Chávez for suspending RCTV's broadcasting license without even mentioning the network's open support of the 2002 coup. Noam Chomsky dissects *The Times'* coverage of Indonesia's 1975 invasion and two-decade occupation of East Timor—supported by Secretary of State Kissinger despite the use of torture, executions and widespread violence—as an example of news media bias (Young, 2008, December 19).

"THE EMPIRE'S" PEON

The relationship between Venezuela and Colombia is too important for their presidents to not on occasion set aside their contempt long enough to pose for the cameras with smiles, handshakes and hugs. Each new crisis, however, gives rise to new flurries of invective. Chávez calls Uribe "imperialism's lackey," a "liar," "cynical" and a "mafia capo," accuses him of bending to Washington's every demand and, in the process, undermining the regional unity other countries are trying to build (*El Universal*, 2008, March 3). With no less acerbity, Uribe accuses the Venezuelan president of legitimizing terrorism, financing the FARC and providing its soldiers refuge inside Venezuelan territory. He threatens to denounce Chávez before the International Criminal Court, and accuses him of harboring expansionist aspirations (*BBC News*, 2008, March 4).

In December 2004, Colombian security forces, operating alongside a bribed contingent of local police and military personnel, kidnap Rodrigo Granda, an international spokesman for the FARC, while he is attending a conference in Caracas. Granda is transported to the border where he is turned over to Colombian authorities. Caracas protests vigorously, accusing Colombia of infringing upon its sovereignty, and bribing members of its military, a violation of Venezuelan law. Chávez recalls his diplomatic corps from Bogotá, and expels the Colombian embassy from Caracas. He closes the border and freezes commercial relations between the two countries.

On January 4, 2005, the Uribe government releases the following misinformation: Granda was "captured" in Cúcuta, a Colombian city near the border with Venezuela. No mention is made of the Caracas operation. Eight days later, the Colombian minister of defense, Jorge Uribe (not a relative of the president) acknowledges that the government paid a million and a half dollars for the capture, but denies that constitutes a violation of sovereignty. Venezuela's vice president, José Vicente Rangel, accuses Uribe of exporting Plan Colombia to the Andean region. He compares the Granda kidnapping to "Operation Condor," a campaign of repression and terror carried out in the 1970's by the military dictatorships of the Southern Cone, who collaborated to assassinate prominent dissidents in other countries. According to Rangel, rather than abducting its target, the Colombian government should have requested his extradition. Uribe, however, cites Venezuela's lack of cooperation in combating the FARC as justification for acting unilaterally.

The Granda kidnapping falls under the category of extraordinary rendition, a practice widely employed by the Bush administration in its war on terror. At the request of the French President Nicolas Sarkozy, Uribe authorizes Granda's release—a necessary step, he believes, in securing the release of Ingrid Betancourt, the French-Colombian former presidential candidate being held by the FARC. The Cuban, Brazilian and Peruvian governments act as mediators in the conflict between Colombia and Venezuela. On February 15, 2005, Uribe and Chávez meet in private, followed by a public show of reconciliation.

In July 2007, Uribe asks Chávez and the Colombian congresswoman Piedad Córdoba, an outspoken critic of his government, to help negotiate a "humanitarian exchange" of FARC prisoners for Ingrid Betancourt and other kidnapped hostages. Assuming that Uribe prefers violent confrontation to peaceful negotiation, many analysts predict the mediation will go nowhere. In November 2007, Uribe abruptly suspends the mediation and accuses Hugo Chávez of violating their agreement by communicating with General Mario

Montoya, the Commander of the Colombian National Army. Chávez takes umbrage and recalls his ambassador, suspends diplomatic relations and calls the Colombian president a "liar" and "cynical." "What we need," Uribe responds, "is mediation against terrorism, not the legitimization of terrorism" (*BBC News*, 2007, November 27).

In January 2008, Chávez secures the release of Clara Rojas, Ingrid Betancourt's former campaign manager, and the ex-senator Consuelo González. In a remote region of the Colombian jungle, the FARC turn the hostages over to a commission of high-ranking Venezuelan officials. The released hostages are flown to Caracas, where they are reunited with their families and meet with the Venezuelan president. The release of these prominent hostages is seen as a victory for Chávez and humiliation for Uribe. In January and February 2008, as a gesture of good will toward Uribe's nemesis, the FARC release six hostages; Venezuelan helicopters pick them up in the Colombian jungle and transport them to Caracas.

As the regional crisis intensifies, the winds of war begin to blow. On March 1, 2008, Colombia launches "Operation Phoenix," a military strike inside Ecuadorian territory to take out Raúl Reyes, after tracking the FARC's second-in-command to an encampment near the Colombian border. President Correa views the incursion, which kills 26 people (the majority guerrillas), as an act of aggression against his country, and suspends relations with Colombia. The assault is condemned around the continent and rejected by the OAS and Rio Group Summit in the Dominican Republic. Offered unreservedly, the only international support comes from the Washington (*El Nuevo Herald*, 2008, March 2). Then a presidential candidate, Barack Obama is among those who defend the operation.

Hugo Chávez characterizes the military strike as a "war crime" and, in a show of solidarity with the Ecuador, breaks off relations with Colombia, deploys army battalions to the border region and warns that any military incursion into his country will be considered a "cause for war." Pledging "full support of Ecuador under any circumstance," he labels the operations a "cowardly assassination" and calls on Venezuelans to "keep in mind the danger [the strike] represents as well as the possibility that Colombia, governed by this mafia, will do anything the 'Empire' demands. It hides behind some supposed right of legitimate defense and claims the authority to bombard neighboring territories, just like Israel." He later dials down the bluster, and professes his aversion to war, but nonetheless withdraws from the UNASUR meeting to be held in Colombia the following March (*El Universal*, 2008, March 3). Chávez is deeply affected by the killing of Raúl Reyes, who for many years had been a key contact in peace negotiations and hostage releases mediated by his government.

Colombian soldiers remove from the encampment the corpses of Reyes and the other slain guerrillas, as well as three laptop computers. That the computers were not destroyed in the bombardment leads some journalists to refer to them as "magical." The Colombian government launches an all-out media blitz against Chávez and Correa, claiming that information retrieved from the computers reveals ties between the Venezuelan and Ecuadorian presidents and the guerrilla leadership. Chávez and Correa deny the allegations. Uribe threatens to bring charges against Chávez before the International Criminal Court for financing terrorism and genocide (*BBC News*, 2008, March 4).

It is Juan Manuel Santos, then minister of defense, who directed "Operation Phoenix." In an interview with *Semana*, Santos claims to have ordered the strike without consulting the president in advance, certain of his approval (Samper Pizano, 2009, February 24). Santos goes on to state that if Ecuador were more cooperative in the war against the FARC, the controversy could have been avoided. According to Uribe and Santos, the strike qualifies as a legitimate act of defense; and yet both go silent when it comes to light, later on, that the guerrillas were killed at dawn, as they slept. The harder Santos insists upon his pretext of "legitimate defense," the more he aggravates the conflict with Ecuador and Venezuela. Uribe bans him from using that defense (*El Tiempo*, 2009, March 4).

There is substantial disagreement over the veracity of the Colombian government's claim of having recovered evidence incriminating Chávez and Correa in the FARC laptops. The

Colombian journalist María Jimena Duzán reports that Interpol found no evidence that the data "had been manipulated or altered by the Uribe government." Nonetheless, she objects to "the government's manipulation of information" and the "politicized media—rather than judicial—noise causing the country to forget the *parapolítica* and Yidis bribery scandals, two investigations that have entered the judicial process and that, with each passing day, prove increasingly compromising to President Uribe. "How else," she adds, "can you explain [the computer data] arriving at *The Wall Street Journal*, *El País* in Spain, *Semana* magazine and the Colombian daily *El Tiempo* before the Attorney General's Office and the Supreme Court, which in two letters to the Ministry of Defense requested that the recovered laptops be sent to them." Duzán criticizes the Ministry of Defense for the "the way it has gone about filtering and manipulating the information" (Duzán, 2008, May 19). An investigation by the NACLA Report concludes that the current media campaign is founded on "evidence at best dubious" and that, without showing them to anybody, the government is using the "magic computers" to divert criticism from the controversy surrounding the strike itself, and to distract the public from other political scandals and justify waging all-out war against the FARC (Denvir, 2008, November-December).

In June 2008, Chávez surprises many when he calls on the FARC to release all its hostages without any concessions in return. "Guerrilla wars have passed into history, and you have now become and excuse for the 'Empire' to threaten all of us.

The day Colombia makes peace," he adds, "the 'Empire' no longer has an excuse" (Sierra, 2008, June 9).

In March 2009, Uribe dispatches Santos, along with his minister of foreign affairs, Jaime Bermúdez, to meet with members of the Obama administration. They visit Secretary of Defense Gates and other high-ranking officials. The Colombian ministers leave satisfied. Santos announces the broadening of military cooperation between the countries; the U.S. will send Colombia aircraft and intelligence satellite equipment, and install new radar devices in the country. To compensate for losing its lease of the Manta military base in Ecuador, Santos offers to station American military personnel in Colombia. And the access will not be limited to a single base: troops and planes will have the full run of whichever bases suit their needs, Santos announces. It is in this tense environment that Colombia's relations with its neighbors, whom Uribe hopes to involve in the conflict, unfold.

INDEFINITE PRESIDENCY?

After two weeks of hard campaigning by the government and opposition, a national referendum on presidential term limits is held on February 16, 2009. Hugo Chávez wins with 54.4% of the votes. The result is received with jubilation by the president and his supporters, who believe they can now fulfill the promises of the Bolivarian Revolution. Congratulations arrive from around the continent; even Álvaro Uribe sends a message.

In spite of a galvanized opposition, considerable progress is made. According to polls the separation between nationwide support for the government and opposition has dwindled to single digits. The country is deeply polarized, and media commentators advise Chávez to reconcile with the opposition he has consistently marginalized throughout his ten years in office. If he wants to govern effectively, the president should seek national unity. Henry Ramón Allup, the opposition leader, calls on his colleagues to stop blaming their electoral defeat on government abuses, as Chávez has prevailed time and again in the past. He points out that popular support for the president has increased; the same cannot be said of the opposition. The time has come, he concedes, for some soul searching. A large portion of the opposition calls on Chávez to "turn the political page" and dedicate himself to resolving the numerous problems the country faces: the economic downturn brought on by the global crisis, the fall of oil prices and rising street crime and insecurity. The violence plaguing many Caracas neighborhoods is a major concern to Venezuelans (*Agencia EFE*, 2009, February 19).

For many Venezuelans, including some Chávez supporters, the prospect of an indefinite presidency is deeply unsettling; it raises fears of a constitutional dictatorship. Having assumed the presidency in 1999, if Chávez is re-elected in 2013 he could end up holding power for two decades. The elimination of presidential term limits is a source of worry outside Venezuela as well. Many fear it will awaken similar ambitions in other leaders around the region. Álvaro Uribe and Daniel

Ortega begin maneuvering to lift restrictions in their own countries. In March 1999, however, the Constitutional Court of Colombia declares the proposed referendum that would permit Uribe to serve a third term unconstitutional.

The most critical issue Chávez must grapple with is economic: the fall of oil prices in the world market; petroleum exports are the source of 90% of Venezuela's foreign currency inflow. In March 2009, he acknowledges, for the first time, that Venezuela could face serious challenges stemming from the global financial crisis, but at the same time promises the Bolivarian Revolution will not be derailed. He announces an austerity plan. "Caution must be taken with every last dollar, every bolívar," he declares, while at the same promising that cutbacks will not affect social programs (*AFD, DPA*, and *Reuters*, 2009, March 9). According to analysts, the president needs petroleum prices to recover for his ambitious social projects to come to fruition.

At the time President Bush leaves the White House relations between Venezuela and the United States have never been tenser. To show solidarity with Evo Morales, Chávez has expelled the American ambassador from Caracas. The Bush administration returns the favor, expelling their ambassadors from Washington. Following Barack Obama's victory in the 2008 election, Chávez remarks that it's a "historical election for a person of African descent to head the most powerful nation in the world. It is evidence of the epochal change emanating from South America, which may now be knocking on the United States' door. From all corners of the earth," he adds, "there is a clamor for new directions in international relations, and for the construction, as the Liberator Simón Bolívar would have said, of a fair world of peaceful and harmonious coexistence." He is willing to dialogue with the incoming American president, but only on a foundation of mutual respect, as equals. Surveying the regional panorama, aside from Cuba and its "historic conflict"—as Raúl Castro refers to the embargo—it is Chávez who most arouses enmity in Washington. Obama inherits the conflict.

THE FUTURE

Going back to the 2008 campaign, Barack Obama has accused Hugo Chávez of "interrupting progress" in the region and affirmed the need to "be firm when we see [...] that Venezuela is exporting terrorist activities or supporting malicious entities like the FARC. This creates problems that are not acceptable." Chávez, however, is quick to fire back: "If any country has been a perverse force disrupting progress, liberty, and life on this continent, that country is the one you will begin to govern" (*Agencia EFE*, 2009, January 19).

A stone in Uncle Sam's shoe, Chávez works indefatigably to strengthen Latin American unity, to consolidate its nations into a bloc and uproot the old colonial order defended by Washington. The region is unlikely to tolerate a repeat in Venezuela of the foreign policy fiasco authored over the past half century in Cuba. The United States accuses Chávez of being a communist, of abolishing private property, and posing a threat to other countries in the region. *The Financial Times*, however, reports that the reality is not quite as the Washington paints it: outside of oil, in the last five years less than 8% of Venezuelan GDP has been nationalized and "Venezuela still has a long way to go before the state has as much a role in the economy as it does in, for instance, France" (Weisbrot, 2010, September 27).

Washington's relentless media campaign against Chávez, going back to his first run for the presidency in 1998, has reached an unprecedented level of intensity and grotesquery, according to the Mexican daily *La Jornada* (Guerra Cabrera, 2010, September 23). The vitriol has also risen in news organizations such as CNN, Fox News, *The Washington Post*, The Wall Street Journal, and the conservative Spanish press. One figure waging a perpetual campaign against the Venezuelan president is Álvaro Uribe: his obsession is so great that, on August 6, 2010, just one day before leaving office, he threatens to denounce his rival before the OAS and International Criminal Court, and reiterates his familiar charges against the Venezuelan leader regarding his supposed alliance with the FARC. Chávez suspends relations with Colombia and causes a headache for Uribe with his UNASUR colleagues.

Scheduled for September 26, 2010, the fifteenth legislative elections since Chávez took office promise to be singularly momentous. This time around, opposition candidates participate. Like previous contests, Chávez converts this one into a plebiscite, fully aware of the popularity of this democratic mechanism and of course record of success in the past. This time around, however, Chávez is not in as strong a position. Things have deteriorated considerably in Venezuela due to falling oil prices. Popular discontent is further aggravated by widespread corruption, economic hardship, soaring inflation (at 30% the highest on the continent), which disproportionately affects the poor, as well as spiking street crime: 16,047 homicides are registered in 2009, and 14,800 the previous year, compared to 4,500 just before Chávez took office in 1998. Adding insult to injury is the discovery of thousands of containers filled with rotten foot and expired medicine, much-needed goods the government should have distributed to the struggling population. For six months the country has endured a water and electricity crisis, leading to the rationing of those vital services, for which Chávez is blamed. His support plummets from 75% in 2006 to 42-44% in 2010 (*Semana*, 2010, September 18). The situation in Venezuela is as dire as it has been in years.

The opposition appears solidly unified. The elections are held without international monitoring. And yet again, they yield solid majorities for the governing coalition—94 seats to the opposition's 60—but the president is denied a two-thirds majority needed to advance the Bolivarian Revolution toward socialism. As was expected, writes Mark Weisbrot in The Guardian, the most of the international press and experts declare the results to constitute a "major blow" for Chávez and predict this election will pave the way for a Chávez defeat in the 2012 presidential elections. "This is exaggerated," Weisbrot writes. The economy moves the electorate, thus the president's popularity is a reflection of economic conditions. It is therefore logical, he argues, that Chávez's popularity would take a hit in the wake of the previous year's recession, which dragged into the first quarter of 2010, as the opposition has no problem diffusing its message through the domestic media (Weisbrot, 2010, September 27).

By February 2011, however, rising oil prices have spurred an economic upswing. The Venezuelan president's position in the region has also improved. Despite clashing with his government in the past, in August 2010 Juan Manuel Santos, now president-elect, invites Chávez to Santa Marta, the Colombian city where Simón Bolívar died. A few days before his inauguration, Santos organizes a warm reception for the Venezuelan leader and reestablishes relations. This unexpected gesture of good will surprises but is well received by the people of both nations, who for several years had to endure nonstop acrimony between the two governments. It is likewise a welcome development for other Latin American governments that also want regional peace. Fearing an American intervention on Uribe's behalf, Brazil and the Dominican Republic had once offered to mediate the escalating conflict between the Colombian and Venezuelan governments. The change of government in Bogotá renews hope for warmer relations with Caracas; the continent celebrates these recent overtures for peace.

BOLIVIA: THE INDIGENOUS VICTORY

A landlocked nation, Bolivia spans 1,098,581 km2, and is populated by nearly nine million people, of which 71% identify as indigenous. Despite its wealth of petroleum, natural gas, tin, lead, silver, gold and zinc—resources controlled by wealthy industrialists and foreign corporations—Bolivia is the poorest, and one of the least stable countries in South America. Since gaining independence in 1825, the country has endured 193 coup d'états, many of them violent. Bolivia has sworn in 75 different presidents (by comparison the U.S. has 44), more than half of whom arose from the ranks of the military. The country is deeply polarized, divided between whites and indigenous, rich and poor. The poorest citizens tend to be indigenous, whose communities have for centuries been enslaved, exploited, humiliated, marginalized by a white, racist elite that has refused to acknowledge their rights and even—in the Media Luna provinces—threatened secede.

In 1952, when Victor Paz Estenssoro is elected president for the first time, this dire socioeconomic and political situation begins to change. Considered the greatest Bolivian statesman, the four-time president (1952-1956, 1960-1964, August-November 1964, 1985-1989) founds the left-wing Revolutionary Nationalist Movement (MNR), and begins to transform the country from a semi-feudal oligarchy to a multiparty democracy. Estenssoro introduces universal suffrage, nationalizes the tin mines (which had been owned by wealthy plutocrats), sets in motion radical agrarian reform and reestablishes relations with Cuba that had been broken, at Washington's insistence, in the 1960's.

In 1992, Gonzalo Sánchez de Lozada, also of the MNR, is elected president after forming a coalition with indigenous movements and other left-wing parties. He enacts a set of reforms to decentralize the country, increases the number of municipalities, holds direct municipal elections in which indigenous citizens participate and adopts other policies that benefit their communities, such as passing education reform allowing for instruction in their native languages. Before completing his second term, however, widespread outrage forces Sánchez de Lozada out of office and into exile after he authorizes an indigenous protest quelled with brute force, resulting in a massacre.

Bolivia is the third largest coca producer in the world and has come under intense pressure from Washington to adopt eradication programs. In the 1980's, during the Reagan Administration, the Bolivian government authorizes American military operations against drug trafficking inside its territory. Despite massive deployments the mission is an outright failure: not even one capo is captured. The DEA devises crop substitution programs in the coca regions, as well as eradication by aerial spraying and manual destruction. Indigenous movements, led by Evo Morales, oppose the eradication programs.

EVO MORALES

Born into the Aymara nation, Evo Morales is a leading champion of indigenous rights and Bolivia's poor underclass. In 1997, Morales founds the leftist Movement Toward Socialism (MAS), a political vehicle that he uses to advance those causes. He calls for agrarian reform, the nationalization and equitable distribution of hydrocarbon wealth, autonomy for indigenous territories, the suspension of coca eradication and other drug-combating operations ordered from Washington, as well as the legalization of the crop. Morales first runs for president on the MAS ticket in 1999, but loses to Sánchez de Lozada by a mere .03% of the vote.

In 1995, Morales is elected to the white-dominated congress with the highest vote tally ever registered. In 2002, legislators from other parties accuse him of irregularities in exercising his congressional duties and he is expelled from the body. The real cause behind his removal—which Morales claims was ordered by the United States—is his ongoing confrontation with the government over the militarization of the country and the indigenous massacre at Chapare, the largest coca-producing region (Zambrana, 2002, January 24). More than once Morales is imprisoned for leading protests and other forms of activism and he endures beatings at the hands of the police.

In 2000, Morales leads a massive protest against water privatization in Cochabamba, which he succeeds in blocking; Bechtel, the American concessionary that had intended to privatize rainwater, is expelled from the country. In October 2003, Sánchez de Lozada responds to growing protests—what becomes known as the "Gas Wars"—with force: sixty indigenous demonstrators are slain at the hands of the police. The ensuing outrage forces the president into exile in the United States. His successor, Vice President Carlos Mesa, enters office amid widespread agitation against government repression and its hydrocarbon law. His government is fiscally austere and respectful of human rights, yet he fails to garner congressional support for a new hydrocarbon law. Mass protests force him to resign, less than two years after taking office, in June 2005. That same year Evo Morales launches another presidential bid. The separatist white minority and Washington view Morales as a threat, and join forces to derail his candidacy.

HIS VICTORY

In spite of powerful domestic opposition and Washington's attempts to sabotage his campaign, Evo Morales is elected president on December 18, 2005 with 53.7% of the vote, cast by 84.3% of the electorate, both unprecedented majorities. In South America, no indigenous leader had ever made it to so high an office. His victory serves as inspiration for indigenous peoples around the continent. Prior to the official state ceremony, Morales travels to Tiwanaku, an archeological site that was once the capital of a pre-Incan civilization, where he is crowned "supreme leader" of the Aymara nation in a ritual attended by indigenous movements and representatives of leftist political parties from Bolivia and around the continent. It is a solemn ceremony, which Morales begins by declaring: "Five hundred years of colonization has ended and the era of indigenous autonomy is beginning." Amid a nationwide frenzy, on January 22, 2006 the indigenous leader is officially sworn in as president. In January 2006, the same month he takes office, Morales begins to stabilize the national economy. He voluntarily accepts a 57% salary cut. Other high-ranking officials agree to similar reductions. Morales announces his intention to end neoliberal programs implemented by previous governments, which he declares to be "based in social injustice and inequality [...] not a humane solution." All around Latin America people are rejecting this development model, which dilutes the role of government. He argues that the state has an important function with regards to oversight, not only of social issues but economic ones too (Morales, 2008, November 18).

His government's policies are nationalist, and regaining control of the country's natural resources and curtailing abuses by transnational corporations is a priority. He nationalizes industries and renegotiates concessions, substantially reducing foreign profits and curbing certain liberties multinationals had previously taken. On May 1, 2006, International Workers' Day, he nationalizes that hydrocarbon industry, the country's greatest source of natural wealth. In an unprecedented move, and without any advance notice, Bolivian troops seize 56 gas and oil fields and show up at the largest in the country, which is controlled by Petrobras and Reposol YPF (from Spain). Morales announces that "nationalization will take place without expropriation" and warns that companies which do not submit to the new terms (taxes levied on production will rise from 50% to 83%) will have six months to leave the country. The companies most impacted are from Brazil, Spain, and Total, from France; to a lesser degree, Argentine and British companies are also affected. Rather than wholesale expropriation, Morales proposes joint ventures: "Though we need partners, we do not want them to be the owners of our resources." Brazil is the country that stands to lose the most. Lula consults with his ministers and proposes a meeting with the presidents of Argentina, Bolivia and Venezuela to discuss the situation. The joint statement they issue, while conciliatory in tone, emphasizes the need to maintain energy supplies to their countries (Weintraub, 2006, May). In May 2006, Morales nationalizes the telecommunications industry, which had been controlled by transnational corporations, and declares, "Public services: telephone, energy, water, and electricity are human rights" (Morales, 2008, May 28).

Morales is at the head of an international campaign for the legalization of coca. In September 2006, he presents coca leaves to the UN General Assembly and speaks of "the historic injustice being committed, the criminalization of this plant, a symbol of the indigenous Andean culture." He points out that, though a legal ingredient in Coca Cola, the plant is banned for medicinal uses. He denounces American pressure to eradicate the crop (Morales, 2006, September 19). As president, he authorizes indigenous communities to cultivate and consume the plant in limited quantities. In July 2008, indigenous farmers in Chapare, Bolivia's largest center of coca cultivation, successfully lobby for the suspension of cooperation with USAID for its interference in internal affairs.

With the assistance of Cuban educators, in 2008 Bolivia declares itself a "territory free of illiteracy." Having pioneered new methods in its "Sí Se Puede" program, Cuba donates 1.2 million textbooks, 30,000 televisions, and other video equipment. Venezuela—the second country to achieve universal literacy—supplies 8,350 solar power systems to impoverished communities that lack electricity (DPA, 2008, November 17).

THE OPPOSITION IN MARCH AND UNASUR

The greatest challenge facing Evo Morales is the violent opposition of the white, separatist minority, led by the governors of the autonomous Media Luna provinces: Santa Cruz (the epicenter of the conflict), Tarija, Beni and Pando. These provinces comprise two-thirds of Bolivia's national territory, and are home to the largest hydrocarbon and mineral reserves, and landed estates, in the country. The elite of these provinces control critical sectors of the economy—banks, factories, vital industries and businesses—and hold a virtual monopoly of the domestic media. Through the media they launch misinformation campaigns against the government, and carry out systematic acts of violence to terrorize the populace and indigenous communities, sowing terror in the streets with coup attempts. They hold illegal referendums on secession, criticize the president's "populist" rhetoric and lambast his relationship with Hugo Chávez, whom they accuse of meddling in domestic affairs.

Leaders of the secessionist provinces, who oppose the president's calls for a constituent assembly, organize protests and marches, block roads, occupy airports and provoke violent clashes with indigenous communities, often resulting in injuries and fatalities. Faced with this escalating chaos and civil unrest, Morales calls for a "recall election on his mandate, as well as those of the vice president's and nine prefects," six of whom belong to the opposition. The election takes place on August 14, 2008 and Morales triumphs with 67.42% of the vote. The vice president and the majority of the prefects are also ratified, though in La Paz and Cochabamba the opposition leaders fall.

In September, the separatist prefects reject the referendum results and unleash a wave of violence throughout the country. They occupy, burn and lay siege to government offices, blockade roads, occupy airports and courthouses, open fire on government vehicles, carry out acts of civil and political disobedience, clash with government forces and attack indigenous citizens. In Pando, men armed with machine guns and machetes slaughter 21 indigenous people. Juan Ramón Quintana, minister of the presidency, categorizes these events as "acts of sedition, of contempt for the government and attempts at a civilian coup d'état," which threaten the stability of the nation. Morales calls on the Bolivian people to defend democracy and its institutions, and invokes the dangers of a potential coup and dictatorship. He accuses the United States of providing financial and other support to the opposition, and promoting their secessionist aspirations. The president, however, still has the loyalty of the armed services, as well as broad popular, and indigenous, support.

Chilean President Michelle Bachelet, presiding pro tempore over UNASUR, calls an emergency summit in Santiago to address the deteriorating situation in Bolivia. In their Declaration from the Palace of the Moneda, ten presidents offer "full and decisive support" to the Morales government, while vigorously rejecting the opposition's acts of violence. UNASUR warns that it will not recognize any coup, or rupture of the institutional order or territorial integrity of Bolivia; it creates a commission to investigate the recent bloodshed and indigenous massacre, while calling on the government to "dialogue" with the opposition. That clause is Lula's suggestion: the Brazilian leader defends the opposition's right, within reason, to express its grievances. Bachelet announces that the commission will be open to any member interested in monitoring the dialogues (Philips, 2008, October 13). Hugo Chávez fails to rally enough support for an official condemnation of American support of the opposition; his offer to send Venezuelan troops to Bolivia is also rebuffed.

A few months later, in December 2008, the commission presents its findings to Bachelet, concluding that the indigenous killings were in fact a "massacre." The report calls on the government to investigate the summary execution of children, clandestine burials and missing people reported by residents of Panda. Furthermore, the report claims that the prefect of that province took part in the disturbances leading up to the massacre. That prefect is detained. The opposition protests and rejects the commission's findings (Agencia EFE, 2008, December 4).

Having played an important role in securing peace, this first action by UNASUR is well received around the continent, but the dialogues between the government and opposition, whose main concern is the new constitution, lead nowhere. Morales pushes for a formal agreement between the parties, but the prefects refuse and broaden the discussions to avoid making any commitments. Morales insists that the autonomy they seek is only possible through constitutional reform.

As Morales rises through national politics, the opposition radicalizes and the country grows increasingly polarized. Though some argue that the opposition was weakened by UNASUR's unanimous support of the government, the violent resistance to the new constitution, and attempts to derail the president's agenda, continue.

In April 2009, in a hotel in the city of Santa Cruz, the capital of the separatist department of the same name, the Bolivian intelligence services foil an alleged conspiracy by foreign mercenaries to assassinate the president, vice president, and opposition prefect of Santa Cruz, according to captured documents. Security forces kill three mercenaries and detain another two. The government asks Interpol to investigate the plot. High-ranking officials suggest that prefects from the Media Luna provinces are implicated.

To the surprise of many, the Supreme Court delegates the investigation to a district court in the opposition stronghold of Santa Cruz, where it is at best questionable that justice will be rigorously pursued. The government threatens to bring a liability suit against the seven magistrates that will make the decision. It has uncovered evidence that the political and business elite of Santa Cruz financed Eduardo Rózsa-Flores, a Bolivian national of Hungarian descent, the commander of the group who was killed in the operation. Video footage of Rózsa-Flores speaking about the conspiracy is aired on national television (Rojas, 2009, April 23).

The government releases the names of leading right-wing figures from several countries who are planning to bring down the president, including the former Spanish Prime Minister José Maria Aznar and his wife, Ana Botella, and Armando Valladares, a Cuban-American CIA agent with a long track record of terrorist activities. Supporters of Santa Cruz's prefect, who is implicated in the plot, as well as relatives of the slain mercenaries, accuse the government of a frame-up.

After a two-year investigation, only 13 of the 39 people originally charged by the attorney general, Mario Soza, are arrested; 18 right-wing leaders go on the lam. One of the most prominent names implicated, Pablo Costas, is the brother of Santa Cruz's prefect, a bitter rival of the president. According to the attorney general, the elite of that province maintained ties with the terrorist group's leader.

WITH AND WITHOUT WASHINGTON

Since the Declaration of Cartagena, signed in 1990 by the presidents of Colombia, Peru, Bolivia, and the United States, anti-drug policy has been the focal point of U.S.-Bolivian relations. Relations with Evo Morales, a former leader of the coca workers union, have been complicated. Washington has frequently taken issue with his opposition to its strategic vision. When Barack Obama enters the White House, relations between the two countries have reached at a new low, culminating in the expulsion of the American ambassador from Bolivia.

Nine days after his election, Morales embarks on an international tour that makes a strong impression on political commentators. Cuba is the first country the president-elect visits. In Havana, he commemorates the 46th anniversary of the Revolution's triumph with Fidel Castro; next he heads to Venezuela, Brazil, France and Spain. He visits Brussels, headquarters of the European Union, and South Africa, and expands relations with China, Russia and Libya. In Tripoli, he attends a celebration of the 38th anniversary of Gaddafi's revolution, establishes diplomatic relations and signs numerous cooperation and exchange agreements with the Libyan leader (*Terra Acutalidad* and *Agencia EFE*, 2006, January 9). In September 2007, he establishes diplomatic relations with Iran and in October of that year is invited to Tehran. These trips are intended to promote trade and secure technical assistance to advance development programs back home.

No indigenous figure enjoys greater prestige or influence in Bolivia than Evo Morales, a socialist, a labor leader opposed to coca eradication, a critic of neoliberal and pro-globalization initiatives enacted under previous governments. Once in power, it often seems he is driving the wrong way up the street. His goals are to free Bolivia from American hegemony and open the country to the rest of the world. He is a friend of Fidel Castro, Hugo Chávez, and Mahmoud Ahmadinejad. Bolivia joins ALBA. Morales supports the regional integration championed by Lula and Chávez; Bolivia becomes a member of the Bank of the South, and signs the PetroAndina treaty with Venezuela to receive petroleum imports under favorable terms.

The Bush administration seeks to undermine his government and when Morales denies Washington's request of diplomatic immunity for its military and civilian personnel, military aid to his country is reduced by 96%. The new constitution, ratified in January 2009, bans foreign military bases in Bolivian territory.

For supporting the violent protests incited by separatist prefects, in September 2008 Morales declares U.S. Ambassador Philip Goldberg persona non grata and expels him from

Bolivia. His intelligence services have filmed the ambassador's frequent encounters with opposition leaders. Morales accuses him of conspiring against democracy and attempting to divide Bolivia (*Reuters*, 2008, September 12). He has proof that the American ambassador gave financial support to white separatists from the Media Luna provinces. Goldberg is the eighth ambassador to be expelled from Bolivia for meddling in the country's internal affairs. Lula da Silva supports Morales and questions the presence of the United States Fourth Fleet off the South American coast, which he considers a threat despite protestations by The U.S. Southern Command that the vessels are only patrolling for drug-related activity. In a gesture of solidarity with Morales, Chávez expels the American ambassador from Caracas. The United States denies any wrongdoing and, as retaliation, expels the Bolivian and Venezuelan ambassadors from Washington.

Morales accuses the DEA of being a politico-military instrument. "Its activities are not related to combating drugs, but rather to conducting espionage against the government," the president declares. "We don't need U.S. control over coca cultivation here. We can handle that internally" (*DERF Agencia Federal de Noticias*, 2008, October 5). Morales proposes a regional anti-drug plan to be directed by the UN instead of the DEA.

Morales openly criticizes Washington's bias in awarding tariff "preferences;" among Andean countries Bolivia has the lowest growth in coca cultivation, a mere 5% (in Colombia and

Peru the rates are 27% and 12%, respectively) according to a UN report (*AP*, 2008, November 2). Morales states that he will never accept conditional cooperation; soon after he cancels USAID programs in Bolivia, citing their political bias, including the agency's assistance to the Center for Strengthening Democratic Institutions (FIDEM), which provides right-wing instruction to politicians and finances the candidacies of the ex-prefects of the separatist provinces of Cochabamba and Pando, with the intention of bringing the president down.

In November 2008, Morales is attending the UN General Assembly when Barack Obama is elected president. Hoping to meet with an advisor to the incoming president, he travels from New York to Washington. During his stay in the capital, Morales states his desire for a "fresh start"—while defending his decision to expel Ambassador Goldberg and the DEA—and describes the fundamental goals of the new constitution as the creation of an egalitarian society that also respects private property, and the codification of public services as human rights. In interviews with the media, he speaks of coca as an ancestral plant and confirms that its limited use by small cultivators is permitted under Bolivian law. Morales reiterates his criticism of Washington's meddling in his country's internal affairs. "Not even a super power has the right to punish or spy on another government under the pretext of combating drug trafficking," he declares (Constable, 2008, November 19).

Morales is unable to gain an audience with Obama's advisors whom, he learns, have engaged in communication with the exiled former president, Gonzolo Sánchez de Lozada, whose extradition request—for corruption and genocide—has received no response from Washington. Nonetheless, Morales leaves behind the message that he hopes for renewed relations between the countries based on understanding and mutual respect. But the covert actions against his government continue.

In 2002, USAID establishes the Office for Transition Initiatives in Bolivia and invests 85 million dollars in decentralization and regional autonomy programs, including separatist and anti-government projects that Morales later suspends for their overt political bias (Golinger, 2009, May 20). In a November 2008 interview with *Democracy Now!*, the president states: "Going back to the first months [of my presidency] the opposition, the far right, the fascists, have tried the obstruct my government. They are convinced that an indigenous man is incapable of governing and they poison the atmosphere with their false accusations, claiming that I am going to end private property, and they believe that in a few months I will be gone" (Morales, 2008, November 18). Nonetheless, now in its third year, the majority of the public continues to support his government.

A NEW CONSTITUTION IS BORN

The government's highest priority is securing passage of a

new constitution that will "refound" Bolivia on a more equitable and fair foundation; one that recognizes the rights of indigenous citizens who, despite constituting the majority of the country, have been largely excluded from the political process since the days of colonization. In this deeply divided nation, guaranteeing constitutional equality, which implies reigning in certain privileges of the elite—who despite being a minority both ethnically and in number have dominated the economic and political life of the country for five centuries—is a tall order. The elite defend by blood and iron their privilege, and with equal vigor oppose new rights for indigenous peoples. The new constitution is anathema to this white minority.

The opposition, however, holds a majority in Congress, and from the outset is determined to torpedo the process. Indigenous and popular movements organize demonstrations in front of Congress and, after months of pressure and several government concessions to the opposition, a bill to call a referendum on a constituent assembly is passed on July 2, 2006. MAS gains the majority of seats in the assembly but falls short of the two-thirds threshold to form a super majority.

Among the issues causing greatest discord are regional autonomy and the permissible size of landed estates, which the government seeks to cap as part of wholesale agrarian reform that landowners, fearing expropriations, staunchly oppose. A new limit for agricultural property is set at five thousand hectares. Obstruction by the opposition ultimately draws the drafting of the constitution's first article out nine months. A year and a half later, in December 2007, the complete text has been agreed upon; each article, however, must be ratified individually in a new referendum. The most important sections address indigenous rights, increased state regulation over the national economy and natural resources, and departmental, provincial and indigenous autonomy. Catholicism ceases to be the country's official religion.

The process, however, stalls again. The opposition blocks the referendum from passing. The government offers additional incentives in the form of regional autonomy. To pressure Congress, indigenous activists organize marches, with Evo Morales at the head. After a 160-kilometer journey they arrive in La Paz, and crowd into the Plaza Murillo, where they wait in front of Congress for the results. By year's end the new constitution is approved. Upon hearing the results Morales proclaims: "Whatever they do, whatever they say, neoliberalism is never coming back. Our new constitution will allow retroactive investigations of former presidents, ministers and members of congress who have robbed the country" (*AP* and *Agencia EFE*, 2008, October 12).

Upon learning that under the new constitution Catholicism will no longer be the official state religion, and that the equality of all faiths (including indigenous ones)—as well as the separation between church and state—will be guaranteed, the Church hierarchy goes on the offensive. In January 2009, it organizes a nocturnal "religious ceremony" in the Mayor de

Sucre plaza, 410 kilometers from La Paz, in which evangelical communities participate, as well as four separatist prefects. The Church has joined the opposition (*AP*, 2009, January 6).

That same month, Congress calls the referendum and the new constitution is ratified with 61.43% of the vote. Latifundia are prohibited and a 5,000-hector limit imposed on agricultural estates. Before tens of thousands, packed into Plaza de Murillo, the political heart of the nation, a jubilant Morales proclaims the rebirth of the nation. "Here the colonial state ended, here domestic and foreign colonialism ended, here neoliberalism ended," he declares. Congress should sanction the constitution in 60 days and the president should call general elections on December 6 of the following year (Rojas, 2009, January 26).

The negative vote (40%) prevails in the Media Luna provinces, a victory the prefects capitalize on to force the government into making a pact. "The pact," Morales explains, "relates to the application of the Constitution, and is not meant to revise or modify it, because the sovereign will of the people must be respected and we are going to respect it" (*La Jornada*, 2008, January 28).

On February 9, 2009, more than a million people—including the Guatemalan indigenous leader and Nobel Laureate Rigoberta Menchú—converge in the city of El Alto for the official proclamation of the new constitution. Morales recalled the founding of Bolivia by Simón Bolívar, and addressed The Liberator: "Here we are, your children, to carry out the second independence, the true liberation of the Bolivian people." He adds, "Only the wisdom of our people, of our social forces, has allowed us to identify, resist and defeat foreign agents, American imperialism. Thanks to this constitution, our ancestor's historic battle and our own can proceed, to defend life, justice, and sovereignty." Upon signing the constitution he concludes: "On this historic day, I officially proclaim the New Political Constitution of the Bolivian State, the birth of the plurinational, socially and economically united state, of Communitarian Socialism (Rojas, 2009, February 8).

The preamble of the new constitution begins with a poetic homage to the land: "In times immemorial mountains arose, rivers spread from one place to another, lakes were formed. Our Amazonia, our swamps, our highlands and our plains and valleys were covered with greenery and flowers. We populated this sacred Mother Earth with different faces, and from that time we understood the plurality existing in all things and in our diversity as beings and cultures. Thus, our peoples were formed, and we never knew racism before we were subjected to it in forlorn colonial times." And further on: "Fulfilling the mandate of our people, with the strength of our Pachamama and gratefulness to God, we found Bolivia anew."

The constitution is made up of five sections and contains 411 articles. One of its novelties is a requirement that the state guarantee "basic services," such as potable water, sewerage systems, electricity, household gas, postal and telecommunications services, though only these last two services may be administered by the private sector. Access to water and sewer systems, however, are "human rights" that cannot be privatized or granted as concessions. Landed estates cannot exceed 5,000 hectares; land cultivation facilitated by any form of servitude is prohibited, as is slavery or semi-slavery in any labor relations. Foreign military bases are prohibited. Indivisible and imprescriptible, natural resources are the property and under direct control of the people. Individual and collective rights to land will be recognized and respected, as well as the rights to use and benefit from natural resources. Regardless of their current state or the state in which they are found, hydrocarbons are also property of the people, in whose name the state—the only entity authorized to commercialize them—will oversee production. Revenues are property of the state. Private initiative and freedom to conduct business are protected; national investment is favored over that coming from oversees; cooperatives and non-profit ventures are also encouraged. The free exercise of religion and creed is protected.

One article in the new constitution addresses coca cultivation: "The State protects coca, a native and ancestral plant as cultural heritage, a renewable natural resource of Bolivia's biodiversity, which contributes to social cohesion and which, in its natural state, is not a narcotic. Its revaluation, production, commercialization and industrialization will be regulated by law." Among indigenous rights codified in the new document are a quota for parliamentary representation, the establishment of a peasant and indigenous judicial system on equal footing the traditional system, and a new Plurinational Constitutional Tribunal that will elect members from both systems; rights to autonomy and indigenous self-governance, and official recognition of their territorial entities and institutions. The resources of indigenous lands are the exclusive property of those communities. Another article declares Bolivia's inalienable and imprescriptible right to sea access and its territorial ocean.

On April 14, 2009, following a five-day hunger strike, Morales manages to push the transitional electoral bill through Congress, which puts a legal stamp on the presidential and congressional elections scheduled for December of that year. The election of prefects (now known as governors) and mayors is scheduled for the following year. After stonewalling for several months, the opposition relents when the government agrees to reduce the number of indigenous seats in Congress from 14 to 7. The concession comes with a political cost: indigenous groups feel betrayed (*Agencia EFE, AP*, and *AFP*, 2009, April 14).

On January 21, 2009, upon finishing his third year in office, and a few hours before ending the campaign for the referendum on the articles of the new constitution, Morales presents a detailed report to Congress on his administration's achievements, highlighting its economic achievements, including annual growth of 5.29% since 2006, record exports totaling

6.2 billion dollars, an increase in foreign-currency reserves to 7.8 billion dollars, and a fiscal surplus 6.2% greater than that of the previous year. The president, however, admits his failure to reign in bureaucracy, corruption and cocaine production, but calls on Bolivians to support the new constitution.

The most vitriolic portion of his speech is directed at the Bush administration, who Morales accuses of sending its ambassador to "conspire" and "carve up" Bolivia. "With the American ambassador expelled, the conspiracy has ended," he declares. He applauds the election of Barack Obama as the new leader of the super power (*Agencia EFE*, 2009, January 22).

HUMANITARIAN CRISIS

Beginning in November 2007, the impact of "La Niña" on Bolivia is nothing short of devastating. Morales declares the country a disaster zone. Torrential rains cause floods, 65 people perish, and 43,000 families are affected. The Media Luna provinces, which make up two-thirds of the country, are hit hardest. Humanitarian aid flows in from the rest of Latin America, Europe, the United States, as well as international relief agencies. Even in the wake of the calamity, the opposition will not suspend its attacks. The prefects accuse the government of responding slowly to the disaster. Morales laments that the prefects continue campaigning for secession even as their provinces are under water with thousands of families impacted (*AP*, 2008, February 14)

International organizations deliver assistance, the Spanish government forgives a debt of 139 million dollars, and the EU promises to increase aid and expand commercial relations; Argentina, Brazil and Venezuela offer the same. Brazil sends 120,000 heads of cattle and donates three million vaccinations against hoof-and-mouth disease to help offset the loss of livestock. Cuba sends 400 doctors to respond to the healthcare emergency.

ON THE WORLD STAGE

The revelation of secret negotiations between the United States and Colombia, granting American military personnel access to seven Colombian air and naval bases, drops like a bomb on the continent. Incensed, Evo Morales accuses Álvaro Uribe of betraying his country. Morales is one of the continental leaders most critical of American hegemony, its military presence in Latin America and meddling in regional affairs. The newly enacted constitutional prohibition on foreign military bases is a clear message to Washington: Hands off Bolivia.

Morales is one of the harshest critics of the U.S.-Colombian pact, which he views as a threat to regional stability. He suggests calling a referendum on the agreement, allowing the Colombian people to decide. Chávez, Lula, Correa and Cristina Kirchner all vigorously oppose Colombia's decision to turn bases over to the United States. Their requests for clarifications from the two governments and guarantees that their sovereignty will be respected go unanswered. According to Morales, the goal of the pact is not to combat drug trafficking—as both governments claim—but rather "South America's 'revolutionary governments'" (*AFP* et al, 2009, November 1). President Chávez and Correa feel the most threatened. Chávez contends that the United States is trying to seize control of the continent's natural resources: petroleum, gas, and water supplies.

On a visit to Spain in September 2009 Morales meets with King Juan Carlos I and Queen Sophia. Addressing a group of business leaders and politicians in the Hotel Ritz, he declares: "We want partners, not bosses." Morales speaks of the recurrent coups in Bolivia and explains that, until recently, the country's indigenous communities lacked the right to represent themselves in Congress, despite universal voting rights (for women, indigenous and illiterate people) being granted in 1952. Natural resources were exploited without any of the wealth generated benefiting the people. But the new constitution, he explains, codifies the national character of these resources. The Bolivian president continues to fume over the U.S.-Colombian military pact, which he describes as "harmful" to democracy, "of which there are abundant examples." He also claims that American forces, stationed in the Soto Cano airbase, are intervening in the political crisis in Honduras (Tejeda, 2009, September 15).

An ALBA summit held in Cochabamba, in October 2009, calls on Colombia to "reconsider" its military pact with the

United States, and concludes with an agreement to impose economic sanctions on the de facto Honduran government until the constitutional president, Manuel Zelaya, is reinstated. Morales sends Obama a message: "If you want to dignify the Nobel Peace Prize, you should lift the economic embargo of Cuba, withdraw troops from Afghanistan and Iraq, and all your bases in Latin America and around the world and, by tomorrow, return democracy to Honduras, as it is your military forces in Palmerola (Soto Cano) that are propping up the coup d'état" (Rojas, 2009, October 18).

THE FUTURE

In the December 2009 general elections, Evo Morales wins an overwhelming majority: 63% of the vote. His term, under the new constitution, will last five years. His political party, MAS, gains the majority of seats in the Plurinational Legislative Assembly (as the new legislature is called) and also wins the governorships of six of the country's nine departments. Morales names ten men and ten women to his cabinet, three of whom are indigenous. The election results provide the president with a clear mandate to continue the process of "re-founding" the country.

Though a political minority, the right wing holds considerable economic power and controls the majority of media outlets; and it has little interest in clearing the path for an indigenous president. Though the country continues to be deeply divided, the election results strengthen the government's position.

In the international arena, Secretary of State Clinton warns Morales and Hugo Chávez to "think twice" about their relationship with Mahmoud Ahmadinejad—whom American officials have described as the world's "greatest promoter and exporter of terrorism"—and "be aware of the consequences." From La Paz, Morales responds: "These warnings don't accomplish anything and we reject them. The United States has no moral authority to speak about terrorism, considering it sends troops to other countries and sets up bases in other regions and continents" (*AFP, Reuters, DPA*, 2009, December 13). Two weeks earlier, Ahmadinejad had traveled to Bolivia, Venezuela and Brazil. All three of those governments support—against Washington's wishes—Iran's right to enrich uranium for peaceful purposes.

In May 2007, with the support of the majority of the people, Morales begins the process of nationalizing the hydrocarbon industry, and the Bolivian economy strengthens. The government continues to nationalize natural resources and renegotiate contracts with foreign corporations, and the influx of foreign currency into the country quadruples from 2 billion dollars in 2005 to 8 billion in 2009.

Formal relations with the United States are yet to be restored, and though Vice President Álvaro García Linera concedes the importance of doing so, he laments Washington's continued adherence to interventionist and destabilizing policies. "Our relations will remain in the freezer," he says. "This healthy and sovereign distance is the least we can do (*AFP, DPA,* and *PL,* 2009, November 23). "We don't want markets in exchange for them telling us who should be minister. We don't want preferential tariffs if in return they tell us what our economic policy should be, because then we would be slaves, we would be another colony, a servile government (*AFP,* 2010, January 5). Morales believes Obama's decision to exclude Bolivia, for the second time, from its preferential tariffs bill amounts to political revenge, considering the U.S. has demanded the revision of certain articles of the new constitution as a condition for renewing preferential tariff treatment. Bolivia compensates for being shut out of American markets by expanding commercial relations with Argentina, Brazil and Venezuela. Morales assures the nation that the economy is progressing and details the considerable advances made since January 2010. "Bolivia is no longer a beggar country, it no longer trails behind international institutions asking for loans. This has ended," Morales declares, as he has regained control of the country's natural resources, and hydrocarbon reserves have risen as a result of nationalization (*Europa Press,* 2009, December 22).

ECUADOR AND SOCIALISM

Ecuador covers 283,561 km2 and has 14 million inhabitants. It's the world's largest banana exporter and third largest petroleum exporter in Latin America. Half of its petroleum is sold to the United States. Ecuador also enjoys large reserves of gold and copper. A country of gaping social and economic inequality, and deep-rooted tensions between white and indigenous citizens—who make up 43% of the population—Ecuador is one of the most volatile democracies on the continent, characterized by the weakness of its presidents: just to complete an entire year in office can seem like a victory. Velasco Ibarra, elected president five times, is deposed four of them. Between 1960 and 2006—when Rafael Correa enters office—17 presidents fail to serve out their terms. Some governments last months. Others weeks. Others days.

In the 1990's, the influence of indigenous movements and organizations in national politics is on the rise; the Confederation of Indigenous Nationalities of Ecuador (CONAIE) grows into a powerful advocacy group for indigenous rights, and against corruption and economic mismanagement. Over a ten-year period, marked by several economic crises, indigenous movements contribute to the overthrow of three neoliberal presidents: Abdalá Bucaram (1996), for incompetence and corruption; Jamil Mahuad (1998-2000), who dollarized the economy and enacted policies that led to the collapse of several banks; Lucio Gutiérrez (2002-2005) is elected in large part owing to progressive campaign pledges and thrown out of office for failing to fulfill them. Criticized for being submissive to Washington and the IMF, ceding to pressure from Álvaro Uribe and becoming entwined in Colombia's armed conflict, popular protests—in which Rafael Correa, then a young economist, takes part—force the

Supreme Court to revoke his mandate. His vice president, Alfredo Palacio, assumes the presidency and names Rafael Correa finance minister. The Bush administration objects to Correa for his left-wing ideology. Petroleum workers force him to void contracts with large transnationals (among them Occidental) and transfer operations to PetroEcuador, the national oil company (Azul, 2006, December 7). Palacio governs for two years, until January 15, 2007.

The presidential campaign takes place in a tense climate of political instability and popular discontent stemming from an economic crisis aggravated by dollarization and pervasive corruption: by naming judges to the high courts, Congress politicizes the judicial system. The primary contenders are Rafael Correa, who enjoys broad popular support for his advocacy, as a member of the Palacio government, of left-wing, nationalist, pro-indigenous and working-class causes, and his opponent on the right, Álvaro Noboa, a banana tycoon, considered the wealthiest man in the country, who has run for the presidency and fallen short on three previous occasions. TV and radio networks support Noboa. Eduardo Tamayo, reporting for Agencia Latinoamérica de Información (ALAI), accuses those media outlets of broadcasting rigged interviews and failing to ask the candidate "uncomfortable" questions, concerning the charges of tax evasion brought against him, and his employment of minors among other alleged workers' rights violations (Tamayo, 2006, November 27).

To launch his campaign, Correa founds a new party, PAIS Alliance, whose official platform—written in the Quechua language as well as Spanish—includes the defense of sovereignty and regional integration, the renegotiation of foreign debt, anti-poverty programs, and the establishment of a "new order" based on equality among ethnic groups and ecologically sustainable development. PAIS Alliance declares itself "part of the current progressive wave in Latin America and the Caribbean whose goal is to restore the country, after 500 years of exploitation." It makes reference to Simón Bolívar's pan-American vision and the fight of native Ecuadorians for their independence (Azul, 2006, December 7). Two key proposals, demanded by his progressive base, define Correa's campaign and subsequently shape his presidency: radical political reform and the drafting of a new constitution. Correa calls for restructuring national institutions and laying a legal foundation for a stronger regulatory role for government over the economy, while dismantling the neoliberal system that has been in place for decades (Conaghan, 2008: 201-202).

Correa defines himself as a progressive Christian and humanist, a proponent of 21st century socialism, and critic of the Washington Consensus and free trade agreements with the United States. In his youth he volunteered for a year in an indigenous community where he learned the Quechua language. He holds economics degrees from the University of Illinois and the Catholic University of Leuven in Brussels; a devout Catholic, his oratory contains references to social

Christian doctrine on poverty, reminiscent of Liberation Theology; he wants to serve like Christ, he declares during his campaign, and help the poor secure access to housing, health and education services, and work, and pledges to prioritize combating social ills in his government. The elections are held on October 15, 2006. Neither candidate obtains a majority, with Correa receiving fewer votes than Noboa, but in the run-off, on November 26, he secures 56.67%. He takes office on January 15, 2007.

PRESIDENT CORREA

President Correa's highest priority is securing passage of a new constitution that will transform the country according to principles of 21st century socialism, which he believes is "the destiny of Latin America, a radically democratic alternative based on fairness, social justice, and humanism" (Calvac Mora and Fernández Lozano, 2009, January 10). Correa preaches the supremacy of work as the end in itself—above capital—of production; and yet, cognizant of the specificities of every culture and society, he rejects the rigidity of dogma.

The disenchantment of the popular classes with the traditional party system, and its endemic instability and corruption, inefficiency and economic mismanagement—often on orders from the IMF and World Bank—favors Correa. As a candidate, he inspires trust and finds widespread support for his campaign pledges: a new constitution, a "Citizenship Revolution," the rebirth of the nation on a more just foundation that responds to the needs of indigenous and other disadvantaged citizens.

The first step is calling a referendum on convoking a constituent assembly. Correa's executive decree requesting that democratic consultation, however, sets off a convoluted political and legal battle involving his administration, public opinion and various government institutions. The majority in Congress opposes the referendum and declares his decree unconstitutional; Correa argues that the current constitution permits Congress to be circumvented in matters of "transcendental importance," and what is at stake is not a constitutional "reform" but rather a wholesale replacement of the constitution, which qualifies as a matter of "undeniable transcendental importance." Correa warns the Supreme Electoral Tribunal that if his decree is struck down, he will create an ad hoc tribunal. The Supreme Electoral Tribunal approves the decree but then sends it to Congress "for its approval and amendments." Correa will have nothing of amendments. He calls on the public to protest Congress and the Tribunal's recalcitrance.

Congress approves the referendum in February 2007, but before it is called Correa changes his terms: the constituent assembly is to possess greater powers to dissolve Congress, a modification approved by the Supreme Electoral Tribunal, but rejected by a congressional majority, which attempts to remove four members from the Tribunal. The Tribunal, in turn, revokes the political rights of 57 members of Congress—from four different parties—who voted against the referendum. Correa supports the Tribunal, arguing that the removals are lawful under the current constitution, as those legislators had acted to "obstruct" the democratic process. Within the halls of Congress the ruling causes an uproar, but out on the streets the uproar is against Congress itself (*RFI*, 2007, March 9; Wikipedia, "Rafeal Correa").

In March 2007, 29 new deputies enter Congress, providing the president's party with a majority: 80 of 130 seats. The referendum is approved the following month with 81.72% of the vote. On September 30, elections for the constitutional assembly are held, and pro-government candidates gain 70% of the seats. The assembly will convene at the end of November. The drafting of the new constitution, which contains 444 articles, takes eight months. Correa pledges to resign from office if it falls short of passage.

On September 28, 2008, a new constitution is ratified with 64% of the vote. "We have fought for a long time and achieved this by democratic means," the president announces. It is his fourth electoral victory and a day of celebration for indigenous people and the working class. A euphoric Correa declares: "This is a historic victory. Today Ecuador has decided to build a new nation and the old structures have been defeated." The new constitution consolidates and expands presidential powers; it allows the president to dissolve Congress one time over a period of four years, and provides the office with greater control over monetary and energy policy, the telecommunications and banking sectors, while curtailing the independence of the central bank. Consecutive presidential terms are also permitted (Lewandowski, 2008, September 29).

For its focus on environmental issues, the new Ecuadorian constitution is considered one of the "greenest" in the world. One of the document's chapters is titled: "The rights of nature or the pachamama, where life flourishes and reproduces itself through caring for biodiversity, natural resources, nature's heritage, rights that are protected under law" (*BBC Mundo*, 2008, October 7). All individuals, communities, peoples or nationalities have the right to demand that the government observe those principles, and public authorities are required to consult with communities prior to carrying out projects that will have an ecological impact. Extraction of non-renewable resources from protected areas is prohibited, although certain exceptions are permitted: the president, with prior declaration of national interest, can authorize it. The constitution recognizes the right to ecological restoration and requires the government to "take precautionary measures and restrict activities that could lead to species extinction, destruction of ecosystems, or the permanent alteration of natural cycles."

Mandatory military service is abolished. Illegal immigrants will receive amnesty and social security and their right to work is guaranteed; the installation of foreign military bases in the country is prohibited. Civil unions between members of the same sex are legalized, though they are still denied adoption rights. Abortion is also legalized. As a devout Catholic, Correa does not personally agree with the aforementioned provisions, which the Church opposes.

Despite a few omissions, the new constitution lays the foundation for a development model that will enforce environmental protections, which are sanctified as legal rights. Ecuador is one of the countries with the greatest biodiversity in the world, home to ecosystems as unique as the Amazon rainforest and Galapagos Islands.

ECONOMIC POLICY

Correa believes that Ecuador's withdrawal from OPEC 36 years earlier was a mistake, and states his willingness to submit to a quota regime, which is necessary to regulate the international price of oil. In Ecuador, petroleum and mineral extraction, historically contracted out to transnationals, has proved to be a constant source of friction and conflict between the government and indigenous communities, who protest the ecological degradation—including water contamination—of their lands. The protests are enormous in scale. In December 2008, CONAIE and other indigenous groups call for a mass mobilization against legislation being studied by Congress concerning large-scale mining projects, which they fear will have dire environmental consequences. They argue that foreign corporations make off with the lion's share of the wealth, and neither impacted communities nor the Ecuadorian people stand to benefit much from these projects.

Hydrocarbon and mineral extraction, however, is vital to the country's development, and though Correa tries his best to assuage fears he characterizes the protests as "infantilism." Nonetheless, he offers to make "small modifications" (*AP*, 2009, January 20).

Correa's politics are nationalist, focused on recovering the country's wealth, increasing the government's control over petroleum revenues, reducing foreign debt, and renegotiating interest payments. He reforms hydrocarbon laws and restructures the petroleum industry and modifies contracts with transnational corporations, which he describes as "real traps for the country." He also accuses foreign corporations of disregarding existing laws concerning the environment and investment. In April, he cancels his debt with the IMF. "The nation," he says, "is regaining its independence to dictate its own economic policy." He expels the World Bank's director in Ecuador and suspends economic policies that had been prescribed by that institution (*BBC News*, 2007, April 26). Washington, the World Bank and IMF, and multinational oil companies grow alarmed. Things are changing in Latin America.

Though Correa is troubled that the dollarization of the Ecuadorian economy (implemented six years prior to his taking office) has led to a rise in consumer good prices—which has hit the poor particularly hard—he believes that abandoning the regime, given the current economic situation, would amount to "suicide."

In December 2008, Correa announces that Ecuador will cease to make interest payments on 10.3 billion dollars of foreign debt, which he describes as "illegitimate" and "immoral," having been contracted by military dictatorships, and tainted by allegations of bribery and other abuses. Correa announces that he will file the necessary lawsuits in international courts. The fall of crude oil prices and unexpected devaluation of government bonds provokes an economic crisis, and conflict with Venezuela, which has invested 800 million dollars in Ecuadorian government bonds. If Ecuador refuses to honor its obligations, Venezuela stands to take a big loss (*AP*, *Agencia EFE*, 2008, November 17; Ayala Samaniego, 2008, December 12).

According to Correa, to continue making interest payments on this debt would be a betrayal of his country. Ecuador has paid 7 billions dollars in interest without reducing its principal. Moreover, a Special Auditory Commission uncovered irregularities in the negotiation of these loans. On January 12, 2009, however, Correa agrees to pay out 30.6 million dollars on other preferential bonds that are not tainted by those irregularities (Ayala Samaniego, 2008, December 12).

FOREIGN POLICY

The primary focus of Correa's foreign policy is consolidating regional integration by broadening political and economic relations with the rest of Latin America. A frequent critic of the Bush administration, Correa is drawn more to the solidarity espoused by Hugo Chávez, whose regional energy agreements—guaranteeing poor nations access to petroleum through barter exchanges—he praises. He is critical of his own country's bilateral investment treaty with the United States, in force since 1997, for the harm it inflicts on impoverished farmers.

Correa is one of the most radical leaders of the New Left, a staunch critic of capitalism, neoliberalism, and the World Bank and IMF. He is a supporter of Cuba and admirer of the Revolution which, during a pomp-filled 2009 conference at the University of Havana, he declares an example for his "Citizens' Revolution" (Calviac Mora and Fernández Lozano, 2009, January 10).

In recent years, Ecuador has expelled multinational oil companies and sued them in international courts. The Palacio government kicked Occidental out of the country for violating its contract as well as Ecuadorian law, while indigenous communities file a suit against Chevron-Texaco claiming 9.5 billion dollars in environmental and other damages—the largest such suit in history. Correa additionally revokes concessions to 587 mining companies. When questioned by the investigative reporter Greg Palast about the recent backlash against foreign corporations, the president responds: "Ecuador is no longer for sale." He further claims, "There are some companies that used to do in our countries things that they will never do in their own countries." While pointing out that the indigenous suit against Chevron has nothing to do with the government, he nonetheless expresses his support, claiming there is a "moral issue" at heart, and if the indigenous win it will set an important precedent (Correa, 2008, February 11).

COLOMBIA LEAPS THE FENCE

Conceived by Presidents Bill Clinton and Andrés Pastrana, one of Plan Colombia's methods of combating the drug trade is the aerial spraying of coca crops, most of which are cultivated in the southern Putumayo department bordering Ecuador. In addition to being a center for cocaine production, clashes between the army, paramilitaries and guerrilla forces are common in this region. Glyphosate sprayings not only affect the health of people and animals but also destroy legal crops in Colombia as well as Ecuador. The armed conflict and fumigations set off an exodus of rural peasants from Colombia into Ecuador, across the same porous border through which paramilitaries and guerrillas also transit. The Ecuadorean government has called on Colombia to halt the aerial fumigations, which affect a 10-kilometer strip along the frontier, to ensure that no toxic chemicals contaminate human habitats inside its territory. Correa has gone so far as to threaten, if necessary, to bring the matter before the International Court of Justice in The Hague (*Agencia EFE*, 2007, June 2). In response to these warning Uribe dispatches his foreign minister, Carolina Barco, with a study issued by the OAS finding that glyphosate, the chemical used in aerial fumigations, poses no health threat to humans. Correa, however, is unmoved. According to investigators, that report is based on secondary sources, and half its data furnished by Monsanto, an American multinational corporation that produces chemical and herbicide products—including glyphosate.

Colombia's armed conflict, waged by the army and paramilitary and guerrilla groups, is most intense in regions that border Venezuela, Ecuador and Panama. The fact that the latter two groups are financed by drug money, and that the United States too is enmeshed in the fight, makes for an extremely volatile and complicated situation. The Bush administration looks to regionalize the war on drugs while Uribe looks to regionalize the war against the guerrillas, hoping to draw Ecuador and Venezuela into his country's conflict, but President Alfredo Palacio González and the Ecuadorian Congress refuse: they see the war as a Colombian affair in which Ecuador should remain neutral. Public opinion and Ecuadorian civic and human rights organizations support that position (PL, 2005, July 1).

THE ARMED INCIDENT

On March 1, 2008, the Colombian army enters Ecuadorian territory, without consulting Quito in advance, to eliminate a FARC commander known by the alias "Raúl Reyes." The attack begins at dawn. After initially bombing the encampment, Colombian troops and police, transported by helicopter, finish off the killing. They remove the corpses of Reyes and another guerrilla, in addition to three laptop computers, from the encampment. That same morning Uribe informs Correa of the cross-border operation, framing it as an act of "legitimate defense" against a guerrilla force that has carried out attacks against the Colombian people. Upon arriving at the scene of the attack, Ecuadorian authorities establish that 26 people were killed, the majority guerrillas, and that the killing transpired at dawn while the encampment's occupants slept; the dead wore undergarments and sleeping attire and others had gunshot wounds in the back. No combat took place; nor was it—as the Colombian government claimed—some sort of "hot pursuit." Correa describes the operation as a "massacre" and accuses Uribe's government of "aggression" and violating Ecuadorian sovereignty; he withdraws his country's personnel from the embassy in Bogotá, and expels the entire Colombian diplomatic mission, including the ambassador, from Quito. Correa dispatches ten thousand soldiers to the border. There are several theories regarding Washington's role in the attack. Some analysts are convinced that U.S. Special Forces, which under Plan Colombia have been stationed in Colombia since the turn of the century, took part (*The Real News*, 2008, May 22). This American contingent has provided military and counterinsurgency training to the Colombian army, and at times partaken in anti-guerrilla operations. Analysts also claim that Reyes was located through American intelligence reports and advanced technology, with support from its Manta military base. Former Israeli generals aided the Ministry of Defense, according to Juan Manuel Santos, the minister responsible for the operation. The American defense secretary, Robert Gates, "applauds" the operation and, when questioned by journalists regarding his own country's participation, responds: "I would say we gave [Colombia] a lot of help" (Lendman, 2008, March 9). In a show of solidarity with Ecuador, Venezuela also breaks ties with Colombia. Around the continent governments condemn the attack; ambassadors to the OAS and Rio Group Summit (convening in the Dominican Republic) "reject" it as a violation of Ecuadorian sovereignty. Colombia nevertheless effectively lobbies against an official condemnation from either group.

The Rio Group confrontations between Correa and Chávez and Uribe are bitter, but the summit concludes with "warm" embraces for the cameras, and plenty of "handshakes" and smiles. And so the "dispute has ended," according to Simón Romero, The New York Times correspondent who routinely files reports biased in Uribe's favor; the incident must have amounted to nothing more than a petty disagreement (Romero, 2008, March 9). Uribe, for his part, hails the cross-border strike as "another blow to terrorism." Defense Minister Santos claims the incident could have been avoided if there were greater cooperation from Quito in hunting down guerrilla groups. Based on information manipulated by the Colombian government, France Press reports: "This is the first time that the Colombian army has slain a FARC leader in combat" (France Press, 2008, March 2).

As usual, when he finds himself boxed in, Uribe goes on the offensive. He orchestrates a media campaign against Corrales and Chávez, alleging that data retrieved from the FARC computers establishes links between both presidents and the guerrillas. The *NACLA Report on the Americas* runs an article on the "magic" computers that the bombardment somehow managed not to destroy (Denvir, 2008, November-December). The Ecuadorian interior minister, Fernando Bustamante, denies Uribe's accusations. "It's very easy," he remarks, "to level accusations based on evidence that has not been inspected publicly or internationally" (Markey, 2008, March 2). Uribe threatens to present the OAS with documents demonstrating that Venezuela and Ecuador aided the FARC in violation of international law prohibiting governments from harboring terrorists. There is no such law, however, only a demand made by President Bush as he wages his open-ended war on terror following the September 11th attacks. More than a few Colombian and foreign journalists see this campaign as an attempt by Uribe to divert attention from the illegality of the cross-border strike and other scandals consuming his presidency. Uribe threatens to take his accusations against Ecuador and Venezuela to the International Criminal Court.

Eight months after the incident, the Colombian foreign minister, Jaime Bermúdez, sends a letter to Ecuador stating the "conditions" required by his government to reestablish diplomatic relations. He calls for "prudence and discretion" on the part of the Ecuadorian government in its public declarations, and the need to "find a mechanism for cooperation to combat drug trafficking, terrorism and border control" (Alsema, 2008, November 21). Correa is dismissive of the letter, and advises Uribe to "get his own house in order before involving other Latin American countries in his problem"; he accuses the foreign minister of lying and suggests he abandon his cynicism: "He should first fix his own government and all its relations with paramilitaries" (*Diario Hoy*, 2008, December 28).

In an official letter dated November 5, 2008, Ecuador vigorously protests the incursion of some 20 heavily-armed paramilitaries, from a group known as the "Black Eagles," into its territory; in pursuing their target, the paramilitaries harass and injure several people, one of whom dies. The letter criticizes Colombia's lack of vigilance along the frontier, and calls for increased border control. It also announces that the incident has been brought to the attention of the OAS. Ecuador's relations with Colombia continue to be severely strained. Its relations with Venezuela, on the other hand, are on the mend.

REELECTION

On January 15, 2009, President Correa, delivers to Congress an assessment of his two years in office and the progress of the "Citizens' Revolution." He singles out the ratification of the new constitution as his greatest achievement, in that it will "allow us to overcome the neoliberal paradigm, this concentrating and servile model that has dominated over the past three decades." The president highlights the reduction in economic inequality—one of the highest, he claims, in the world—through raising salaries, issuing bonds, and creating jobs. For the first time social investment exceeds payments toward servicing foreign debt, which he refers to yet again as "immoral." He reiterates his support for regional integration and desire to bring about a "new world order" based on a greater respect for sovereignty. The president's approval rating surpasses 70% (*PL*, 2009, January 17).

Three days later, before a large crowd of supporters in Independence Square, the president invokes a threat looming over his government. He informs the people listening that the opposition ("those who do not want the country to advance") will stage a march the following day and goes on to warn of "agitations" talking place within certain military circles, including rumors circulating about unrest within the armed forces; the possibility of an "illegal play," Correa claims, cannot be dismissed. He refers to the indigenous shutdown in response to the mining law as "absurd, irrational and terrible," and, calling for continued support of his political agenda, exclaims: "Not even one step backwards with the Citizens' Revolution!" (*Prensa Web YVKE*, 2009, January 19).

The demonstration to which the president refers is not the first the opposition has organized in Guayaquil, the largest city in the country and capital of the Guayas province, a wealthy agricultural center whose aristocratic landowners, similar to those in Bolivia's Media Luna provinces, are conservative and separatist (though nonviolent in their methods). They protest the new constitution's prohibition on splitting up the country and the enhancement of presidential powers. Under the new constitution the state will exert greater control over the petroleum and mining industries, as well the budget for social programs. Among the elite there is also discomfort with new laws that seek to curb tax evasion, which, according to the president, is detrimental to the economy and country.

Guayaquil's conservative mayor, Jaime Nebot, a member of the Social Christian Party (PSC), leads the opposition. A respected figure in the province, he enjoys widespread support not only among the middle and upper classes, which tend to share his hostility towards the president, but also among workers and the poor, who have benefited from various social programs the mayor has implemented. Nebot's opposition activities are a source of concern, even though the pro-government portion of the population comprises a clear majority.

Supported by his party, PAIS Alliance, Correa launches his reelection campaign. On January 28, 2009, his party triumphs in 21 of 24 governorships. On April 26, in general elections Correa is reelected in the first round of voting with 52%, despite his government's ongoing disagreement with indigenous groups. His opponent, the former colonel and president Lucio Gutiérrez, whose previous government was brought down in April 2005, only obtains 27% of the vote. It is a decisive victory: the Citizens' Revolution and 21st century socialism gain new momentum. "The Revolution is marching forward and nothing, nobody will stop us," the president proclaims. He pledges to renew his commitment to the poor. Though his term ends in 2013, under the new constitution he could be reelected for a second time (Ayala Aamaniego, 2009, April 27).

Opposition leaders refuse to acknowledge the election results, arguing that the election was "unequal"; they cite Correa's use of government resources, including the presidential jet, for campaigning around the country. Over the past year, Jaime Nebot has been calling for complete autonomy in Guayas. The mayor holds illegal referendums—approving autonomy by 95%—which he attempts to make the government recognize (Ayala Aamaniego, 2009, April 27). He threatens to continue waging his anti-government campaign, but Correa can still count on the majority.

THE STORY CONTINUES

For decades the nations of South America have enjoyed peaceful relations; Colombia's conflict with Ecuador and Venezuela, therefore, casts an unfamiliar, ominous shadow over the geopolitical panorama. Following the 2008 cross-border strike, Correa refuses to reestablish the relations with Colombian before its government turns over additional information and videos pertaining to the operation, as well as the hard drives recovered from the encampment. Ecuador also seeks clarification regarding the role of the United States in the attack. Colombia's foreign minister, Jaime Bermúdez, in an interview with the Ecuadorian newspaper *El Comercio*, discards the possibility of turning over those hard drives, insisting that Quito has already received all the relevant information (Telesur, 2010, March 7).

By the end of the first decade of the 20th century, leftist governments are in control of the majority of Latin American countries. In 2009, Rafael Correa and Evo Morales win reelection by wide margins. Their political parties gain majorities in their respective legislatures and register gains in the provinces. By the time the 2010 legislative elections come around, however, Hugo Chávez and his Bolivarian Revolution have lost some steam. Economic hardship is widespread, oil prices have fallen, inflation continues to be the highest on the continent, accusations of government corruption and incompetence are mounting, and rates of homicide and violence continue to soar. Discontent is high and the government's approval rating takes a dive. Nevertheless, the president manages to preserve a substantial majority in the National Assembly (95 of 165 seats), despite losing his two-thirds majority. The opposition gains more than a third of the total vote, a development that garners much attention in the local media.

In Colombia, meanwhile, a presidential change occurs. After eight controversial years Uribe's time in office comes to an end and his former defense minister, Juan Manuel Santos, is voted in to succeed him. To the surprise of many, one of the president-elect's first acts is to invite Hugo Chávez to Colombia; he welcomes the Venezuelan leader in an emotional ceremony in Santa Marta, the city in which Simón Bolivar died, where there is a monument to his legacy. His message seems to be: with Uribe out of office, there is no reason our countries can't patch things up. Santos goes on to mend relations with Ecuador, a move that is supported by the people of both countries as well as observers around the continent. There is a general feeling that regional harmony has been restored.

Upon completing his second term in 2010, Lula leaves office with enormous prestige; the void he leaves behind will be large. Dilma Rousseff, his former chief of staff, is the candidate to succeed him. After initially trailing José Serra, the governor of São Paulo, Dilma closes the gap after Lula officially throws his support behind her, and eventually rallies to overtake her opponent. Some supporters, however, fear her administration will tack to the right. In Chile, a change of course is all but certain. Despite leaving office with an approval rating surpassing 80%, Michelle Bachelet's party loses the election to succeed her. Sebastián Piñera, a conservative business tycoon, whom some media commentators presume will be continuation of the Pinochet regime—which continues to be viewed favorably by large segments of the populace—triumphs. The situation in Argentina, meanwhile, is unstable. Cristina Kirchner's term is marked by achievements but also failures, and by 2010 her approval rating has fallen to 35%. Her Justicialist party is progressive, and she maintains close ties to the labor movement, and enjoys substantial popular support, but her adversarial relationship with the media harms her government's image around the country. Her term ends in 2011 and it is difficult to predict which way the pendulum will swing.

In El Salvador, some fear that President Mauricio Funes, of the FMLN, will fail to curtail the violence plaguing the country, and that the government will fall back in the hands of the same conservative forces that have historically dominated it.

In Paraguay, the former bishop Fernando Lugo, succeeds in ridding himself of cancerous tumors, but not of the constant threats from the military and conservative elite. Prior to his election, the Colorado party had governed for 61 years. Lugo's term ends in 2012.

Alan García, who over the course of his political career migrated from the leftist Peruvian Aprista Party to the far right, ends his term in July 2011 with the lowest approval rating a president has ever registered. Of the four contenders vying to succeed him—including Keiko Fujimori, daughter of the former president—Ollanta Humala's candidacy appears to be the strongest. In the first round of voting he fails to gain a majority, but in the run-off, held on June 3, 2011, he is elected president with 51.45% of the popular vote. The former military officer and founder of the Peruvian Nationalist Party, Humala opposes free trade agreements with the United States, favors the convocation of a constituent assembly to bring about constitutional reform, advocates fiscal austerity, and reigning in the expenditures, privileges and immunity of legislators. These proposals are the same ones he put forth during the 2006 presidential campaign. His supporters hope he will stick to his campaign pledges.

Progressive governments around the region continue to be targeted by powerful right-wing interests both at home and abroad. Despite his natural propensity towards optimism, Fidel Castro predicts that by the time Obama finishes his term there will be six to eight right-wing governments on the continent (*AFP*, 2009, November 13).

In December 2009, at Georgetown University, Secretary of State Clinton outlines U.S. foreign policy toward Latin America, which is based, she explains, on three axes: "Democracy, development, and broad dialogue with its partners." She reiterates her support for the Honduran elections, a controversial position that contradicts the majority of Latin American governments, which are critical of the U.S. president's overall erratic response to the military coup. Secretary Clinton reiterates her criticisms of Hugo Chávez, which are the same as those leveled by President Bush and Condoleezza Rice. "We have expressed our concern for Venezuela and for Nicaragua," she says, and declares her desire to see a "democratic Cuba" in the future. She warns Venezuela and Bolivia against "flirting with Iran" and suggests that should their governments continue to deepen those ties "they will have to face the consequences." From La Paz, Evo Morales responds that those threats "don't accomplish anything and we wholly reject them. The United States has no moral authority to speak about terrorism, considering it sends troops to other countries and sets up bases in other regions and continents" (*AFP, Reuters, DPA*, 2009, December 13). Secretary Clinton omits any mention of Brazil, though Lula maintains broad relations with Iran and its president, and supports its right to develop a nuclear program for peaceful ends—a position that is anathema to Washington and its allies—and opposes the economic sanctions advocated by the United States in the UN. Other Latin American leaders are also critical of Clinton's threats. Despite not having a close relationship with Iran, Christina Kirchner voices her disapproval of the Secretary of State's interference in the internal affairs of other countries.

President Obama faces a continent drifting out of Washington's orbit, a region no longer willing to engage in asymmetrical relations based on submission and dependence. The collapse of the global financial system discredits the Washington Consensus and many countries begin dismantling failed neoliberal programs. Obama inherits strained relationships with Bolivia and Venezuela. Morales has expelled President Bush's ambassador, as well as the DEA and its agents for interfering in his country's internal affairs and conspiring against his government, and the relations are yet to thaw.

During his first term in office, Obama makes little effort to bridge the gap between his country and Latin America. Washington continues to carry out activities—both declared and covert—aimed at destabilizing inconvenient or hostile governments. In 2009, the presidents of Ecuador, Bolivia, Paraguay, Cuba, and Venezuela all denounce covert actives in their countries. Despite these continued strains, the prevailing sentiment around the region favors forging a relationship with the United States based on mutual respect and understanding; there is continued hope for a policy change towards the region, and Cuba, and an easing of tensions with Venezuela. Many are grateful for the solidarity shown by the Venezuelan leader, his willingness to lend a hand and dedication to achieving progress for the region as a whole.

According to Mark Weisbrot, an American economist, the creation of the Community of Latin American and Caribbean States—a Lula initiative—is the most significant geopolitical development of the past decade, in that it affects not only the region but also the rest of the world. Disillusion with President Obama, he contends, has provided additional incentive for Latin America to consolidate its independence, and points to Brazil's opening to Iran, and the emergence of Latin America as a more unified block pursuing its own agenda (Weisbrot, 2010, February 25). It is unfortunate, to many, that two years into President Obama's first term, and despite all the promises made, relations between the United States and Latin America continue so fragile.

5

Obama's World

A HISTORIC CANDIDACY

In light of its well-documented struggles with racial inequality, and global standing as the most powerful nation on the planet, the election of Barack Obama to the presidency of the United States is a transcendental event, a historical milestone for Americans as well as people around the world. For African-Americans, it is an affirmative victory, a crowning achievement after their centuries-long fight for equality. It is also a triumph for the progressive movement after decades adrift in the political wilderness.

Obama catapults into the political spotlight when he is invited by Senator John Kerry to deliver the keynote address at the 2004 Democratic National Convention. A new breed of national politician, the likes of which the country has never known, Barack Obama is the son of a Kenyan economist who was "raised in a small village [and] grew up herding goats, went to school in a tin-roof shack" and a white woman from the American heartland. He defines the "greatness" of the nation not by "the height of our skyscrapers, or the power of our military, or the size of our economy; our pride is based on a very simple premise, summed up in a declaration made over two hundred years ago: 'We hold these truths to be self-evident, that all men are created equal, that they are endowed by their Creator with certain inalienable rights, that among these are life, liberty and the pursuit of happiness.'"

Obama becomes the third African-American elected to the U.S. Senate after serving three terms in the Illinois Senate. A few years later, he launches his presidential campaign with the slogan: "Change We Can Believe In." The campaign breaks with the traditional modes of doing politics, harnessing the power of the Internet to galvanize support among people of all ethnicities, social classes and, most of all, the young, many of whom are participating in the political process for the first time.

The Obama campaign declines public funding and instead capitalizes on grassroots enthusiasm and its Internet savvy to raise millions of dollars from small individual donors. The campaign focuses on the economic crisis, the unpopular war in Iraq—which costs the country hundreds of millions of dollars every day—and the dysfunction of the healthcare system. Obama pledges to withdraw troops from Iraq and criticizes the excessive influence of corporate interests in Washington. He accuses his principal rival in the Democratic primaries, Hillary Clinton, of representing the same old brand of politics.

Despite attempts to leave the issue of race out of the campaign, when video footage surfaces of Obama's former pastor at the Trinity United Church of Christ, Jeremiah Wright, delivering incendiary comments in the way of the 9-11 attacks, the candidate has no choice but to respond. "We bombed Hiroshima," the Reverend Wright was recorded saying, "we bombed Nagasaki, and we nuked far more than the thousands in New York and the Pentagon, and we never batted an eye…and now we are indignant, because the stuff we have done overseas is now brought back into our own front yards. America's chickens are coming home to roost." Wright's sermons are subjected to intense media scrutiny and political commentators wonder if Obama's close relationship with the outspoken pastor implies a tacit agreement with the controversial views expressed in the videos. Obama denies being present when the sermons in question were delivered, and condemns the inflammatory statements, but critics continue to zero in on his relationship with the pastor. On March 18, 2008 at the National Constitution Center in Philadelphia, the candidate delivers one of the defining speeches of his political career: "A More Perfect Union." He remarks that some people are attempting to polarize the campaign with the issue of race, and declares that the views Reverend Wright expressed have "the potential not only to widen the racial divide, but […] denigrate both the greatness and the goodness of our nation." While restating that his campaign has never been about race, he concedes it is an issue the country cannot afford to ignore:

> We do need to remind ourselves that so many of the disparities that exist in the African-American community today can be directly traced to inequalities passed on from an earlier generation that suffered under the brutal legacy of slavery and Jim Crow. Segregated schools were, and are, inferior schools; we still haven't fixed them, 50 years after Brown vs. Board of Education, and the inferior education they provided, then and now, helps explain the pervasive achievement gap between today's black and white students [...] For the men and women of Reverend Wright's generation, the memories of humiliation and doubt and fear have not gone away; nor has the anger and the bitterness of those years.

The candidate concludes the speech on a more upbeat note: "America can change. That is true genius of this nation. What we have already achieved gives us hope—the audacity to hope—for what we can and must achieve tomorrow."

Political analysts hail the speech as masterful, and it helps Obama finally put behind him the controversy that threatened to sink his campaign. In a close and hard-fought primary he defeats Hillary Clinton, and moves on to confront a Republican ticket of John McCain and Sarah Palin in the general election. With only a couple months to go before the November election, economic disaster strikes: the financial system teeters on the brink of collapse. The economy becomes a focal point of the presidential campaign. Amid the confusion and distress caused by the demise of several financial institutions, and the growing number of unemployed nationwide, Obama declares that, while his government will not be able to resolve every problem, his administration will do what it can to attend to the needs of all Americans, regulate the economic justly, guarantee clean air and food, and ensure that the sick have access to healthcare and the young to education (*The New York Times*, 2008, November 5).

On November 4, 2008, the Obama–Biden ticket triumphs with 53% of the popular vote. In his acceptance speech, the president-elect remarks:

> If there is anyone out there who still doubts that America is a place where all things are possible, who still wonders if the dream of our founders is alive in our time, who still questions the power of our democracy, tonight is your answer [...] It's the answer spoken by young and old, rich and poor, Democrat and Republican, black, white, Hispanic, Asian, Native American, gay, straight, disabled and not disabled. Americans who sent a message to the world that we have never been just a collection of individuals or a collection of red states and blue states. We are, and always will be, the United States of America.

The president-elect pays tribute to the American soldiers serving overseas as well as ordinary families struggling to get by in hard economic times: "Let us remember that, if this financial crisis taught us anything, it's that we cannot have a thriving Wall Street while Main Street suffers. In this country, we rise or fall as one nation, as one people."

Obama is sworn into office on a winter morning, January 20, 2009. It is a day of celebration for tens of millions of Americans, and many more around the globe. David Sanger of *The New York Times* renders the scene as such:

> There were middle-aged veterans of the civil rights movement for whom this seemed the crowning achievement of a lifetime of struggles. And there were young Americans — and an overwhelming number of young African-Americans — with no memory of the civil rights movement or of the cold war, for whom Mr. Obama was a symbol of an age of instant messaging, constant networking and integration in every new meaning of the word (Sanger, 2009, January 21).

The rest of the nation follows the ceremony from their television sets, the largest audience that medium had ever registered. From the Washington Monument to Capital Hill, the mall overflows with people from all walks of life, who have journeyed from all corners of the country to greet the incoming president. Never before, the media reports, has the capital seen a crowd so large and enthusiastic. All the living former presidents, as well as the cupola of the outgoing Republican administration, dignitaries of every stripe, judges, legislators, Washington insiders, war veterans and Hollywood luminaries share the podium with Barack and Michelle Obama and their young daughters. Jesse Jackson, the civil rights activist and two-time presidential candidate, remarks: "All of us are feeling the joy of redemption, reconciliation and renewal" (Blackmon and Pérez, 2009, January 21).

In his inauguration address, President Obama declares:

> Forty-four Americans have now taken the presidential oath. The words have been spoken during rising tides of prosperity

and the still waters of peace. Yet, every so often the oath is taken amidst gathering clouds and raging storms. At these moments, America has carried on not simply because of the skill or vision of those in high office, but because We the People have remained faithful to the ideals of our forebears, and true to our founding documents […] That we are in the midst of crisis is now well understood. Our nation is at war against a far-reaching network of violence and hatred. Our economy is badly weakened, a consequence of greed and irresponsibility on the part of some but also our collective failure to make hard choices and prepare the nation for a new age. Homes have been lost, jobs shed, businesses shuttered. Our healthcare is too costly, our schools fail too many, and each day brings further evidence that the ways we use energy strengthen our adversaries and threaten our planet. These are the indicators of crisis, subject to data and statistics. Less measurable, but no less profound, is a sapping of confidence across our land; a nagging fear that America's decline is inevitable, that the next generation must lower its sights. Today I say to you that the challenges we face are real, they are serious and they are many. They will not be met easily or in a short span of time. But know this America: They will be met. On this day, we gather because we have chosen hope over fear, unity of purpose over conflict and discord.

He goes on to speak of the nation's diversity:

We are a nation of Christians and Muslims, Jews and Hindus, and nonbelievers. We are shaped by every language and culture, drawn from every end of this Earth. And because we have tasted the bitter swill of civil war and segregation and emerged from that dark chapter stronger and more united, we cannot help but believe that the old hatreds shall someday pass; that the lines of tribe shall soon dissolve; that as the world grows smaller, our common humanity shall reveal itself; and that America must play its role in ushering in a new era of peace.

He highlights the importance of the moment:

This is the meaning of our liberty and our creed, why men and women and children of every race and every faith can join in celebration across this magnificent mall. And why a man whose father less than 60 years ago might not have been served at a local restaurant can now stand before you to take a most sacred oath.

In an editorial, *The New York Times* remarks:

There was no shortage of powerful imagery on Barack Obama's Inauguration Day, starting with the confident man who defied all political conventions — that he was too young, too inexperienced, too black or not black enough — to stand on the steps of the Capitol and take the oath of office in a city and a country that are still racially divided in many shameful ways (*The New York Times*, 2009, January 21)

The editorial revels in the excitement of the people around the country, despite the myriad challenges confronting the nation, and notes that in his inaugural address the president provided "the clarity and the respect for which all Americans have hungered. In about 20 minutes, he swept away eight years of President George Bush's false choices and failed policies and promised to recommit to America's most cherished ideals. It filled us with hope," the editorial concludes, "that with Mr. Obama's help, this battered nation will be able to draw together and mend itself."

The Times also notes that the new president's words signaled "a commitment to remake America's approach to the world and embrace pragmatism, not just as a governing strategy but also as a basic value. It was, in many ways, exactly what one might have expected from a man who propelled himself to the highest office in the land by denouncing how an excess of ideological zeal had taken the nation on a disastrous detour" (Sanger, 2009, January 21). A photograph of the helicopter escorting ex-President Bush and his family back to Texas accompanies the article. The image seems to pronounce the end of a sinister decade, one marked by fear and distrust and despair. Around the world millions let out a sigh of relief as that helicopter departs from the nation's capital.

PRESIDENT OBAMA

There is, indeed, much work to be done, and damage to be undone. The country is mired in the worst economic crisis since the Great Depression; according to Paul Krugman of *The New York Times*, the economy is in "free fall" (Krugman, 2009, February 6). That national debt has risen to eleven trillion dollars, the armed forces are bogged down in a pair of ruinous and unpopular wars, and the country's image has taken a hit around the world. The new administration's priority is responding to economic hardship on the domestic front: extending a lifeline to ailing financial institutions and the automobile industry, creating new jobs for the growing ranks of unemployed (two million are sacked in the first months of 2009 alone) and helping families who have lost their homes. Immigration is another issue the new administration must address. There are eleven million undocumented workers in the country—the majority Hispanic—an unsustainable situation that is further aggravated by the economic downturn.

On the diplomatic front, President Obama must mend tattered relations with European allies, as well as Russia and the Muslim world. The Bush administration has allowed the Israeli-Palestinian conflict to stagnate and fester, a toxic conflict with ripple effects throughout the region. President Obama has to deal with wars in Iraq and Afghanistan, manage the fraught relationship with Pakistan, combat the continued threat of Al Qaeda, the Taliban and other terrorist groups; navigate international disputes with Iran and North Korea over their nuclear programs, the political quagmire surrounding Cuba, and diminished relationships in Latin America, Washington's traditional sphere of influence.

In outlining his administration's foreign policy, President Obama pledges to withdraw troops from Iraq in sixteen months and, on his first day in office, orders the Pentagon to begin planning a "responsible," gradual withdrawal of the 140 thousand troops stationed in that country. Despite his stated desire to wind down the war in Afghanistan as well, the president authorizes an additional 30 thousand troops to that country. The "surge" is seen as a success; after eight years of combat, however, the Taliban once again controls two-thirds of the country. In the first interview that Obama grants as president is to the Arab news agency *Al Arabiya*, he delivers a message to the Muslim world that Americans are not their enemy and "if countries like Iran are willing to unclench their fist, they will find an extended hand from us"—a declaration repeated from his inaugural address.

Obama sends a video greeting to the Iranian people on the Persian New Year, but not without a warning: "The United States wants the Islamic Republic of Iran to take its rightful place in the community of nations. You have that right—but it comes with real responsibilities, and that place cannot be reached through terror or arms, but rather through peaceful actions that demonstrate the true greatness of the Iranian people and civilization." He speaks of a "season of new beginnings" and establishing "constructive ties" between the two nations. In Mashad, speaking before thousands assembled in a plaza, Ayatollah Ali Khamenei dismisses the president's overtures, noting that there is not even any change in the rhetoric of the new president, whom he accuses of insulting the Iranian people by claiming they support terrorism and are constructing nuclear arms—even in a supposedly friendly greeting. The Ayatollah recites a long list of American aggressions over the past three decades and reiterates that his country's nuclear ambitions are peaceful in nature. He leaves the door open, however: "If you change, our behavior will change as well" (Skbar Dareini, 2009, March 21).

Obama has professed his support for the creation of a Palestinian state, and the Israeli government is not sold on his commitment to supporting its interests, and troubled by his overtures to Iran, which it views as the greatest threat to Israel's existence; it sees an Iran equipped with nuclear arms as a threat to the entire region. Hillary Clinton's first trip to the Middle East, during which she voices American support for a Palestinian state, receives positive reviews in the international media, as do the new administration's overtures to the region as a whole. Though he receives some flack from the right wing, opinion polls show the majority of the country approves of the president's emphasis on open diplomacy.

The world economy is the focus of the G20 conference in London, to be held in April 2009, and among the world's economic powers there are a wide spectrum of views on how to best mitigate the crisis. In the run-up to the meeting, the British prime minister, Gordon Brown, travels to several countries—including Chile and Brazil—to drum up support for his position. Obama's attendance at the summit generates high expectations among its participants. The international media covers the American president like a rock star during this first tour of Europe. Obama visits Strasbourg, France and Kiel, Germany to celebrate the 60th anniversary of NATO, and then the Czech Republic for the European Union Summit. Aware of his country's battered reputation in Europe—both for its role in spawning the economic crisis and his predecessor's foreign misadventures—Obama describes the United States as "just another actor in the global community" that, rather than always leading, will listen, exchange ideas, and act collectively with an emphasis on cooperation and diplomacy over military supremacy (Scherer, 2009, April 3).

At the G20 summit a wide range of solutions to the crisis are bandied about. The United States and United Kingdom favor providing stimulus to revive the world economy; France and

Germany, on the other hand, believe the focus should be on implementing more stringent regulation, cracking down on tax havens and demanding greater transparency in the banking system. The participants approve 750 billion dollars in aid to help prop up economies in distress; 250 billion to stimulate trade through the IMF, and 100 billion for development banks and the Third World economies most impacted; it is also agreed to crack down on tax havens, enact anti-protectionism measures, and strengthen regulation of the financial markets.

Prime Minister Brown declares the Washington Consensus dead, and argues that a new consensus must be forged to take collective action in solving the economic crisis. Governments of developing countries criticize the summit for allocating resources that will triple the IMF's lending capability, despite that organization being viewed by many as one of the culprits in the current crisis (Herrera Beltrán, 2009, April 3). According to the London police, 35,000 people participate in protests of the summit. Their slogans include: "We won't pay for your crisis," "Put the people first," and "Jobs not bombs."

Evo Morales is one of the summit's high-profile critics. "There is no way," he argues, "that the capitalist agencies that provoked the crisis are now its solution." He lambasts the "monetary injections" through the IMF and World Bank agreed upon without any corresponding reform to those institutions. "It's like turning money over to the wolf," he quips, "for the wolf to care for sheep he will devour" (Rojas, 2009, April 4).

OBAMA AND LATIN AMERICA

Latin Americans hope that President Obama's progressive worldview and cultural sensitivity will redefine Washington's relationships with foreign governments, but his foreign policy, for the most part, has followed the signposts laid out by the Bush administration. With a host of pressing matters both at home and abroad, Latin America does not rank among the new president's priorities. The White House's relations with the region remain substantially unchanged; the president offers gestures, however, to show he cares. He names a conservative Chilean-American, Arturo Valenzuela, a former Georgetown University professor, the new Assistant Secretary of State for Western Hemisphere Affairs; he also names Sonia Sotomayor, of Puerto Rican descent, to the Supreme Court. Congressional Republicans oppose her nomination, but ultimately yield and she is confirmed on August 6, 2009.

Influential business leaders and political leaders from both sides of the aisle petition President Obama to revise U.S. policy toward Cuba and lift the embargo. European allies and Latin American governments also support a new course. In his first hundred hours as president, Obama lifts two restrictions imposed by the Bush administration. Cuban-Americans will once again be allowed to travel to Cuba as well as send remittances to the island. The new president moreover authorizes the sale of agricultural and food products, but for all intents and purposes the embargo remains in place.

The U.S. naval base on Guantanamo Bay has always been a source of heated debate. From the outset, the Cuban Revolution has demanded its restitution. The United States has leased the territory since 1903, after defeating Spain in the Cuban war of independence. Since then the military installment, administered by the U.S. Southern Command, has been critical to U.S. interventions in the region. Beginning in the 1960's, at the height of the Cold War, with guerrilla movements proliferating throughout the region, Fidel Castro rails against the naval base for its role in American provocations and interventions throughout the region, such as the invasion of the Dominican Republic in 1965, Panama in 1989 and Haiti in 1994. The Cuban government has continually requested the return of Guantanamo Bay, and criticized the senior George Bush's administration for turning it into a "concentration camp" for Haitian refugees, while his son's administration has used it as a detention center for presumed terrorists. Washington's response to Havana's persistent protests against its military presence on the island is that the issue is not a "priority." Obama states that returning the territory to its "owners" would be contingent upon his own country's security plans, as well as concessions from Havana. Fidel Castro claims that imposing conditions for the territory's return would constitute an "act of bribery and an abuse of its immense power against a small country" (*BBC Mundo*, 2009, January 30).

A clamor can be heard around the region for Cuba's reinstatement to the OAS. Secretary-General Miguel Insulza describes the 1962 resolution that suspended the island as "obsolete." In June 2009, in Tegucigalpa, Honduras, the OAS Assembly General approves Cuba's reentry into the organization with no preconditions, despite Washington's attempts to impose some. When the Honduran foreign minister, Patricia Rodas, president of the Assembly, announces the decision, the audience breaks out in cheers. In Havana, hours earlier, Fidel Castro declared that his country has no interest in returning to the OAS, and Cuban officials and media outlets unleash a barrage of criticism against the organization. Two months earlier, during the Summit of the Americas, President Obama expressed his hope that Latin America would help bring about change in Cuba (*Agencia EFE* and *AFP*, 2009, April 19); apparently, the region is moving in the opposite direction.

Relations between Venezuela and the United States continue to be tense. Obama's anti-Chávez rhetoric is similar to that of his predecessor: "I have great differences with Hugo Chávez on matters of economic policy and matters of foreign policy. His rhetoric directed at the United States has been inflammatory. There have been instances in which we've seen Venezuela interfere with some of the countries that surround Venezuela in ways that I think are a source of concern." When the two leaders meet for the first time in Port of Spain, however, their exchange is polite and Obama accepts his counterpart's offer to reestablish diplomatic relations and send a new ambassador to Washington. Earlier in the year, after Chávez succeeded in abolishing presidential term limits, a manuever widely criticized in the United States and around the region, Washington refrained from meddling—as was its custom in years past. The State Department declined to comment, referring to the matter as an "internal" one pertaining to Venezuela. Analysts view this gesture as a subtle but significant change of tone and many applaud Washington's restraint.

In security matters—including military agreements and covenants, training programs and joint exercises—most of the region continues, as if by inertia, to follow in lockstep behind the Pentagon. Going back to the Reagan administration, U.S. anti-drug policy in the Andean cocaine-producing countries has been highly militarized. Around 80% of the billions of dollars funneled into Plan Colombia and the Mérida Initiative—or Plan Mexico as critics refer to it—goes toward military assistance. The right-wing governments of Álvaro Uribe and Felipe Calderón wage low-intensity wars against internal enemies: in Colombia, the guerrillas and drug-traffickers; in Mexico, organized crime, drug cartels and the social and indigenous movements branded subversive by the state. In both countries, however, the results are disappointing. Colombia continues to be the epicenter of the drug trade, cocaine continues to enter the United States by the ton, and the regions that historically cultivated coca continue to do so. Mexico, for its part, continues to be the principal cocaine transit route to the United States, its locally produced marijuana continues to flood the U.S. market, and criminal violence within its borders reaches levels unprecedented in the hemisphere.

LATIN AMERICA AND THE ECONOMIC CRISIS

At the end of 2008, the Council on Hemispheric Affairs (COHA), an independent NGO based in Washington, joins the discussion on the impact of the world financial crisis and economic downturn on the capitalist powers; it predicts that the effects will be felt most acutely in Latin America and the developing world—despite financial sectors that are for the most part stable—as the credit crunch will slow growth and development, especially in countries that are most dependent on U.S. markets, such as Mexico and Central America. It predicts a slowdown in growth, high inflation, a credit crunch, a fall in export prices, widespread layoffs and a perilous spike in unemployment, resulting in instability, including popular and labor protests. Similar difficulties will face economies that depend on tourism and remittances from overseas (Cuba, for instance, could lose a billion dollars).

The economic crisis endangers more than a dozen Venezuelan projects, including the continental oil pipeline, construction of eight refineries from Jamaica to Uruguay, and petroleum pacts signed with different regions. Chávez has no choice but to make cuts to these programs, which will diminish his sphere of influence. In 2008, the government invested

70 billion dollars abroad, but by 2009 that figure has fallen to six billion.

The news, however, is not all bad for Venezuela. Chávez pledges to maintain the same level of social spending, which already exceeds that of other countries in the region. His Bolivarian Missions benefit millions of the country's most disadvantaged citizens. Through international assistance, the Venezuelan leader maintains influence over the fifteen nations of Central America and the Caribbean, in addition to ALBA's six members. The Bank of the South, one of his most ambitious initiatives, continues to move forward (Romero, 2009, May 20). In May 2009, the Bank's members set their annual contributions: Venezuela, Argentina and Brazil will contribute two billion dollars every year, while Bolivia, Ecuador, Paraguay and Uruguay will be responsible for 100 million dollars until reaching their two-billion dollar requirement. Though the bank is yet to commence operations, the initiative has become a reality, according to Venezuela's foreign minister, Nicolás Maduro.

To counter the effects of the economic crisis, several Latin American countries look for new markets, broadening diplomatic and commercial relations with China, Russia, and the Middle East. The Brazilian, Argentine and Chilean governments subsidize exports.

By April 2009, the American economy begins to show modest signs of recovery, and many countries hope Washington will extend additional aid, as the United States continues to be the world's largest economy, despite the pain inflected by the financial meltdown. The IMF's director declares that the "the beginning of the recovery is coming and will continue to come from the United States," but concedes that "the crisis is far from being overcome and months of economic hardship are still to come." Many analysts believe that the American and Chinese economy—which has continued to grow throughout the crisis—will be the first to recover (Hill, 2009, April 26).

SUMMIT OF THE AMERICAS

In December 1994 Bill Clinton inaugurates the first Summit of the Americas as a forum to resolve regional issues—despite the OAS serving that same function for the previous fifty years. The selection of Miami as the host city, some commentators suggest, could be seen as a nod to the anti-Castro groups that exert considerable influence over Washington's hemispheric policy. At this first summit, the creation of a free-trade zone spanning the entire region is proposed. In the 2001 summit in Quebec, the FTAA is created. Lula da Silva opposes the agreement, arguing that it contains protectionist clauses that will be harmful to Latin America. At the Fourth Summit, in November 2005, the agreement is scuttled. President Bush's presence at the summit, which is held in Mar del Plata, generates a wave of protests historic in scale.

There is a certain degree of unease on both sides leading up to the first encounter between President Obama and the Latin

American and Caribbean heads of state; countries with closer ties to Washington take steps to settle the atmosphere. Vice President Biden is invited to a couple comparatively low-profile summits: the first, a meeting of "Progressive Leaders" in Chile, on March 27, called by Michelle Bachelet to discuss and align positions on the economic crisis prior to the upcoming G20 summit in London—despite the fact that Chile and other invitees, such as Norway and Uruguay, are not even members of that group. In the final resolution the attendees "commit" to arriving in London with "a united vision that will create a new economy in which prosperity will be widely shared"–a very broad goal that is left unexplained. Hugo Chávez, who was not invited to the conference, accuses Bachelet of undermining South American unity by inviting "two representatives of the 'Empires'" (*AFP*, 2009, March 31).

The second summit, to be held in Costa Rica on March 30, is called by President Óscar Arias for his Central American colleagues. After learning of Joe Biden's plan to attend, Daniel Ortega and Manuel Zelaya announce they will send representatives in their stead. Zelaya publishes an open letter to Barack Obama, who is yet to take office, criticizing Washington for interventionism, and "inappropriate" statements from its Latin American ambassadors; he also calls for the elimination of covert ops from its policy toolkit. The summit addresses topics as far ranging as the global economic crisis, the war on drugs, and immigration without reaching any conclusions. "It's not the ideal moment," Vice President

Biden admits, "to deal with immigration reform in Congress," and asks for patience. Cuba is not discussed, but the vice president assures journalists that the United States will not lift the embargo. "We hope for a transition," he states, and a "firm commitment from Cuba to democracy and human rights"—demands similar to those made by the Bush administration (*AFP, DPA,* and *Reuters,* 2009, March 31; Gutiérrez, 2009, March 29).

The perception of the United States as a champion of human rights deteriorates even further following the release of photographs taken in the Abu Ghraib prison that depict American soldiers humiliating and torturing defenseless Iraqi prisoners; moreover, international human rights organizations, such as Amnesty International and Human Rights Watch, denounce the use of torture in the Guantanamo detention center, military prisons in Afghanistan and CIA "black sites."

In preparation for the summit in Port of Spain, Chávez convenes ALBA's six members in Cumaná, Venezuela, to reach common ground on certain issues. The heads of state of Nicaragua, Honduras, Bolivia, the Dominican Republic, and Cuba all participate, in addition to the presidents of Paraguay and Ecuador, as special guests. The attendees declare "unacceptable" the goals elaborated in the Fifth Summit's final resolution for excluding Cuba, failing to respond to the global crisis, and attempting to impose on the world solutions adopted by exclusive groups like the G20; if these concerns are not addressed they pledge to exercise their veto power

(*DPA* and *Reuters*, 2009, April 18). From Mexico, where he is meeting for the first time with Felipe Calderón, Obama calls Lula da Silva to ask for help in avoiding a crisis (Petrich, 2009, April 18).

President Obama receives a warm reception in Port of Spain. The international media paints a picture of a cordial atmosphere fostered by the new American president's simple and open style, including towards his country's critics. Newspapers print photographs of his jocular encounter with Hugo Chávez, whom he greets in Spanish: "Como estás?" To which Chávez responds in English: "I want to be your friend." He tells Daniel Ortega: "Pleasure to meet you," and smilingly greets Evo Morales, another critic of his government. During the opening session, Chávez approaches the American president, gives him a pat on the back and presents a copy of Eduardo Galeano's *The Open Veins of Latin America: Five Centuries of the Pillage of a Continent*, a landmark historical study of the political and economic dominance exerted by his country and European powers over Latin America (*AP*, 2009, April 18; *AFP*, *DPA* and *Reuters*, 2009, April 18).

In his speech, Obama professes his desire to begin anew with Cuba: "I know it's a long road to overcome decades of distrust." He goes on to state that his country should not be blamed for all the problems afflicting Latin America, and he has not come to "debate the past, but rather address the future;" he does however, mention that Washington is willing to "acknowledge mistakes"; he wants his country to be viewed as a "friend" and "comrade" and hopes to open "a new chapter of dialogue" on a plane of "mutual respect, common interests and shared values" (*AFP*, *DPA* and *Reuters*, 2009, April 18). According to Evo Morales, Obama's speech contains positive elements, but he disagrees with the American leader's insistence on forgetting the past. "We cannot forget our history, which should be corrected, and interventionism done away with," he says (*AFP*, *DPA* and *Reuters*, 2009, April 18).

Cristina Kirchner, who inaugurates the conference, calls on Obama to lift the embargo and not allow a historic opportunity to construct new hemispheric relationships pass by. Alluding to the defeat of the FTAA, a pet policy project of several U.S. administrations, she reminds those in attendance that the previous summit, held in her country, marked an "inflection point" in hemispheric relations (*AFP*, *DPA*, y *Reuters*, 2009, April 19).

There is no mention of the Cuban embargo in the final resolution. "In 67 pages and 97 epigraphs the countries reaffirm their commitment to a broad range of issues and problems, all of which are important, none a priority; there is an inflation of thematic references and devaluation of specific commitments. In their current state, the summits have lost their reach, focus and consensus," opines the Argentine sociologist Juan Tokatlian (2009, April 22). Felipe Calderón criticizes the declaration's failure to address the economic crisis; Rafael Correa dismisses it as "irrelevant and inconsequential;"

in light of so many reservations, Patrick Manning, the president of Trinidad and Tobago, signs the final resolution on behalf of all, stating "it is a compromise that receives the approval of some, but not of others; we adopt it acknowledging that it was not unanimous (*DPA*, 2009, April 19).

In a press conference, Obama states that the summit has "served to establish a new era of respect among the sovereign and democratic countries of the continent, despite differences of opinion." He notes that there have been positive signs in the relationships between the United States and Cuba and Venezuela that constitute at least an opportunity for "frank dialogue" on a wide range of issues, including democracy and the defense of human rights, in all the hemisphere." For some of its participants, the summit is "historic" and "extraordinary"; Lula christens it the "summit of Obama" and Chávez suggests that the summit "came close to perfection" as "cordiality reigned, and it concluded with a new climate, opening the gates for a new era of relations for all the countries of our continent;" he also affirms that the topic of Cuba was present "from the beginning to the end" of the meeting. This is the first Summit of the Americas to conclude without participants signing a final resolution, but there was no acrimony either, as Obama's cordiality proved disarming to all (*AFP*, *DPA*, and *Reuters*, 2009, April 20).

In his weekly *Granma* column, titled "Delirious Dreams," Fidel Castro ridicules the euphoria of certain Latin American leaders who described the summit as the "most extraordinary that has ever taken place," while taking a jab at the OAS. Judging from the euphoria at the summit, he writes, one would think a miracle had occurred, like the "discovery of the philosopher's stone," when in fact it was just the OAS "saving us all"—as was established in 13 of 97 epigraphs of the final statement (Castro, 2009, April 21). The Cuban leader continues with a tongue-in-cheek rumination:

Can it be the OAS is the protector of the independence and integrity of the Latin American people? Always! Has the OAS ever intervened in the internal matters of a country in the hemisphere? Never! Is it true that it's just a docile instrument of the United States? Not at all! Has even one Latin American or Caribbean person ever died on its account? Not one, that is just slander of Castro-communism emanating from Cuba, a country expelled from the OAS for declaring itself Marxist-Leninist, where there has never been an election, nobody votes or is elected, and where a tyranny, which has had the gall to confront a docile, defenseless and poor country like the United States for the past half century, reigns.

Republican leaders waste no time in criticizing the friendly exchanges between Presidents Obama and Chávez. Senator John Ensign of Nevada accuses the president of being "irresponsible" for laughing and joking with "the most anti-American leader in the world." Obama responds that a short conversation and handshake with Chávez "hardly puts the strategic interests of the United States in danger" (Barrionuevo and Stolberg, 2009, April 20). Chávez later remarks: "It was with pleasure that I extended my hand to Obama, however the 'Empire' is alive and well" (*Agencia EFE*, 2009, April 24).

IN MEXICO FOR THE FIRST TIME

Between March and April of 2009, Secretary of State Hillary Clinton, Secretary of Homeland Security Janet Napolitano, and Attorney General Eric Holder visit Mexico in preparation for the first meeting between Presidents Obama and Calderón. The cabinet members address sensitive issues concerning both countries, such as drug trafficking, NAFTA, and the millions of undocumented Mexicans living north of the border. Secretary Clinton acknowledges the "insatiable" demand for illicit drugs that fuels the drug trade, not just in the U.S. but throughout the region, and expresses disappointment with the inability of her country to crack down on the activity of Mexican crime syndicates beyond its borders. Wars between drug cartels also claim the lives of police, soldiers and civilians. The parties agree to collaborate in the war on drugs and enhancing border security, a responsibility Secretary Clinton affirms should be shared (Landler, 2009, April 18).

Drug trafficking and immigration are critically important issues to both countries. Their shared border extends over three thousand kilometers, demarcating a volatile region traumatized by violent territorial wars between drug cartels, arms trafficking, and money laundering. President Bush orders the construction of a fence spanning the entire border and the installation of a security network of border guards, canines and helicopters. But tens of thousands of undocumented workers, and tons upon tons of illicit narcotics, continue streaming over the border; arms trafficking and money laundering, likewise, proceed unabated. Clandestine alliances form between cartels from both countries looking to maintain their hold on the billion-dollar business. Obama also must address a trade war between the countries: the U.S. Congress, in violation of NAFTA, bars the entrance of Mexican trucks; Mexico, in retaliation, imposes a billion dollars in tariffs on American goods. There are also disagreements concerning the prosecution of the drug war: the U.S Congress withholds 15% of economic aid until the State Department certifies that Mexico has put in place certain human rights protections, a response to past violations by its security forces.

The levels of violence spawned by the Mexican cartels have no precedent. In the corridors of Congress, organized crime and public insecurity in Mexico is seen as a threat to national security. Around 90% of firearms confiscated by Mexican authorities originate up north, purchased with revenues from U.S. drug sales, estimated to be between 12 and 15 billion dollars per year. Security issues—in particular firearms trafficking—dominate the first meeting between the two presidents.

In June 2008, the United States and Mexico formalize their cooperation in the war on drugs. The Bush administration signs the Mérida Initiative, which covers Central America and the Caribbean as well, for an initial period of three years. That same month, U.S. Congress approves 400 million dollars in military aid to Mexico for the purchase of 412 helicopters, two Cessna airplanes and a small surveillance aircraft, in addition to police and military training and judicial system reform. All other countries are assigned 65 million dollars. As President Obama arrives in Mexico, drug cartels are locked in a bloody territorial dispute in the border region. Homicides rise to 7,300 in 2008, with an additional thousand in the first months of 2009. On the eve of the American president's arrival, a clash between drug-traffickers and police leaves 16 dead in the state of Guerrero. Obama offers to beef up the Mérida Initiative and, in 2009, Mexico receives an additional 450 million dollars, and Central America and the Caribbean 100 million more. Like Secretary Clinton, Obama acknowledges the correlation between demand for drugs in the U.S. and the spate in criminality south of the border, and once again calls for joint efforts between the two countries in the war on drugs, illegal arms trafficking, money laundering and terrorism. He claims to be reviewing the possibility of dispatching troops to the border, as some governors in that region have called for, but which the president has been reluctant to militarize.

Calderón dispatches 45,000 troops and a thousand police—trained by the United States—to the country's most bloody regions. Complains of abuses and brutality follow. According to Human Rights Watch, "the Mexican armed forces commit grave human rights violations, forced disappearances, assassinations, torture, sexual assaults, arbitrary detentions, abuses committed with impunity"; the organization furthermore claims that military justice "does not work, it is broken, and hardly transparent" and "there is not one single documented case of military personnel accused of these violations being tried or sentenced" (Ballinas, 2009, April 30).

Obama and Calderón also discuss illegal immigration to the United States. In 2008, 81% of immigrants taken into custody after entering the United States illegally are Mexican. Though Obama reiterates his desire to "pull them out of the shadows" and grant undocumented workers the opportunity to legalize their status, he stops short of committing to push the wholesale reform he promised through Congress.

In April 2009, the Mexican navy participates for the first time in the UNITAS Gold multinational maritime exercises, organized by the United States, with Latin American, German, and Canadian militaries also participating. The Commander of the U.S. Naval Forces Southern Command applauds its participation as "one of the most important strategic elements" of those exercises, whose purpose, he states, is maritime security and combating the drug trade. In UNITAS Gold 2004 Mexico had participated only as an observer.

In an editorial published April 21, 2009, the Mexican daily *La Jornada* characterizes Mexico's participation as "worrisome and improper" when taking into account that "the doctrines, objectives and values of the two nations are distinct and even conflicting;" the editorial rails against the "predominantly aggressive [nature] of the American military apparatus, which turns it into a systematic violator of national sovereignty, spawning 'monstrosities' of preventive wars." This military cooperation is a "historical anomaly," considering that since its independence Mexico has been the object of American "expansionist and interventionist designs," which are incompatible with the southern nation's values in the international sphere (*La Jornada*, 2009, April 21). Mexico's historical commitment to national sovereignty and independence, and the country's centuries-long resistance to its powerful northern neighbor, is now a thing of the past, relegated to the realm of nostalgia. Dating back to the neoliberal government of Carlos Salinas de Gortari, which negotiated NAFTA, Mexico's foreign policy has undergone a radical makeover; Salinas surrendered the country to Washington.

PRETTY WORDS, VAGUE PROMISES

The contours—and main objectives—of the Obama administration's policy towards Latin America remain ill defined. Aside from vague promises of "social inclusion" through free enterprise, renewed dialogue on equal footing, and cooperation with democratic governments and "new beginnings," there have been few substantive changes in Washington's relationship with the region; tensions with Venezuela remain high, policy change with respect to Cuba only benefits Cuban-Americans and their relatives on the island; the embargo—and hostile rhetoric—continues.

In May 2009, at the annual conference of the Council of the Americas, an American business association whose goal is promoting free trade and enterprise throughout the region, James Steinberg, Deputy Secretary of State, addresses U.S. policy in Latin America (Brooks, 2009, May 14). The priority of the administration, he concedes, is getting the nation's economy back on track; he does tout, however, the president's trip to Mexico, his participation in the Summit of the Americas, Lula da Silva's invitation to the White House, the attendance of Vice President Biden at two Latin American summits, and Secretary Clinton's visits to Mexico, Haiti, and the Dominican Republic.

In this same forum Hillary Clinton broaches some controversial issues. Free enterprise and globalization, she claims, will not be the only lodestar of U.S. policy; social inclusion and the "equitable distribution of prosperity" will be focal points as well. Though it may not be the poorest region in the world, Latin America has the most unequal income distribution. Clinton also acknowledges the "process of sub-regional integration," praising UNASUR's contributions to the hemispheric agenda (Brooks, 2009, May 14).

U.S.-Venezuelan tensions continue under the new president. During the 2008 campaign, Obama accused Chávez of "impeding progress in the region" and "exporting terrorist activities and supporting 'malicious' entities like the FARC," which, he added, "we cannot accept." As president, Obama repeats the same criticisms (El Espectator, 2009, January 18). Judging from those statements, his administration's policy towards Cuba and Venezuela will likely amount to more of the same.

Obama's claim of having revised Washington's policy toward Cuba is belied by his rhetoric: he calls on the Castro government to change and adhere to the Inter-American Democratic Charter. As a conciliatory gesture, however, Washington removes the electronic ticker from the top of its interests section in Havana, which had scrolled pro-democracy slogans from the likes of Abraham Lincoln and Martin Luther King, much to the chagrin of Fidel Castro (Hirsh, 2009, August 1). In its August 1 edition, *Newsweek* asks: What happened to the new policy towards Cuba? Four months have passed since the Obama administration announced it was lifting of the restrictions imposed by his predecessor, but no measures have yet been taken. Cuban-Americans Ileana Ros-Lehtinen and Robert Menendez, and many other Republican legislators, fervently oppose any overtures to the Castro brothers.

To avoid confrontation with European governments, Obama, like his predecessor's, temporarily suspends (for a period of six months, beginning August 1, 2009) Section III of the Cuban Liberty and Democratic Solidarity Act (also known as the Helms–Burton Act) which imposes sanctions on non-U.S. companies that do business with Cuba, and authorizes American citizens to sue anyone making use of property that was confiscated by the Revolution. European countries have threatened to challenge the law in the International Court of Justice, on the grounds that its extraterritorial clauses violate principles of free international commerce and interfere in the internal concerns of other nations (*Agencia EFE*, 2009, July 15). Its temporary suspension, however, does not bring any tangible benefit to Cuba.

ARIZONA SENATE BILL 1070

In 2010, Obama again proposes wholesale immigration reform, despite the hostile political climate and nationwide polarization. The country is still feeling the effects of the financial crisis, with several critical industries ailing and high unemployment. Republicans blame the Obama administration. Despite the steadfast Republican obstructionism, Democrats continue fighting to push their agenda forward. Towards the end of February, when he goes before Congress to present his plans for job creation, bank bailouts, healthcare reform, as well as education, social security and energy initiatives, Obama makes no mention of immigration. His silence is telling. In April 2010, the topic of undocumented immigrants and the urgent need for reform is thrust into the national debate by the murder of a prominent Arizona rancher, Bob Krentz, near the Mexican border; rumors circulate that the assassin was an illegal immigrant, presumably Hispanic. The crime stokes anti-immigrant backlash in border states: governors request federal troops and law enforcement agents to crack down on illegal crossings. In Arizona, a border state with a high percentage of undocumented immigrants, the legislature responds by passing the nation's toughest law against illegal immigration. Arizona Senate Bill 1070 authorizes the police to interrogate individuals if there is "reasonable suspicion" that they are undocumented, and criminalizes the failure to carry valid identification within the state. Individuals unable to prove their legal standing are subject to detainment and deportation. Applying for a job without a visa is also criminalized. Arizona's Republican governor, Janet Brewer, signs the bill into law. Latinos denounce the law as racist and one unjustly targeting their communities. Reactions both for and against the polarizing legislation are swift in coming; expressions of intolerance and xenophobic sentiment proliferate. Economic hardship and high unemployment fan anti-immigrant phobias; undocumented residents are accused of taking jobs from American citizens. Congressional Republicans advocate stripping the children of undocumented immigrants born inside in the U.S. of their citizenship, despite the constitutional guarantee; others call for mining the border.

Latino and progressive activists organize large demonstrations and marches in Phoenix, as well as other cities around the country, to protest SB 1070. On May 1, 2010, International Workers' Day, demonstrations are staged simultaneously in 70 cities, including Miami, Boston, Chicago, Detroit, Los Angeles, New Jersey and New York.

Hispanic communities feel persecuted and there is widespread frustration with Obama's management of immigration reform; after unveiling proposals in both 2009 and 2010, the president has given no indication that he will push for reform in 2011. The issue continues to inspire heated debate: Republicans oppose the "legalization" of undocumented immigrants, a central facet of Obama's vision, and refuse to grant any concessions before their border security demands are met. Amid the urgent cries for reform they have made it clear where they stand. On July 1, Obama dedicates an entire speech to immigration, in which he describes the current system as "fundamentally broken" and urges congressional action. Obama must somehow accommodate both Republican demands for enhanced border security and his own base's clamoring for a clear path towards citizenship. Yet the Republican idea of fencing off the entire border, and dispatching federal troops to guard the frontier, the president dismisses as fantasy. He criticizes Republicans for standing in the way of critical reform, and calls for bipartisan cooperation moving forward.

Many dismiss Obama's speech as nothing more than political gamesmanship, a play for Latino votes in the upcoming election (Baker, 2010, July 2). Republicans describe the strategy as demagogic, and argue that with 15 million Americans unemployed it is not the right time to ease the rules for millions of immigrants who are already illegally in the labor force. Taking into account the urgent legislation currently swamping Congress, and the political polarization in Washington, the White House indicates that the transformational immigration reform envisioned by the president would be unlikely to secure passage.

Hoping to woo Latino voters, who could prove decisive in the upcoming elections, Senate Democrats circulate a 26-page "compromise" proposal they hope will garner bipartisan support: they propose expediting a bill that would bolster border security prior to granting legal status to undocumented immigrants. Even if Congress adopts the proposal, its implementation would take several years. Experts point out the similarities between the Democratic proposal and Bush's "zero tolerance" policy with respect to illegal border crossings. In proposing more stringent anti-immigrant measures, Democrats are appropriating policies typically championed by Republicans; they go so far as endorsing mandatory national identity cards, which they had previously opposed, to win over Republican support.

Obama publicly criticizes Arizona SB 1070 for usurping federal powers. Attorney General Eric Holder challenges the law in an Arizona federal court in an attempt to block it from taking effect on July 29. Though the administration's challenge is intended to serve warning to other states, some 150 towns pass similar laws, and 13 states intend to follow in Arizona's footsteps. "The Constitution and the federal immigration laws do not permit the development of a patchwork of state and local immigration policies throughout the country" the suit says (Preston, 2010, July 6). Polls show that 59.4% support the government's legal challenge and 40.6% support the right of states to adopt their own immigration laws (*The Guardian*, 2010, July 7).

Latinos see SB 1070 as a direct consequence of the government's failure to implement immigration reform. It is not enough for the Obama administration to challenge the law in court; preventing future attacks on immigrant communities will require systemic reform and an order for the Department of Homeland Security, under Director Janet Napolitano, to suspend roundups, detentions and deportations of undocumented residents, which tear families apart and devastate communities. In 2009, some 400,000 undocumented immigrants are deported, an astounding number not even reached during the Bush years.

GLOBAL WARMING

During his campaign, Obama raises the possibility of reviving the Kyoto Treaty and bringing to an end U.S. isolation resulting from the previous administration's unilateralism. President Bush withdrew the country from the treaty in 2001, and his administration's inflexibility throughout negotiations stalled critical progress in this area. Despite pro-forma declarations of support for international treaties and cooperation, Bush clearly turned his back on Kyoto. At an October 2009 climate change conference in Bangkok, a precursor to the December summit in Copenhagen aimed at bolstering the Kyoto Treaty, the U.S. uses its influence to undermine this critical mechanism for collective action, reducing the responsibility of developed countries, global warming's primary culprits (Klein, 2009, November 2). At the 2009 United

Nations Climate Change Conference, the first opportunity in a decade for the world's governments to come together and agree on a unified approach to global warming, there is optimism that progress can be made after previous negotiations were hampered by the Bush administration. Yet the industrial powers, led by the United States, succeed in thwarting the aspirations of the Third World, which faces their own set of challenges. Western Europe, however, has committed itself to greater reductions in greenhouse gas emissions, of which the United States is the world's largest producer. The summit begins amid intrigue caused by the circulation of a document drafted in secret by a handful of industrialized countries, which they intend to submit as the summit's final resolution. The so-called "Danish document," in effect, cuts the UN out of future negotiations on climate change, and departs from the principles outlined in Kyoto Treaty, setting per capita caps on carbon emissions, which would vary for industrialized and developing countries. According to a senior Western diplomat, the terms are unfavorable to developing countries. Authored by the United States, United Kingdom and Denmark, the document is circulated among a handful of countries with similar interests (Vidal, 2009, December 8). Latin American leaders criticize the industrialized countries for standing in the way of an agreement. In an impassioned speech, Lula da Silva voices his frustration with the collective inability to draft an agreement whose goal is nothing less than saving the planet, and calls on world leaders to take concrete actions to spare poor countries from bearing the burden of climate change, including providing economic and technical assistance; he declares that Brazil is ready to do its part. Lula calls on the developing world to set more ambitious goals, including a 25-40% reduction in CO_2 emissions by 2020, the target recommended by the Intergovernmental Panel on Climate Change (IPCC). Lula urges industrialized countries to adhere to the Kyoto Treaty and reduce emissions in the way many developing countries already are doing, despite not being required to by the terms of the treaty. He calls for collective action to save humanity before it's too late (Act of Copenhagen, 2009, December 18).

Hugo Chávez lambasts the existing imbalance in which 7% of humanity is responsible for 50% of worldwide emissions. The Venezuelan president repeats the slogan reverberating outside the summit: "Don't change the climate, change the system." He inveighs against the capitalist system, accusing wealthy nations of destroying the planet. "If the climate were a bank," he quips, "they would have saved it by now." He refers the "top secret" Danish document, of whose existence many are still unaware, declaring that Venezuela and the ALBA member states will neither accept nor sign it. Evo Morales argues that rich nations owe poor ones billions of dollars in "climate reparations" and calls for the creation of a climate change court to deal with polluting countries (Kakissis, 2009, December 12).

The summit goes on for two weeks and discussions are bitter and agitated; the secret machinations of wealthy nations contribute to a toxic environment. Meanwhile, outside the Centro Belle, where the summit is being held, tens of thousands of protestors, mainly young Europeans, demand an agreement that will halt global warning; their placards accuse the world's leaders of being "climate criminals." Though their protests are peaceful the police clash with demonstrators and thousands are arrested.

The most significant conflict at the summit involves the United States and China, the two largest emitters of CO_2 gases. Their disagreement revolves around international monitoring and verification of greenhouse emissions. The U.S. insists on strict verification of Chinese compliance to which the Asian power will not consent. Absent this control Washington is unlikely to sign on to an agreement. A clandestine recording of the final session, made in the early morning of December 18 and later published by *Der Spiegel*, captures the standoff between representatives from the United States, Great Britain, Germany and France, and China—which is supported by India—all the contention and frustration bubbling to the surface, the result of China's determination to block any agreement involving mandatory reductions. Without such an agreement, however, the ability of the world to control emissions and stave off dangerous levels of planetary warming will remain in limbo (Adam and Randerson, 2010, May 7). The summit is "neither a huge success nor a complete disaster," according the editorial page of *The New York Times*, which goes on to praise the Obama administration for his hard negotiations with China (*The New York Times*, 2009, December 21). On the other end of the spectrum, Cuba's foreign minister, Bruno Rodríguez, describes the summit as a "solemn failure," a step in the wrong direction that fell far short of the international action needed to mitigate the global warming's negative effects—a view shared by Third World countries. The summit, for all intents and purposes, concludes without the adoption of any binding resolution. The industrialized countries were unwilling to take on the commitments called for by the developing world: a 40% reduction in CO_2 by 2020 and the transfer of the technology and financial aid needed by poorer countries to cut toxic emissions. The Cuban foreign minister criticizes the "ambiguous and misleading deal" made by Obama and a handful of other industrialized countries, behind the backs of the rest, as an attempt to impose their own final resolution for the summit. He makes clear that ALBA countries and Sudan, which holds the chairmanship of the Group of 77, reject that document and, after long and painstaking negotiations, they convince the rest of the delegates to recognize the controversial text as expressing a position held by only a group of 25 countries (out of 193 in total).

The United States, China, India, Brazil and South Africa draft a final resolution on their own, without input from any other countries, which they hope the entire summit will adopt. The text recognizes climate change as one of the gravest challenges facing the world and calls for collective action to maintain temperature increases under 2°C, without imposing legally binding requirements for carbon emission reductions.

The text is ultimately adopted, but after fifteen days of vigorous debate, is left virtually toothless.

The principle Chinese negotiator argues that, at this stage of its development, his country "cannot and will not" enforce too low a cap on greenhouse emissions and, moreover, given China's short history as an industrialized nation, its contribution to this global problem is not so great. Along with the United States, however, China is one of the largest producers of greenhouse gases (Lan Lan, 2010, February 25). In light of their lack of commitment, many commentators suggest that international pressure—including sanctions—will be needed to bring the United States and China into binding agreements.

In Copenhagen, Obama offers to reduce greenhouse emissions at most 17% by 2020 and extend 100 billion dollars in aid to poor countries (a third of what Europe is offering), pending congressional approval. The administration's negotiator, Todd Stern, concedes that American credibility at the next round of negotiations now hangs on Congress taking action. In February 2010, the House of Representatives passes a climate change bill, unblocking the largely stalled measure on greenhouse emissions and establishing a new set of caps. In April, Senators John Kerry and Joe Lieberman present an outline for compromise between the House and Senate (Cowan, 2010, April 11)

Foreseeing another collective failure, Evo Morales suggests that the next climate summit, scheduled for December 2010 in Cancún, Mexico, should be cancelled. "It would be devastating if the great capitalist powers put their economic interests over the survival of humanity, and a major blow to the prestige of the UN," the Bolivian president argues. At the European Union, Latin America and Caribbean (EU-LAC) Summit in Madrid, he advocates an international campaign to apply pressure before the summit convenes. "As a whole," he claims, "Europe is most responsible for climate change." He further proposes an EU-Latin American alliance in defense of life and the rights of mother earth (Cowan, 2010, April 11).

THE IRAN-LATIN AMERICA ALLIANCE

The Iranian nuclear program turns into a point of conflict between Obama and Latin America, most of all with Lula. Certain leftist governments refuse to go along with Washington's policy of isolating Tehran. Lula, Hugo Chávez, Evo Morales, and Daniel Ortega all invite President Ahmadinejad to their countries and each, in turn, receives an invitation to visit Tehran. Cooperation agreements in several different areas are signed. Other Latin American countries, including Argentina, Cuba, Costa Rica, Chile, Ecuador, Mexico, Peru and Uruguay also maintain economic ties with Iran. Only Colombia and Paraguay fall in line behind Washington. This diplomatic pivot is yet another indicator of Washington's diminished clout in its traditional sphere of influence, and the extent to which new partnerships are squeezing out the former master from the north.

Before the UN can begin debating the fourth round of sanctions against Iran, Lula takes the matter in hand. After criticizing Western leaders for seeking sanctions against a country without first engaging its leadership in dialogue, he announces: "I will do it." Brazil and Turkey, both non-permanent members of the UN Security Council, oppose sanctions. Lula suggests to Turkish Prime Minister Recep Tayyip Erdoğan that they travel to Tehran to negotiate a solution directly with President Ahmadinejad. After a long day of negotiations in the Persian capital the parties sign a tripartite agreement: Iran agrees to send the majority of its enriched uranium to Turkey in exchange for fuel rods for a medical research reactor. The terms of this agreement are identical to those Obama proposed, eight months earlier, in a letter to Lula. They must, it should follow, be acceptable.

On May 24, prior to the adoption of a fourth round of sanctions, Lula returns from Tehran proclaiming "a victory for diplomacy," touting his trip as proof that "dialogue is the best way to resolve conflicts" (*La Nación*, 2010, May 17; Eyler Reid, 2010, June 4). Western nations, including American allies, applaud the tripartite agreement. The Brazilian and international media also praise Lula's initiative, with some commentators describing it as his greatest achievement in the international arena. The negotiation, they argue, has cemented Brazil's position as a global power. Washington, nonetheless, wastes no time downplaying the achievement. A State Department official dismisses it as "too little too late"; Jackson Diehl, the Deputy Editorial Page Editor of *The Wash-*

ington Post pens an opinion piece titled: "Has Brazil's Lula Become Iran's Useful Idiot?" Hillary Clinton accuses Brazil and Turkey of attempting to ease U.S. pressure on Iran, and reiterates her demand that Iran immediately halt enriching uranium or face sanctions (Eyler Reid, 2010, June 4). The White House fears the positive worldwide response could sway China and Russia to withdraw their support for sanctions.

Obama continues to push for sanctions and on June 8, 2010 the UN Security Council adopts a 10-page resolution with 12 votes in favor of sanctions (including Russia and China), 2 against (Brazil and Turkey), and one abstention (Lebanon). The resolution orders Iran to suspend its nuclear program and allow inspectors from the International Atomic Energy Agency (IAEA) to enter the country. Hillary Clinton describes the new sanctions are the harshest yet approved by the Security Council. The Iranian Ambassador to the UN laments that the United States has opted for the path of confrontation and Ahmadinejad remarks that the resolution isn't worth a dime, just a piece of paper for the wastebasket. His country will continue enriching.

Lula predicts that the passage of new sanctions will prove to be a "Pyrrhic victory" for Washington. Incensed, he publishes the letter Obama sent him eight months before his trip to Tehran stating the demands which, one by one, Iran consented to in the tripartite agreement, including the transfer of part of its enriched uranium to Turkey in order to "build trust and reduce regional tensions." That exact term appears in the tripartite agreement that the White House now rejects. Some analysts take the president to task for his inconsistency while others are more willing to give him a pass, noting that easing sanctions in an election could have left Democratic candidates vulnerable to conservative attacks of going soft on one of the world's major "exporters of terrorism." For others, his decision to disregard the agreement represents a lost opportunity for greater understanding with Iran.

With each passing day the Iranian question further complicates the geopolitical panorama for the United States; the new alliances forming between its principle Middle Eastern rival and governments in its own backyard are unsettling. In Latin America, Washington's diminished influence is increasingly evident. In an article published in *The NACLA Report on the Americas*, Samantha Eyler cites Lula's diplomacy in arguing that much of Latin America, in the realm of foreign policy, has become independent from Washington, a geopolitical realignment that goes beyond mere rhetoric (Eyler Reid, 2010, June 4).

REELECTION PANDEMIC

On June 28, 2009 there is a military coup in Honduras. The constitutional president, Manuel Zelaya, is abducted and taken to Costa Rica. This is the first Latin American crisis Obama faces: regional leaders await the new president's response. The coup's leaders, right-wing elites acting in cahoots with high-ranking military officers, cite as one of their motivations the referendum Zelaya had been preparing that would allow him to run for reelection. The White House issues no formal opinion of Zelaya's political ambitions, and ultimately comes to support the post-coup government.

The entire region, it seems, is in a reelection state of mind, with several presidents pushing through constitutional reforms, often by way of referendum, to prolong their stays in office. The new constitutions of Ecuador and Bolivia permit consecutive presidential terms, and in Venezuela a constitutional amendment lifts term limits all together. Álvaro Uribe and Daniel Ortega both seek reelection through constitutional reform. In July 2009, addressing a crowd of supporters on the thirtieth anniversary of the Sandinista victory, Daniel Ortega declares his intention to run for reelection in 2010 by reforming the 1995 constitution, which prohibits consecutive presidential terms while also enforcing a maximum of two terms (*AFP*, 2009, July 21).

The day after the coup in Honduras, the first one-on-one meeting between Álvaro Uribe and Barack Obama takes place in the White House. In the press conference that follows, a journalist questions Obama about his Colombian counterpart's quest for a third term. Obama responds: "Our experience in the United States is that two terms work for us, and after eight years, typically, the people want change." He cites the example of George Washington, who "could have been president for life," but decided to "step aside and return to civilian life." To alleviate any subsequent awkwardness on the part of his Colombian counterpart, Obama adds: "We stand on the side of democracy, sovereignty and self-determination" (Gomez Maseri, 2009, June 30). This unexpected statement from the sitting U.S. president delights Colombians who adamantly oppose a third Uribe term; they hope that Obama has pulled the rug out from under their political bête noir.

The reelection bonanza in Latin America is not an entirely new phenomenon: in the 1990's, similar situations were seen in Peru and Guatemala, what became known as the self-coups of Alberto Fujimori ("Fujimorazo") and Jorge Serrano Elias ("Serranazo"), both of whom attempted to prolong their presidencies by circumventing democratic institutions. Two years after entering office, Fujimori shuts down Congress and dissolves the Supreme Court, forming a Government of Emergency and National Reconstruction; he later pushes for a constitutional amendment allowing him to run for a consecutive term. After securing passage of the amendment, he wins a third term in 2000, but an economic downturn and widespread opposition to his government force Fujimori to flee to Japan only 117 days into his third term, and on November 19, 2000 he faxes his resignation from Tokyo. Eying a political comeback, the exiled president later relocates to Chile. In 2007, however, the Peruvian government secures his extradition, and the Supreme Court sentences him to 25 years in prison for a slew of serious crimes.

Jorge Serrano Elias's political trajectory bears certain similarities to Fujimori's. On May 25, 1993 he too dissolves Congress, the Supreme Court and other government institutions, announcing that he will govern by decree; the Constitutional Court subsequently rules against his attempted takeover. Ten days after the self-coup, having failed to secure the support of the military, Serrano flees to Panama, where he establishes himself as a businessman.

In that same decade, Carlos Menem, a right-wing Peronist pushes for reform to modernize the Argentine constitution, which dates back to 1853; the new constitution sanctions consecutive presidential terms, which had been barred under the previous one. Menem is reelected the following year, and in 1999 tries for a third term, though his bid is ultimately ruled unconstitutional.

In his first trip to Africa, in July 2009, Obama visits Ghana and, in Accra, voices his disapproval of the dubious attempts made by some heads of state to perpetuate their terms. "History," he says, "is [...] not with those who use coups or change constitutions to stay in power. Africa doesn't need strongmen, it needs strong institutions," and warns that respect for the democratic process will be considered when extending future aid to the continent (*AFP*, 2009, July 12).

Despite announcing that sanctions will be imposed against governments that prolong their rule in violation of democratic principles, Obama accepts as legitimate the elections held by the military usurpers in Honduras, and recognizes their victor. His previous statements about respecting democratic institutions as a sine qua non for gaining Washington's support ring hollow.

THE STORY CONTINUES

So what can the world expect from Obama? From the first days of his administration, the president has created an atmosphere of openness and possibility that was nonexistent during the previous administration. His European allies encourage this constructive approach, as it breeds greater cooperation even with ongoing differences in both focus and substance—a dynamic that was on display at the G20 summit in London, and again later in the year at a summit in Copenhagen on climate change and the Afghanistan war.

Throughout his campaign Obama pledged to shake things up in Washington, but upon taking office he faces a fierce right-wing opposition that denies or distorts his government's achievements. Obama, to be sure, has failed to make good on certain campaign pledges: the detention center at Guantanamo Bay, for instance, remains open; despite promising to engage hostile regimes in dialogue, tensions with Iran have not abated; nor has the new president reached out to the Cuba, despite its government's professed willingness to engage in constructive talks; there has been no renewal of Israeli–Palestinian peace negotiations and Prime Minister Netanyahu has ignored the White House's modest request that Israel freeze construction of Jewish settlements in the

West Bank. On the other hand, relations with Washington's old rival, Russia, show signs of improving.

Obama's record in Latin America is disappointing. Although many remain hopeful that Washington will open its arms to the region, especially after the president's promising speech in Trinidad and Tobago, thus far no substantive changes have materialized. There have been two high-level visits to Mexico, White House invitations extended to several Latin American leaders, a lifting of restrictions on Cuban-Americans visiting and sending remittances to the island, but little else. Furthermore, the president is widely criticized for his handling of the Honduran coup. The military pact negotiated with Colombia for access to seven of its military bases, all but ensuring an oversized American military presence in that country, also provokes widespread indignation. Hispanic groups in the U.S. are frustrated with the stalemate on immigration reform, which the president had promised to work on his first year in office. In an editorial published on June 19, 2009, *The New York Times* calls for immigration reform to be expedited, as "inaction and the passing of time have only increased the frustration of those who have been counting on" the president; the newspaper reminds Obama of the "overwhelming" Hispanic support he rode into the White House.

6

U.S. Militarism in Latin America

FROM DRUGS TO MILITARISM

The bleakest and most confounding problem on President Obama's Latin American agenda is the war on drugs, a challenge Washington has historically confronted with force. In 1986, at the height of the crack and cocaine epidemic, Ronald Reagan declares the drug trade a threat to national security and revises the function of the armed forces to assume the leadership in that fight—the official beginning of the drug war's militarization. Jim Wright, a Democratic congressman, calls for a "war with no frontiers against drugs," and succeeds in drumming up overwhelming bipartisan support (Youngers, 2006: 108-109). Washington demands military action and the U.S. Southern Command will lead the charge.

Under the pretext of the war on drugs a new ignominious

chapter in the history of U.S. military encroachment in Latin America is written. Washington is determined to replace the Panamanian bases it had to dismantle under the Torrijos–Carter Treaties, which required the United States to vacate the Canal Zone by December 31, 1999. Its departure marks the end of nearly a century of an overwhelming U.S. military presence in Panama, whose government takes control of the Canal, recuperating the zone that has been partitioned since Theodore Roosevelt's administration. The Pentagon loses its principle military enclave in the region.

A BRIEF HISTORY

In the 19th century Latin America gained its independence from European powers only to fall into Washington's sphere of influence. The Monroe Doctrine (1823) served warning to the European powers that attempts to colonize or intervene in any part of the Americas would be seen as a direct aggression against the United States. "America for the people of the Americas" goes Washington's cri de guerre. "America for the Americans," is what everybody else is thinking.

The U.S. expansion begins in earnest in 1902 with Theodore Roosevelt's historic declaration: "I took Panama." Roosevelt constructs the canal connecting the two oceans, and for ten million dollars purchases the Canal Zone, a strip 8.1 kilometers wide on each side of the waterway; he goes on to builds a network of military installations for its defense. The United States begins to expand its economic, political, and military domination of Latin America and the Caribbean. Over time, the objectives and function of the Canal-based forces evolve, which is reflected in its name changes from U.S. Troops, Panama Canal Zone in 1915 to the Caribbean Defense Command (CDC) in 1941 to the Unified Combatant Command (UCC) in 1946 and finally, in 1963, the United States Southern Command.

The Southern Command, which incorporates ground, air and maritime forces, is the backbone of U.S. security policy in Central America, South America and the Caribbean, including continental landmasses, islands as well as territorial waters; it administers the twelve bases in the Canal Zone and the naval base in Guantanamo Bay. The United States Fourth Fleet also falls under its command. Created in 1943 to defend the Canal during World War II, but subsequently dissolved, after the cessation of hostilities, in 1950, the U.S. Fourth Fleet is resuscitated—behind the backs of Washington's regional allies—by President Bush in the summer of 2008. The presence of this mighty fleet, which includes aircraft carriers, submarines and nuclear missiles, navigating off the South American coast alarms the governments of Brazil, Argentina and Venezuela, which protest and request clarifications regarding its objectives, while warning that its encroachment in their territorial waters will not be permitted. The Brazilian congress condemns the patrols and the foreign minister, Celso Amorim, criticizes Washington's lack of transparency in reactivating the fleet after 58 years without notifying its regional allies in advance. Evo Morales labels it an act of aggression, and Fidel Castro predicts a new era of "gunboat diplomacy." Commentators suggest that Washington's goal is to intimidate South America's left-wing governments. To assuage continental fears and stymie criticism Washington announces that the fleet's main objective is combating the drug trade.

Aside from military operations, the Southern Command administers joint naval and military exercises around the region, the training of local forces in situ or on U.S. soil, military assistance and arms sales; it provides political orientation and controls the fifteen radar installations mounted in 1999 (the majority in Colombia and Peru). Its most essential function, however, according to current and former officers, is establishing personal relationships with commanders of other armed services. Out of those connections the military coups, so frequent in decades past, emerge.

At the onset of the Cold War, Harry Truman institutionalizes the inter-American system, ensnaring the entire region; he creates the OAS, signs the TIAR, and globalizes the Monroe Doctrine under the slogan of "containment" (of international communism). The notorious School of the Americas, founded in 1946 and installed in the Canal Zone, in Fort Amador, plays an key role, training military and police officers from around the region, and indoctrinating them with an anti-Communist ideology. The history books are replete with graduates of this school going on to lead military coups, and repressive dictatorships that commit heinous crimes against their people, often enlisting death squads to fight their dirty wars in order to avoid soiling their own hands. Many of these coups gestate in Washington, with the CIA and Southern Command taking part, and later propping up the dictatorships that emerge.

Throughout the 1960's, the clash between capitalist and socialist ideologies intensifies and armed guerrilla movements proliferate. At the epicenter of this regional upheaval is the Cuban Revolution, which becomes the first communist state in the Americas, and sparks an explosion of pro-Castro revolutionary movements throughout the Andean nations; civil wars break out in El Salvador, Guatemala, and Nicaragua; the neo-fascist military dictatorships (adhering to National Security Doctrine) wage war against determined guerrilla organizations: the Montoneros and the People's Revolutionary Army (ERP) in Argentina, the Tupamaros in Uruguay, as well as weaker movements in Brazil. "Operation Condor," a clandestine campaign orchestrated by the Southern Cone dictatorships expands the dirty wars beyond their borders. Conspiring with other authoritarian regimes they pursue, kidnap and assassinate political opponents overseas.

To stymie this growing revolutionary fervor, and the spread of communism throughout the region, President Kennedy sets in motion a new counterinsurgency strategy in Latin America. Under pressure from Washington, Latin American militaries take on functions relating to law and order that fall outside their constitutional mandates. Kennedy promotes militarism around the region, urging countries to give their armed services a more prominent role in national development plans, an approach that is met with immediate and widespread backlash, as military coups have long been the scourge of the region. What Kennedy proposes—giving military authorities preeminence over civilian ones—is antithetical to democratic rule, an abomination that in the past has been all too prevalent throughout the region.

Kennedy's counterinsurgency strategy transforms national armies into occupation forces; the militarization of law and order leads to increased violence and egregious human rights violations. National armies wage internal warfare not only against revolutionary insurgents, but also popular movements, organizations and protests, labor, student and indigenous movements, left-wing political parties and dissident politicians classified as subversive. The military authorities order assassinations, extrajudicial executions, torture and disappearances of internal "enemies" in what becomes known as the "Dirty Wars." The victims include tens of thousands of innocent men, women and children. Southern Cone and Central American nations suffer some of the most horrific human rights violations in the region's history. In Guatemala, where a revolutionary movement takes up arms in the 1960's, Washington puts its counterinsurgency theory into practice. This internal war against the Guatemalan population (of which 66% is indigenous) leads to genocide—an ethnocide—one of the worst atrocities in Latin American history.

In response to these revolutionary movements, the School of the Americas begins to focus on counterinsurgency and jungle warfare; it provides military intelligence instruction with Pentagon manuals. In September 1997, Lisa Haugaard of the SOA Watch, an NGO that lobbies for the closing of the School of the Americas, publishes a report about seven of those manuals that have been declassified (more than 1,100 pages remain broadly censured). The manuals provide instruction on repressive techniques, interrogation methods including the use of torture, disappearances, extrajudicial executions, reward payments for political killings, false imprisonment, and other extreme practices that violate human rights. The Pentagon distributes these manuals to military commanders throughout the region. In the 1970's and 80's, neofascist dictatorships in the Southern Cone put into practice the brutal methods, as do the genocidal Central American regimes. According to Haugaard, between 1987 and 1991 the SOA trains military personnel from Bolivia, Colombia, Costa Rica, the Dominican Republic, Ecuador, Guatemala, Honduras, Mexico, Peru and Venezuela using those manuals (Haugaard, 1997, September).

Year after year, Father Roy Bourgeois, founder of SOA Watch, organizes peaceful protests in front of the School of the Americas to call attention to the vile repression techniques and methods of social control being espoused there. At several peaceful demonstrations, thousands of people carry crosses with the names of victims of military dictatorships led by graduates of the School. Father Bourgeois is locked up in federal prisons for trespassing and spends months behind bars. He also visits several countries appealing to their governments to stop sending their soldiers to the notorious school.

It is through SOA pupils (who are carefully selected and later assigned to high military and political positions in their native countries) as well as joint military exercises that the Southern Command forges close bonds with the region's military establishments, often times behind the backs of their own governments. Without applying for visas or even presenting passports U.S. military personnel enter and leave other countries as if they owned them. In his 1982 report on the U.S. military bases in Panama, Gregorio Selser, a prominent Argentine intellectual and professor at the National Autonomous University of Mexico (UNAM), chastises Drew Middleton, *The New York Times* military correspondent, who reported on the coup that ousted Salvador Allende. "Spread throughout South America and the Caribbean, " Middleton wrote, "more than 170 graduates of the School of the Americas are today government leaders, cabinet ministers, chiefs of staff, intelligence bosses." He reports, with apparent satisfaction, that the Chilean coup leaders participated in six courses at that institution (Selser, 1982, November-December).

Disturbed by the SOA's insidious influence in the region, in 1984 President Jorge Illueca expels it from Panama. Relocated to Fort Benning, Georgia, where it is renamed the Western Hemisphere Institute for Security Cooperation, the school continues to carry out the same mission. Between 2003 and

2006, more than 68,000 Latin American military and police officers are trained and indoctrinated in its classrooms, nearly 40,000 of them Colombian.

In December 1989, the Southern Command leads a full-scale invasion of Panama, its declared objective the detention of General Manuel Noriega, who is accused of drug trafficking, despite having collaborated with the CIA in the past. Christened "Just Cause," the operation's aerial and ground assaults inflict vast destruction in residential neighborhoods, leaving tens of thousands dead. Weeks earlier, swarming clouds of American paratroopers descended upon various sections of Panama City with the goal of terrifying the population. These humiliating acts, abusive acts are entirely uncalled for. Washington's real objective, it is said, has less to do with arresting Noriega than installing a puppet regime that will disavow the Torrijos-Carter Treaties, allowing the U.S. to maintain its military forces in that country. In an outrageous show of heavy-handedness, the commander of the U.S. Southern Command swears in Guillermo Endara as the new Panamanian president on a U.S. base in the Canal Zone.

AMERICAN MILITARY PENETRATION

After 1999, Washington begins the process of replacing the military bases it lost in Panama with Forward Operating Locations (FOL)—already existing bases and airports in foreign countries to which the Pentagon gains operational access without signing a lease or maintaining an expansive permanent presence. In these sites U.S. forces, including fighter planes and military personnel and civilian contractors, can be stationed. Under the pretext of the war on drugs, Washington signs renewable agreements for ten years with Honduras, El Salvador, Ecuador and a few Caribbean governments. In El Salvador, they gain access to the Comalapa base; in Honduras, Soto Cano (previously Palmerola); in the Caribbean, the Queen Beatriz airport in Aruba and Hato Rey in Curaçao; in Ecuador, the Pentagon acquires the Manta base, which becomes the most controversial site of all. That same year Plan Colombia is conceived: 800 military personnel and 600 contractors enter the country on a more permanent basis. They are granted diplomatic immunity as well as access to several military sites. Though no one in Colombia speaks of these FOLs, they are present.

These FOL agreements tend to be one-sided in Washington's favor, allowing U.S. forces access to foreign sites at no cost other than upgrading the facilities themselves; the local governments renounce their rights to sue for material damages and human losses, and grant diplomatic immunity to U.S. military and government personnel. FOLs allow the United States to save hundreds of millions of dollars while serving the same function that a base of their own would; as an added bonus, they are seen as less intrusive, and generate scant resistance in the host countries. Around the globe, FOLs are utilized by Air Expeditionary Groups capable of intervening in any regional hot spot within 24 hours, and provide runways that can accommodate C-17s, large military aircraft capable of transporting thousands of troops. Other bilateral arrangements involve "lily pad" bases, foreign facilities with little or no permanent U.S. personnel presence that can be utilized for logistical purposes and contingency access. The Pentagon considers these sites important for the enhanced mobility they afford its forces on intelligence-gathering missions (Lindsay-Poland, 2010, January-February).

With FOLs in Central America, Ecuador, and Colombia, three anti-drug bases in the Peruvian Amazon (two on the border with Brazil and Colombia and another, administered jointly with the DEA, on the border with Ecuador); three permanent bases in Puerto Rico, the naval base in Guantanamo Bay and other "lily pads," the United States has the Caribbean and Venezuela encircled and, virtually free of charge, is positioned within striking distance of any country in the region.

In 2002, President Bush withdraws the United States' intent of ratification of the Rome Statute of the International Criminal Court (originally signed by President Clinton) and launches an international campaign against the ICC. To ensure that U.S. government and military personnel posted abroad will not have to answer to the International Criminal Court, Washington demands their diplomatic immunity. Human Rights Organizations criticize the campaign for violating fundamental tenets of international law. The treaty enters into force on July 1, 2002. In August, as U.S. officials crisscross the globe pressuring small and vulnerable countries into signing immunity agreements, European allies criticize Bush's actions for being heavy handed, and threaten to bring a complaint before the International Court of Justice. More than 45 countries, including several from Latin America, refuse to sign the immunity agreements. In a letter addressed to Secretary of State Colin Powell, Human Rights Watch raises objections to Washington using its leverage as a super-power to coerce small countries into signing "illegal and irrational" agreements, and criticizes the penalties imposed on those who refuse, including cutting off military, economic and development aid. Washington knows how to strike where it hurts most. After considerable protest, NATO members are exempt from signing these one-sided accords (Vann, 2002, October 12).

THE HISTORY OF MANTA

The Clinton administration tries its utmost to hold on to the Howard Air Force Base in Panama, which is regarded as a critical outpost in Central and South America, a launching pad for anti-drug operations that also played a key role in the invasions of the Dominican Republic (1965), Grenada (1983) and Panama (1989). President Clinton proposes converting the base into a multinational anti-narcotics command center, but is unable to persuade the Panamanian government. In 1999, he signs an agreement with Ecuadorian President Jamil Mahuad to occupy the Eloy Alfaro air and naval base, located on the Pacific Coast in Manta, rent-free for ten years (with the possibility of future renewal). The agreement includes unrestricted access to Ecuadorian airspace. American military personnel (which numbers around 500) and government officials are granted diplomatic immunity and can enter and leave the country without visas or passports; they are furthermore exempt from paying taxes, including on any property acquired. The U.S. government establishes its own mail service, installs satellite communications for its exclusive use, and obtains free, unregulated access to radio and television stations. Ecuador renounces its right to bring injury or death suits, as well as claims for damages, losses and destruction of government property. President Mahuad ignores the constitutional requirement to submit the agreement to Congress, nor does he pursue any other constitutional avenues for approval. The contract, therefore, is illegal.

In Quito, indigenous and popular protests, amid allegations of widespread corruption and mismanagement, ultimately bring down the government. Mahuad doesn't even last a year in office. His vice president, Álvaro Noboa, assumes the presidency. When new elections are held, the former army colonel Lucio Gutiérrez, running on a progressive platform, triumphs with broad popular support. Like the previous two presidents, however, Gutiérrez ultimately bows to Uncle Sam. After taking office, he travels to Washington where he meets with Secretary of State Colin Powell and, upon returning to Ecuador, announces that he will extend the Manta contract. The opposition grows and after two years Gutiérrez meets the same fate as his predecessor: popular revolt boots him out of office.

When the Pentagon takes possession of the Manta base its runways are dilapidated, broken into pieces of cement the size of "tennis balls," the result of poor drainage and illumination and the absence of security. Wild animals roam the site. The control tower is obsolete (Branhé, 2005, July 24). Though the agreement the countries signed was for an FOL, the Pentagon proceeds to invest 86 million dollars in repairing and upgrading the base, as well as constructing new facilities. The refurbished base, capable of conducting electronic and satellite espionage throughout the continent, is called an Advanced Operations Center, the most sophisticated in the region, hosting E-3 Sentry (AWAC) and P-3 Orion aircrafts—which can be deployed for surveillance and espionage—as well as 475 troops (Ballvé, 2008, June 6).

Manta is a twenty-minute flight from Colombia's southern frontier, a coca- and petroleum-producing Amazonian region contested by the army, paramilitaries and guerrilla forces. The Colombian conflict affects Ecuador in several ways, not only the aerial fumigations, but also the influx of Colombian refugees fleeing the violence, and guerrilla and paramilitary cross-border incursions. Neither country is able to exert much control over the frontier that divides them.

The Pentagon's acquisition of the Manta base, and expropriation of 24,000 hectares to expand the facility, along with the privatization of roads for military purposes affects local inhabitants, who lose their land and have no choice but to leave the region. The militarization of Manta's port also harms local fishermen left without work. Many inhabitants are forced to migrate as unemployment and poverty increase (Ballvé, 2008, June 6).

The United States' decade-long control of Manta has been an unsavory and all-around humiliating experience for Ecuador. Within its armed services discontent arises from the presence of foreign troops in its territory and the second-class treatment it receives. American aircraft do not limit their activity to monitoring drug trafficking: in violation of national laws they detain fishing boats in search of migrants heading for the United States, or pursue and sink them without paying compensation or facing justice thanks to the diplomatic immunity they enjoy. Ecuadorian authorities register upwards of 300 criminal offenses—from the sinking of ships to paternity cases and property damage—to which Washington refuses to respond.

From Manta, American military personnel provide logistical and intelligence support to the Colombian army in its operations against the FARC. In Ecuador, among government and military authorities, there is widespread discomfort with the base functioning as the "eye and ears" of Plan Colombia.

COLOMBIA AND MEXICO: DRUGS AND MILITARISM

Prior to the dismantling of U.S. bases in Panama, President

Clinton signs a five-year renewable agreement with President Pastrana, in December 1999, which becomes known as Plan Colombia. Eight hundred American military personnel and 600 contractors soon arrive in that country, bringing with them an arsenal of warplanes and armed helicopters. The Pentagon installs five radar towers in strategic locations, to be operated by its own personnel, and occupies the Tres Esquinas and Larandia bases—in the southern petroleum-rich Caquetá department—as well as the Apiay base in the Meta department. Under Plan Colombia, the DEA also sets up shop in the country, installing one of its two most important bases in the world, the other being in Afghanistan. Colombia becomes Washington's principal strategic ally in Latin America.

It is widely believed that President Pastrana would like to make peace with the FARC and implement a sort of Marshall Plan for depressed rural areas; he has stated that coca cultivation is a social problem and that the inequality fueling the violence must be addressed. Washington, however, modifies the plan and the agreement is ultimately signed on its terms, with priority given to combating the drug trade militarily, eradicating coca crops and destroying clandestine cocaine laboratories throughout the country. Eighty percent of Plan Colombia aid funds those missions; a billion dollars over a five-year period is allocated toward military and police training, the purchase of warplanes and helicopters, and intelligence support. The terms of Plan Colombia seem to suggest the permanent presence of foreign troops in Colombian territory, as such the government should be constitutionally obligated to submit the agreement for congressional approval, but Pastrana proceeds without consulting the legislature, and there is scant protest against this military commitment negotiated behind its back.

In the wake of the September 11th attacks the United States finds itself in the unfamiliar position of feeling vulnerable. The Bush administration invades Afghanistan and launches its war on terror; a palpable climate of fear and apprehension envelops the world. In 2003, at the height of the anti-terrorist paranoia, the United States, driven by its insatiable hunger for petroleum reserves, invades Iraq. That same year a new Colombian president, Álvaro Uribe, pushes for an extension of Plan Colombia to combat terrorism—that is, the FARC, which he and the Bush administration both view as a "terrorist organization." Uribe's foremost priority is obliterating the guerrilla forces. With ruthless determination he leads the country into a low-intensity counterinsurgency war with logistical, military and intelligence assistance from the United States and Israeli agents, and succeeds in bleeding the guerrilla forces. In the Arauca department, American soldiers guard the Occidental Petroleum Corporation's Caño-Limón oil pipeline against ELN attacks.

Washington praises the Uribe administration for its achievements in the security sphere and blows dealt to the FARC while turning a blind eye on a human rights rap sheet that includes political assassinations, massacres, disappearances, and ethnic cleansing. In 2009, the XI Forum of the Permanent Committee for the Defense of Human Rights in Colombia presents documentation of 14,000 political assassinations between 2002 and 2008, the majority at the hands of paramilitaries and the military (September, 12, 2009). Similar findings are reported by the Center for Investigation and Popular Education (CINEP), a Jesuit institute for social investigation. Each documents and condemns the targeted assassination of labor leaders, disappearances and massacres of rural peasants carried out by paramilitaries acting in cahoots with the Colombian army (Cinep y Programa Por la Paz [PPP], 2010, August) A study sponsored by the UN finds that, after Sudan, Colombia is the country with the largest number of people internally displaced by violence (*BBC Mundo*, 2008, April 17). There is no humanitarian crisis more tragic in Latin America.

Considering the magnitude of the military aid given to Colombian, the spike in human rights abuses is a cause for concern on Capitol Hill. In 2003, Congress "decertifies" Palanquero, the primary air base in the country, following the 1998 bombardment of Santo Domingo in the Arauca, in which 17 civilians (including a child) were killed. Although the Air Force initially tries to attribute the attack to the FARC, it is eventually established that the type of bomb used was exclusive to the military. The United States cuts back aid and suspends military training programs. Alarmed by another scandal—euphemistically referred to in Colombia as "false-positives"—the U.S. Congress requests more information from the government and sanctions the army battalions accused of rounding up young men from poor communities with the promise of work, and taking them into guerrilla-controlled areas where they are slain; the soldiers then present their victims as rebels killed in combat to claim government rewards offered for the "death of enemies." Executions of more than 1,700 civilian "false-positives" come to light in February 2009, but neither the president nor defense minister is held accountable.

Disillusioned by Plan Colombia's disappointing results—despite the seven-billion-dollar investment—some American legislators call for the suspension of the program. Coca cultivation continues at the same level as fifteen years ago when the fumigations were initiated; the drug trade continues to flourish.

Following denunciations of Plan Colombia made by 45 human rights and religious organizations, which called on the U.S. government to acknowledge the atrocities being committed by the Colombian military against the civilian population, President Obama—in a February 2009 joint House and Senate session—pledges to review the federal budget line by line and ax ineffective and superfluous programs. The winds, however, are blowing in the opposite direction: Uribe opens the door wider for the U.S. military in Colombia, turning over seven of the country's most strategic bases. Whether or not Plan Colombia is working, whether or not it will ever come to an end, is irrelevant if Washington deems that the country's military interests take precedence over the war on drugs and respect for human rights in an allied nation.

Signed by George W. Bush in the homestretch of his presidency, the Mérida Initiative is intended to address the deteriorating situation in Mexico as well as Central America. Like Plan Colombia, it prescribes a military solution to the illicit drug trade. Its initial budget is 1.6 billion dollars over a period of three years. The relationship between the United States and its southern neighbor is complex. Mexico produces and exports tons of marijuana to the United States, while also serving as a transit route for cocaine originating in South America; its drug trade is controlled by powerful cartels operating in the border region, which also traffic in arms and launder illicit funds. According to the DEA, these cartels earn between $12-13 billion a year from exports to the United States. Despite a fence spanning the length of the border, and military and police vigilance—including helicopters and canines and sophisticated sensors, radar and surveillance equipment—illegal narcotics continue flowing into the United States.

Felipe Calderón initiates a far-reaching war, not only against drug cartels but also indigenous and popular movements and organizations he classifies as "terrorist." Human rights organizations in Mexico and abroad denounce these abuses, which they contend are committed with regularity and impunity by the armed forces against the civilian population. Territorial wars between cartels in the border region result in tens of thousands of deaths. The U.S. Congress grows alarmed by the escalating violence.

RUMSFELD IN LATIN AMERICA

No U.S. Defense Secretary has paid more visits to Latin America than Donald Rumsfeld. He disembarks in the region to drum up support for the global war on terror—pressuring governments to send forces to Iraq—establish new military footholds, shore up support for Washington's Cuban policy, lash out against Hugo Chávez and derail Evo Morales's presidential campaigns.

Washington remains under a perpetual terror alert—a tactic intended to bend other countries into submission. "Those who are not with us are with the terrorists"—President Bush's theatrical declaration in the wake of the 9-11 attacks—sets the tone for the coming decade. Around the globe his surrogates trumpet the dangers of the drug trade and terrorism, and the Pentagon floats fantastical theories of Islamic terrorist cells operating in the tri-border region of Argentina, Brazil and Paraguay, where it hopes to establish a military outpost. The Guaraní aquifer, the largest subterranean water reserve in the world, also happens to be located in that region.

The Pentagon touts its base in Manta as critical to combating the drug trade in South America. During its initial honeymoon phase with the Ecuadorian government, the Pentagon selects Quito to host the VI Defense Ministers Conference of the Americas in November 2004. Rumsfeld's goal for the summit is to push for the regionalization of the wars on drugs and terrorism. Once again, he invokes Islamic terrorist cells operating in South America, supposedly financed by the drug trade; the only way to combat this threat, he argues, is through broad regional cooperation. Rumsfeld also praises President Lucio Gutiérrez, who threw his full support behind the Manta agreement, as a valuable friend and ally.

Things don't go as smoothly for Jorge Uribe, the Colombian defense minister, in Quito. Despite Rumsfeld's support, the majority rejects his proposals, which include drafting a list of Latin American terrorist groups to be combated through the OAS. Uribe is hoping to garner regional support for his fight against the FARC; it's a matter of "hemispheric security," he argues. No one is convinced. Uribe proposes the creation of a multinational force to confront the conflict, but the majority, once again, is opposed. Thus Uribe departs Quito empty handed. The idea of a multinational regional army, under the Pentagon's command, is not a new one. The United States has proposed it in a number of forums for a variety of different reasons, but has never garnered enough support.

In Quito, the principal objector to Colombia's aspirations is Nelson Herrera, the Ecuadorian defense minister, who finds himself at odds with his own president, an ally of the Colombian government. *El Comercio*, the oldest newspaper with largest circulation in Ecuador, applauds Herrera's independence (*El Comercio*, 2004, November 20).

In August 2005, on his fifth visit to Latin America, Rumsfeld returns to Ecuador to visit the military forces in Manta and formalize military assistance agreements with Gutiérrez. The Defense Secretary then travels to Peru, which hosts FOLs in Iquitos and in Nanay (in its Amazonian region). In Paraguay, he meets with President Nicanor Duarte Frutos of the right-wing Colorado Party; the press describes it as a meeting of allies. The Colorado Party has governed Paraguay for 61 years, 35 of those under the repressive dictatorship of Alfredo Stroessner. Rumsfeld and Duarte discuss "mutual concerns." Rumsfeld reiterates the need for a military facility in the Triple Frontier to combat Islamic terrorist cells; he expresses concern over instability in several parts of the continent and asks the Paraguayan leader to support democracy in Bolivia and prevent Evo Morales, who is supported by Cuba and Venezuela, from being elected (White, 2005, August 17).

Duarte Frutos opens his country's doors to joint military exercises and, at the Pentagon's insistence, grants diplomatic immunity to American personnel. Every year hundreds of American military servicemen rotate, in groups of 10 to 20, in and out of Paraguay, remaining for a maximum of 45 days. The public grows wary when the Senate, on December 30, 2003, authorizes the entry of American forces into Paraguay to "carry out training courses in the fight against drugs and terrorism, as well as joint operations with the national navy"; rumors once again circulate that Washington has designs on a military outpost in the Mariscal Estigarribia base in the tri-border area.

Argentina and Brazil grow alarmed. In July 2005, the Argentine daily *Clarín* reports that months earlier the Paraguayan Senate granted diplomatic immunity to American military personnel and authorized the entry of 400 troops over an 18-month, renewable period. Both governments deny that Mariscal Estigarribia base exists (Aliscioni, 2005, October 11). In April 2008, the Brazilian magazine *Carta Capital* reports the same. One of its reporters visits the base and interviews Paraguayan military personnel as well as residents of the region, and all confirm that they have not seen American soldiers. They only report having seen them in 2005 and 2006, during the annual joint exercises with Paraguayan forces. The State Department denies that they have a base in Paraguay and claims that its military personnel never remain in the country for longer than 45 days.

THE SEVEN BASES BOMBSHELL

The steadily advancing U.S. military penetration of Latin America continues under the Obama administration. On July 1, 2009, the Colombian magazine *Cambio* publishes an explosive report: the U.S. and Colombia are engaged in secret negotiations to relocate American military personnel from Manta to seven Colombian air and naval bases. These forces are scheduled to leave Ecuador when the contract expires at the end of the year; Rafael Correa has already stated that he has no intention of renewing it.

Cambio analyses both the content and reach of the one-sided pact. The United States will be allowed to utilize seven bases dispersed throughout the country. The exposé examines the characteristics of the bases that "have already been selected" and the role they will play in the Colombian conflict; it notes that in March 2009 the American ambassador, William Brownfield, informed the Colombian government that the Palanquero base would be "recertified"—a first step towards utilizing it. The article describes the types of surveillance aircraft that will arrive (AWACs and P-3 Orions) and calls attention to other terms of the agreement bound to "raise hackles." For instance, operations will not be restricted to Colombia, but rather "will include autonomous actions" by U.S. forces against drug trafficking and terrorism throughout the continent. Operations undertaken outside Colombia will not be limited to the Pacific region, as was the case with Manta; some will extend into the Caribbean. Furthermore, U.S. and Colombian forces will carry out "joint" missions against drug trafficking and terrorism—against the FARC, that is—an "internal security matter," the magazine points out. The agreement contains the usual clause granting diplomatic immunity to all military and U.S. government personnel operating in Colombia and the magazine points out that "since they don't intend to interfere with Colombian command on the bases, they will be sure to assert the autonomy of their own officials for operations carried out beyond the country's borders." *Cambio* reports that, despite a few remaining issues in the negotiations, the deal is as good as done (*Cambio*, 2009, July 1).

The revelations have the rest of the continent fuming. The presidents of Brazil, Argentina, Bolivia, Ecuador and Venezuela all express deep concern, and demand assurances that military operations—presumably targeting drug trafficking and terrorism—will not extend beyond Colombian borders. They fear that the United States will take advantage of its foothold in Colombia to intervene in other parts of the region. Brazil asks for guarantees in writing. In November, Lula and Cristina Kirchner issue a joint statement declaring the presence of extra-regional troops in South America to be "incompatible with the principles of respect for sovereignty and the territorial integrity of the region" (*AFP* and *DPA*, 2009, November 19).

At Uribe's insistence, the negotiations are carried out in secret, behind the backs of the public and legislatures of both countries. After the full extent of the region's ire becomes clear, and criticism of Washington proliferates in the international press, the White House regrets having not conducted negotiations openly, as much of the backlash might have been averted.

The Uribe administration unleashes a propaganda offensive aimed at influencing perceptions abroad. Around the continent critics accuse him of surrendering his country's sovereignty. In Colombia, senior military officers, political leaders and pro-government news organizations weigh in on the side of the president. William Brownfield, the U.S. ambassador appointed by Bush and kept on by Obama, insists that the agreement is "only an expansion of what already exists," and promises that there will be no attempts to undermine Colombian sovereignty, and all military operations will be "directed" by the Colombian army. According to the political analyst Claudia López, "These claims diverge from reality, with the government denying in public what has been agreed to in private" (Lopez, 2009, July 7).

President Obama also claims that the two countries are merely updating and expanding a bilateral agreement, which has been in place for many years, to "assist" in the war against drugs, and he has no intention of dispatching a "large number of additional troops" to South America. In essence, the plan is not to "create" new bases but rather "utilize" and upgrade already existing ones. These new FOLs will replace, free of charge, the bases lost in Panama.

THE NEGOTIATIONS

For the United States, relocating its forces from Manta to Colombia is the most sensible option: Colombia is a bi-coastal nation that borders five countries. Moreover, Uribe is Bush's only ally in South America. The embattled American president rewards Uribe's loyalty with the Medal of Liberty, a high distinction bestowed for service rendered to the country. After Israel and Egypt, Colombia is the country that receives the most U.S. military aid in the world. Washington already has Colombia and Uribe in the palm of its hand; the only question, now, is how to expand its foothold?

Obama inherits the negotiations initiated by his predecessor for the relocation of American forces from Manta to Palanquero. His administration pushes the talks forward and Uribe ultimately offers six additional bases, dispersed throughout the country and on both coasts. According to one analyst, Uribe is ensuring that Washington will continue to fund Plan Colombia after the U.S. Congress, put off by the poor results, announced that it would reduce its budget (Schumacher-Matos, 2009, August 14).

In March 2009, sources in Colombia's Ministry of Defense release information on the American contingent expected to arrive in the country: a fleet of surveillance planes capable of detecting small aircraft—as well as the rudimentary submarines and boats utilized by drug traffickers—within a radius of hundreds of kilometers; Air Force, Navy, Coast Guard and border patrol personnel, including 200 pilots with flight and support crews, for a total of 500 servicemen (*El Tiempo*, 2009, March 15). Ambassador Brownfield casually states that Washington would also "be interested" in utilizing the naval base in Málaga Bay, on the Pacific Coast.

According to comments by senior Washington officials published in *The Economist* on December 3, 2009, the military pact with Colombia, source of so much consternation around the region, wasn't even necessary, considering that for ten years—under Plan Colombia—U.S. planes had enjoyed access to Colombian bases and hundreds of American troops had operated in Colombia; the actual agreement, therefore, was just "cooked-up bureaucracy" drafted at Uribe's insistence, and intended to dissuade Venezuela from future aggressions against Colombia. Using Venezuela to justify this unusual pact is a new and disturbing dimension, political observers note, given the animus between Washington and Caracas.

Neither the Ecuadorian nor Colombian government seeks approval from its national legislature prior to signing controversial military pacts with the United States. In circumventing this legal obligation, both governments hope to avoid unseemly and unconstitutional concessions coming to light. Uribe argues that the "Complementary Agreement for Technical Assistance in Defense and Security" is a continuation of already existing agreements and therefore does not require congressional approval. The Council of State disagrees: it finds no relation to any previous agreement and therefore, under the constitution, should be submitted to the legislature. Despite these presidential abuses, the majority of Colombians remain silent.

CONTINENTAL UNEASE

The military agreement granting the U.S. access to seven Colombian bases is, and will continue to be, a controversial issue around the continent. For the Brazilian foreign minister, Celso Amorim, the guarantees given by both governments—that third countries will not be affected—do not go far enough. "I am not satisfied," he says, "this issue has not died, and the conversations must continue" (*El Espectador*,

2009, December 26). Amorim is critical of Washington's lack of clarity in its relations with Latin America, citing Obama's dubious managing of the Honduran coup and the secret negotiations leading up to his unpopular agreement with Colombia.

In Latin America there is deep resentment of Colombia and distrust of its president: Uribe operates in secret, creates dangerous situations that affect other countries, undermines regional unity and disseminates falsehoods and misinformation. "Our policy cannot be reversed. We have to defeat [the guerrillas] totally and this is a step in the right direction" he proclaims (Brooks, 2009, August 21). His justifications for turning over the seven bases, however, are seen by many as glib. Lula points out that over the past decade Colombia has received a prodigious amount of U.S. aid (6 billion dollars) to combat the drug trade and terrorism, and yet continues to be the largest cocaine producer in the world; the guerrillas, likewise, have not been defeated. Many observers are unnerved by the fact that, in a supposed democracy, the president can single-handedly mortgage the future of the country and surrender its sovereignty to a foreign power without civil society or the high courts even protesting. This collective sheepishness reflects a shocking distortion in public opinion: 80% of Colombians support Uribe and barely utter a word in protest amid the accumulating scandals casting a grim pall over his government. In the face of an egregious surrender of its sovereignty the country simply rolls over.

Despite Uribe and Obama's public declarations that their agreement is strictly bilateral and aimed exclusively at combating the drug trade and terrorism, Hugo Chávez remains convinced that the pact constitutes a new phase in Washington's geopolitical strategy whose ultimate goal is seizing the continent's natural resources.

Colombia's willingness to turn over seven bases to the United States represents a devastating blow to regional unity and independence, and the plans for increased integration and multilateral cooperation promoted by Lula da Silva and Hugo Chávez. Evo Morales announces that he will ask UNASUR to adopt a resolution prohibiting foreign military bases on the continent.

It is regrettable, disgraceful even, that despite all the alarm, protest and recriminations coming from governments that feel threatened by the pact—not to mention political commentators, high-profile politicians and personalities as well as ordinary citizens—nothing changes. Uribe pompously declares that his decision is "irreversible." The explanations, clarifications, promises and guarantees issued by both governments do nothing to assuage continental fears as to what the superpower has up its sleeve with the complicity of its ever bellicose—and kowtowing—Colombian ally.

Obama and the Seven Bases

In June 2009, three months after the Colombian base scandal

blows up, the Obama administration requests 46 million dollars from Congress for the construction of a Cooperative Security Location (CSL) in Palanquero, the most important air base in Colombia. CSLs are counterinsurgency and anti-narcotic training institutions, as well as sites from which operations into other countries can be launched. The Government Accountability Office (GAO), however, raises certain questions before dispensing the funds, including the prohibition in the Colombian constitution against the "permanent presence" of troops in that country without congressional approval and the "certification" required of any base receiving funding; it also requests a signed agreement from Colombia not to interfere with the Southern Command's anti-narcotics operations. A Pentagon official explains that the requested funds will go towards upgrading runways and other facilities in Palanquero, assuming negotiations end satisfactorily (*El Tiempo*, 2009, June 19).

Though the White House insists that the new pact merely "formalizes" an existing agreement, and that it will not bolster the military's offensive capabilities in the region, the Pentagon confirms just the opposite: it requests congressional funding to enhance its capability to carry out operations in all of South America, expand its capacity to wage expeditionary warfare, and combat the threat of anti-American governments. Palanquero will be a launching pad for "contingency" operations targeting the rest of the continent; the airbase will host C-17 aircraft enabling the rapid transportation of large contingents of troops. The Pentagon will modernize the bases, extend runways and station marines on them, along with surveillance aircraft, private contractors and intelligence operatives unaccounted for in the public record.

According to John Lindsay-Poland, a political analyst, after receiving congressional approval for the Palanquero funds, the Air Force presented a revised budget to justify the resources requested. For instance, Lindsay-Poland claims, references to combating anti-American governments were excised from the new document, as well as the term "expeditionary war," which raises hackles in Latin America. Less clear is to what these modifications are owed: whether the Obama administration has reversed the Bush Doctrine of preventive warfare or if it simply covering up the Pentagon's true intention of expanding its military reach to cover the entire continent (Lindsay-Poland, 2009, January-February).

The military pact signed by the United States and Colombia in October 2009 gives rise to new animus towards President Obama, whose regional policy many see as indistinguishable from that of his predecessor. Venezuela and Ecuador feel the most threatened. Chávez believes that Washington—with Uribe's complicity—will attempt to invade his country.

The clandestine manner in which the bilateral negotiations proceed spawns unease on Capitol Hill. Influential Democratic senators, such as Patrick Leahy and Christopher Dodd, complain that they were not consulted or even notified in advance. They request explanations from the administration about the pact's implications and express concern over deepening relations with Colombia, whose military is accused of egregious human rights violations. The Democratic senators are unconvinced by the responses provided by Uribe's government to the slaughter of innocent people at the hands of soldiers: the "false-positives." The Colombian government's objective is to demonstrate the efficacy of its flagship policy: "Security Democracy." Senators Leahy and Dodd are also concerned about the widespread repudiation of the pact as a potential complicating factor in U.S. relations with the rest of region.

The uproar around Latin America, coupled with concerns expressed by influential legislators and other domestic critics, compels the Obama administration to provide periodic explanations and justifications for its mission in Colombia. The United States will not, the White House claims, install new bases in that country, but rather utilize existing ones (as FOLs). Rankled by the criticism of his administration, Obama sounds off on the "traditional anti-Yankee rhetoric" being "played up" by certain regional leaders (Reuters, 2009, August 7). "Where there are American military bases," Evo Morales declares, "there are military coups" (*El Espectador*, 2009, September 13).

The public declarations made by President Obama, Secretary Clinton and Philip Crowley, the Assistant Secretary of State for Public Affairs, that the agreement with Colombia is "strictly bilateral" in scope, are intended to assure critics that the pact will not affect them (*AFP*, 2009, August 15). But the condemnations, complaints, and criticism refuse to die away.

Tammy Baldwin and Jan Schakowsky—influential legislators on Latin American issues—along with fellow Democrat James McGovern pen a "Dear Colleague" letter alerting members of Congress to the dangers they see in the military pact with Colombia, and the "arduous regional controversy" it has generated. They fear that Plan Colombia's lackluster results will lead to increased support of the Colombian military rather than development aid, while undermining U.S. commitment to human rights abroad. They annex a letter from the Colombian Support Network NGO making a similar request of President Obama (Gómez Maseri, 2009, September 8). "Dear Colleague" letters are a method of exerting pressure. After receiving enough signatures in Congress, they are forwarded to the president in hope that he will take action.

On September 11, 2009 the United States announces that it "legally certifies an improvement in Colombia's record in the area of human rights," a decision considered outrageous by many who see no such improvement in the country's abysmal performance (*AP*, 2009, September 12). Washington is well aware that over the course of Uribe's presidency five hundred labor leaders have been assassinated, upwards of 195 teachers and two thousand civilians as part of the "false-positive" scheme. The International Trade Union Confederation classifies Colombia as the most deadly country in the world for trade unionists and defense lawyers.

Some commentators believe that Washington's motive for turning a blind eye on Colombia's human rights violations is to pave the way for its military pact. "Certification" allows Congress to release millions of dollars being held up by human rights concerns, and the Pentagon can resume its military assistance to the Colombian army. The certification is seen not only as high-handed, but deeply insensitive to the victims of state, guerrilla and paramilitary violence—a green light to the atrocities and human rights abuses that continue unabated.

UNASUR on Red Alert

President Uribe announces that he will not attend the UNASUR summit in Quito on August 10, 2009, citing the broken relations between his country and Ecuador. Instead, he embarks on a whirlwind tour of the continent, visiting seven countries in an attempt to ease tensions following his controversial military pact. The retired American general and National Security Adviser, James Jones, accompanies him (*DPA* et al., 2009, August 11).

Uribe leaves his meetings empty handed: the presidents of Argentina, Bolivia, Brazil, Chile, Uruguay, Peru and Paraguay one by one reject the U.S. military presence in Colombia and question his assertion that Washington's "assistance" is limited to combating the drug trade and defeating the FARC. Cristina Fernández expresses unease with the combativeness it has unleashed in the region, which she characterizes as "unacceptable and unprecedented" (*DPA* et al., 2009, August 11). Michelle Bachelet suggests that the U.S.-Colombian pact should be discussed at the upcoming UNASUR summit in Quito. The only foreign leader supportive of the Colombian president is Alan García.

At the Quito summit, which had been scheduled prior to the scandal erupting, Rafael Correa, UNASUR's pro tempore president, announces that the matter will not be on the agenda, but will be the central topic of the upcoming South American Defense Council summit scheduled for August 24. Hugo Chávez, nonetheless, refers to the controversy while underscoring the urgency of the moment: "The winds of war are blowing," he declares. The Venezuelan leader later circulates a letter among his colleagues alerting them to the threat looming over South America's socialist governments and calls for an emergency UNASUR summit to discuss in depth the U.S.-Colombian military agreement (*DPA* et al., 2009, August 11).

With the continent's second largest armed forces (400,000 strong), and the ability to enhance its military facilities through its relationship with the United States, Correa argues that Colombia has become a regional threat. Clemencia Forero, Colombia's deputy foreign minister, who is representing Uribe at the summit, assures those in attendance that the bases in question will remain under Colombian jurisdiction (*DPA* et al., 2009, August 11). Lula demands immediate dialogue with the United States on the matter, and Cristina Kirchner offers to host the emergency summit requested by Chávez in Bariloche, so as to ensure Uribe's participation.

On August 27, 2009, the twelve Latin American presidents, convene in Bariloche to discuss Colombia's military pact with the United States. In a tense, uninterrupted session lasting seven hours, Uribe is put on the defensive: several attendees request explanations and guarantees that future military operations will be restricted to Colombia. They also demand to see the text of the agreement, which has not yet been signed, but which Uribe refuses to share "without the authorization of the United States." When asked if he will undertake military incursions in other countries, similar to the one recently launched in Ecuador, Uribe's responses are evasive. The majority of attendees underscore the importance of both governments clarifying the scope of the agreement and providing guarantees that other countries will not be affected. They warn that the matter is not over, and continue to be a source of great concern in their countries. Colombia has radically altered the geopolitical panorama.

Uribe justifies the pact based on the need for "assistance" in bringing his country's armed conflict, which has raged on for decades, to an end (Barrionuevo and Romero, 2009, August 29). Lula and Correa argue that this new agreement will not, as the Colombian president hopes, result in the end of the drug trade or the guerilla movements; Colombia continues being the largest producer of cocaine in the world despite enormous U.S. military aid under Plan Colombia. Lula wonders if it is not time to rethink those strategies all together, rather than amp them up. The Argentine newspaper *Página 12* publishes Cristina Kirchner's criticism of Uribe on the grounds that military bases don't "help" in combating the drug trade, as that is carried out with intelligence and counterinsurgency operations (Miguez, 2009, August 29).

At Uribe's insistence, the Bariloche summit is televised live. One by one, the heads of state in attendance put forth persuasive arguments against the presence of the U.S. forces on Colombian military bases (Miguez, 2009, August 29).

Alan García, a supposed Uribe ally, argues that the agreement's text should be made public and leads a petition for UNASUR to inspect the Colombian bases. The proposal, however, doesn't gain traction. Colombia argues that if its bases are to be subject to inspection the same should go for all bases in which the U.S. has a presence. "I thought we lost him," writes the Colombian columnist María Isabel Rueda, commenting on García's unexpected position at Bariloche (Rueda, 2009, August 29). Some insist on meeting with President Obama, for the American president to clarify his intentions in the region, but that demand is omitted from the final resolution. Uribe argues that the most appropriate forum to dialogue with the United States is the OAS.

In a detailed presentation, supported by statistics and other data, President Correa recounts Ecuador's difficulties with the Manta base, which the Pentagon controlled for a decade.

He recalls the impossibility of controlling and tracking its aircraft, the repeated abuses and environmental damage wrought. He warns Uribe: "You cannot control them" and "this represents a grave threat to peace in Latin America" (Forero, 2009, August 29).

Hugo Chávez reads excerpts from "The White Paper on Air Mobility Command Global En Route Strategy," a document dated May 2009 that details the Pentagon's strategy in the region, revealing it goes far beyond the stated anti-drug and terror operations. The Colombian bases are part of a broader strategy to facilitate the movement of troops and military equipment throughout the continent. The document also reveals that Palanquero will be a CSL (*Agencia Bolivariana de Noticias*, 2009, August 28) hosting C-17 transportation aircraft that can cover half the continent without refueling. Since the document details military and covert plots to destabilize the Venezuelan government, Chávez requests that the Council of South American Defense deliberate on it during the meeting scheduled for September 25, and release its findings. This request is left out of the final resolution.

Correa does not miss the opportunity to confront Uribe over the latter's allegation that the Ecuadorian government provides a safe haven for guerrilla soldiers and drug-traffickers. Denying the accusations, Correa claims that "Ecuador is the victim" and adds: "Colombia does nothing to solve the problem inside its borders and is the principal drug producer in the region." He claims that coca is being cultivated in a Colombian military base near the border and protests the extortion of Ecuadorian citizens by Colombian guerrillas and drug-traffickers operating along the frontier (Miguez, 2009, August 29).

On multiple occasions Chávez has cited peace in Colombia as imperative for regional security, and called attention to the conflict's negative effects on neighboring countries. He is critical of the Colombian president's contorted excuses for refusing to initiate peace talks with guerrilla leaders. The United States, he believes, takes advantage of the conflict to justify its presence in the region. In June 2008, Chávez called on the FARC to unconditionally free all its hostages and demobilize, declaring that the era of guerrillas had passed. At the time, some Western media outlets commented favorably on that public declaration. And in Bariloche he introduces a proposal that unsettles Uribe. He calls on "UNASUR to begin to deliberate peace in Colombia" and asks: "When will this war end?" Visibly flustered, Uribe, as is his custom, goes on the attack. He retorts that peace will only be achieved when the "bandits" are "defeated" before concluding with a jibe aimed at both Chávez and Correa: "The armed conflict will be resolved as long as the guerrillas don't find shelter in third countries." At the end of the session Correa, echoing the Venezuelan leader, declares: "I believe that peace can be achieved through dialogue, but Uribe wants war" (Miguez, 2009, August 29; Barrionuevo and Romero, 2009, August 29).

The final resolution at Bariloche reaffirms the organization's commitment to the "principles of international law pertaining to friendship and cooperation between States, and the UN Charter"; it declares that "military cooperation agreements should be governed by a strict respect for the principles and goals of the UN Charter and the fundamental principles of UNASUR's constitutive treaty"; it recommits to the principles for sovereignty, territorial inviolability and the right of people to determine their own fates free from outside interference; it declares that "foreign military forces, with their means and resources directed towards their own objectives, cannot threaten the sovereignty and integrity of any South American nation and, by extension, peace and security in the region"; it pledges to redouble cooperation in the fights against terrorism, the illicit drug trade and other forms of organized crime, and rejects the presence and activity of illegal armed groups; it calls on foreign and defense ministers to hold an extraordinary meeting, in the first two weeks of September, to examine the controversial military pact; there is neither any condemnation of Colombia nor support for Uribe; the conflict with the FARC continues to be treated as an exclusively Colombian issue; it is acknowledged that Colombia's military pact with Washington is an internal matter that affects the entire continent.

The live transmission of the Bariloche summit keeps Colombians glued to their television sets. María Jimena Duzán, a columnist for *Semana*, accuses the influential daily *El Tiempo* of reporting on the debates with a pro-Uribe bias, distorting events and attributing nonexistent triumphs to the administration. She cites the newspaper's conclusion that "it has become clear that the agreement is bilateral and, as Uribe claims, does not affect the region." Never mind that UNASUR has concluded just the opposite. Duzán points out that not even Alan García, a supposed Uribe ally, is coming forward with full support and that all the region's leaders agree that UNASUR is the appropriate forum to debate the issue, despite Uribe's insistence on "elevating the OAS above it." She makes note of Uribe's failure to convince his counterparts—with the exception of the Peruvian president— to classify the FARC as a "terrorist" organization. "But one has to acknowledge," she adds, "that Uribe speaks for more than half the country that wants the same. If we pay attention to the polls, today Colombians want the bases and do not feel that their sovereignty is being threatened, a reality that remains worrisome. The feeling it leaves you with," she concludes, "is that Colombia can no longer confront the drug-traffickers, or the FARC, or Chávez, or anyone else without the presence of the Americans. That conviction is underpinning this entire situation" (Duzán, 2009, August 22).

In a meeting of the Council of South American Defense, held in Quito the following month, the primary topic once again is the U.S.-Colombian pact. Uribe attempts to divert attention from that controversy by claiming to have uncovered "new evidence" of Venezuela's ties to the FARC, this time in the form of Swedish weapons captured from the guerrillas which, he claims, were purchased from Venezuela. Sweden denies having sold any arms to Venezuela since 2006, and Venezuela's interior minister denies that his government or any Venezuelan entities are furnishing "criminal or terrorist organizations" with arms. "That yarn is laughable," he concludes. "It resembles a cheap movie made by the U.S. government" (CNN.com, 2009, July 27).

The Colombian defense minister, Gabriel Silva, and Jaimie Bermúdez, its foreign minister, arrive in Quito with their own peculiar agenda. Despite their government's engorged military budget, and the hefty economic and military aid coming from Washington, they find it appropriate to criticize the recent arms purchases of other countries for threatening regional peace. They allude to the presence of terrorist groups in Latin America and FARC soldiers in Venezuela. They also invoke the threats of drug trafficking and the rise in drug flights departing from that country. Both ministers jockey to have those topics included on the agenda, but their isolation is soon apparent. On the matter of the Swedish weapons allegedly sold by Venezuela to the FARC, Celso Amorim, the Brazilian foreign minister, points out that as many arms end up in the hands of Colombian guerrillas as drug dealers in Rio de Janeiro favelas, a trivial matter compared to turning over military bases to the United States. The recent arms purchases, he adds, do not justify the presence of foreign troops on the continent. Other ministers likewise criticize the Colombian stance; an irked Gabriel Silva warns that if the matters he would like to discuss are not included on the agenda his government could go so far as to withdraw from UNASUR. "Colombia has not understood the sensitivities that its agreement involving military bases has caused," Amorim remarks (Tamayo, 2009, September 17). From Bogotá, Uribe pledges not to withdraw Colombia from UNASUR.

Argentina, Bolivia, Brazil and Venezuela all criticize Uribe's lack of transparency; the Colombian president is yet to make good on the promise he made in Bariloche to divulge the text of his country's military pact with the United States. The Brazilian defense minister, Nelson Jobim, insists that Colombia and the United States should provide legally binding guarantees that their bilateral treaty will not result in the presence of foreign troops in third countries. The Quito conference comes to a close without any consensus. According to the foreign ministers of Bolivia and Ecuador (David Choquehuanca and Fander Falconí, respectively), the failure to reach an agreement is the result of the Colombian ministers' intransigence, and insistence on "consulting a third country" prior to divulging the text of the military pact (*AFP*, *DPA* and Reuters, 2009, September 17).

Hello to Arms!

In mid-September 2009, at the height of the continental uproar over the seven Colombian bases, media reports emerge of large-scale arms purchases by South American governments, which some commentators attribute to fear stemming from the controversial military agreement. Brazil, Venezuela, Ecuador, Chile and Bolivia purchase fighter jets, submarines, helicopters, and a wide range of weapons and military technology from Russia, South Africa, France, Sweden and Brazil. According to Washington, these acquisitions constitute a dangerous outbreak of militarism in the region. The largest purchases are made by Brazil from France. Several Brazilian newspapers report that the government has acquired 36 fighter bombers (along with ancillary technology), from the French company Dassault, and that Lula has proposed transferring part of the manufacturing process to Brazil. He purchases 51 helicopters, and four conventional submarines, as well as one that is nuclear powered. Lula defends Brazil's right to develop its own nuclear technology and, along with other Latin American countries, supports Iran's right to do the same (*AFP* et al., 2009, November 24).

In defending his government's recent military expenditures, Chávez insists that his hand was forced by the "Yankee" presence on Colombian bases. Venezuela, after all, is surrounded by American bases, and purchasing Russia weapons to protect the country's petroleum reserves is a sovereign right. Russia extends 2.2 billion dollars in credit to help finance those purchases, which include 92 T-72 tanks and an S-300 long-range surface-to-air missile system. He also accepts Iran's offer of assistance in nuclear transfers [?]; alongside other regional leaders, Chávez remains adamant that all countries have the right to develop nuclear energy for peaceful purposes. Ecuador purchases 24 Super Tucano combat planes from Brazil, as well as radar equipment, helicopters and unmanned aircraft; it also negotiates the purchase of 12 combat planes from South Africa, 14 Mirage 50 planes from Chile and accepts, as a gift from Venezuela, another 14. Ecuador modernizes its armed forces and bolsters its military presence along the the Colombian border.

Though analysts have repeatedly attributed this military buildup to Colombia granting the U.S. access its bases, Washington and Uribe react with surprise and concern. Gabriel Silva, the Colombian defense minister, with another heavy dose of hypocrisy, decries the burgeoning militarism in neighboring countries, which he characterizes as "unnecessary" and a "threat to regional stability" (*El Tiempo*, 2009, September 29).

Colombia allocates 4% of its GDP toward military expenditures, the highest such percentage in the region (Tamayo, 2009, September 17). In 2008, the country purchases 13 Kfir combat aircraft from Israel, as well as Black Hawk helicopters and warships from the United States. The government repeatedly uses the guerilla threat to justify the size of its armed forces—the second largest on the continent—and bloated military budget.

Alarmed by the militaristic wave sweeping over the continent, Alan García addresses a letter to UNASUR's foreign and defense ministers alerting them to the economic impact of these expenditures. He urges them to tamp down on the spending binges, and presents figures on South American military expenditures over the previous five years, which total 156 billion dollars (in addition to 23 billion in non-military budgets). The Peruvian president conveniently omits any mention of factors that could be causing the rise in military expenditures, nor does he name the countries responsible for pushing the region towards war (Tamayo, 2009, September 17).

At a November 2009 conference sponsored by the Inter-American Dialogue, 60 experts from a variety of think tanks and research centers discuss the recent arms surge. Román Ortiz, of the Security and Defense Study Group at Los Andes University, argues that there is no arms race as "there is no homogenous pattern" and the purchases correspond to "specific necessities." "Brazil and Chile seek to maintain the status quo; others to update their arsenals; Colombia and Mexico are motivated by internal security, while Venezuela breaks the mold, having in recent years invested 7 billion dollars in arms, as it seeks to alter the status quo and has the means to do so." Adam Isacson, of the Center for International Policy (CIP) concurs: though there is no arms race, the military pact between Colombia and the United States "has escalated tensions in the region" and "created an atmosphere of distrust." Michael Schiffer, of the same institution, views Venezuela's arms purchases as a defense strategy against the United States while Brazil, he claims, is "defending the Amazon and projecting itself as a power" (Gómez Maseri, 2009, November 3). Lula da Silva has, on multiple occasions, called attention to the need to protect offshore petroleum reserves.

Hugo Chávez has been a White House target going back to the Bush years; now the Obama administration and its surrogates renew the attacks with a similar zeal. Following the surge in arms purchases Venezuela is called out as a threat to regional peace. Meanwhile, the White House continues to ignore the continental outcry over its military pact with Colombia. Hillary Clinton criticizes Venezuela's arms purchases for "exceeding" the level of other countries in the region. Through spokesman Ian Kelly, the State Department expresses its concern over the purchase of Russian and Spanish weapons and makes clear that Washington will follow closely the plans for nuclear cooperation with Iran (*AFP* and *Reuters*, 2009, September 15). The Western media likewise focuses on Venezuela in its coverage of the Latin American arms purchases. What these reports fail to mention is that Washington refuses to sell Venezuela replacement parts for its planes and other American military equipment, leaving Caracas little choice but to acquire them through other channels. Venezuelan Vice President Ramón Carrizales maintains that the arms purchases are for defense only, and offers to provide UNASUR with any pertinent information.

Washington is disturbed as much by the escalating arms purchases as by the fact that the purchases are not being made, as historically has been the case, from U.S. manufacturers. Latin America is attempting to distance itself from Washington, whom it fears and distrusts. More than one government expresses dismay that Obama's promises of change and rapprochement remain unfulfilled. The American leader has, for the most part, adopted disappointing, and sometimes alarming, positions.

Consumatum Est

In October 2009, in a modest closed-door ceremony held at seven in the morning in the San Carlos Palace, headquarters of Colombia's Ministry of Foreign Affairs, Jamie Bermúdez, the foreign minister, Fabio Valencia Cossio, the interior minister, and Gabriel Silva, the defense minister, add their signatures to the agreement that will surrender Colombian sovereignty to the United States for at least ten years, and perhaps longer. William Brownfield, the American ambassador from Texas—appointed by President Bush in 2007 and kept on by the Obama administration—signs for the United States. Following this discreet ceremony (to which access is strictly limited), the Colombian press records the foreign minister's euphoric proclamations concerning this agreement whose text nobody has seen. Bermúdez pledges to release the document to the public, as well as all the region's foreign ministers in the interest of "better relations and finding mechanisms for cooperation," and "to make clear that the sole aim of the pact is to rid Colombia and neighboring countries of the drug trade and terrorism. To the extent that Colombia is successful in this fight," he adds, "it will benefit not only Colombians but the entire region and world" (*AFP*, 2009, October 31).

According to *Prensa Latina*, Colombia has become a Yankee aircraft carrier. An editorial published in *La Jornada* argues that, owing to its privileged geographic position, Colombia now represents an unprecedented threat to the rest of the continent, especially its left-wing nationalist governments. A former Colombian president, Ernesto Samper, criticizes the "almost clandestine manner" in which the two countries carried out the negotiations, and asserts that Uribe has neglected his obligation to submit the agreement to Congress and the Constitutional Court for approval; Samper also bemoans the "futility of pursuing drug traffickers and fumigating coca." Uribe has entangled Colombia's foreign policy for the foreseeable future and compromised the country's relations with its neighbors, the former president concludes (*Cuba Debate*, 2005, November 5).

The Venezuelan foreign minister, Nicolás Maduro, lambasts the agreement as "an embarrassment in our continent's history." He adds, "No one really knows what's in this document, not the Colombian Congress, or general public, or the entirety of the Colombian government, or U.S. Congress" (*El Espectador*, 2009, November 3). For Fidel Castro, the pact is tantamount to the annexation of Colombia, with the ultimate goal being to "crush the Bolivarian Revolution, as Washington tried to do with Cuba in the Bay of Pigs invasion." He dismisses as "cynical" Uribe's characterization of the pact as a "necessity in the fight against the drug trade and international terrorism" (*AFP*, 2009, November 7).

Even Ambassador Brownfield, following the finalization of the agreement, concedes it was a mistake ("that all acknowledge") to have carried out the negotiations in secret, which "gave rise to clamor and continental protest, and domestic as well as outside criticism." He remains adamant, however, that there is "nothing new" in the agreement and the "changes will not be many"; the uproar, he dismisses, as a "tempest in a cup of tea," considering that Article IV, paragraph 3 of the agreement "expressly prohibits carrying out operations that go beyond [Colombian] borders." That particular article, however, refers to something else and in no part of the agreement is any such intervention "expressly prohibited." Brownfield maintains that "cooperation against drugs, terrorism and international criminality is the same as before, only modernized" and he reiterates: "We are not going to see any change" (*El Tiempo*, 2009, October 31).

In equal measure candid and patronizing, the ambassador reveals that over the past decade American forces have been operating openly in six of the seven bases included in the agreement. "The only one in which we have not previously had a presence," he claims, "is Palanquero." The ambassador insists, "There will be nothing different than what has been done over the previous ten years, intelligence missions, information gathering and joint maritime missions, perhaps more sophisticated than before." He attempts to reassure critics that the U.S. cannot "participate in military missions in Colombia, given the legal restrictions imposed by [the U.S.] Congress" (*El Tiempo*, 2009, October 31). Two months earlier, however, on August 18, *El Tiempo* quoted the ambassador seemingly suggesting the opposite: "The FARC will be the target of joint missions carried out under the new military agreement: Brownfield" (Peña, 2009, August 18). No one, however, challenges the silver-tongued ambassador's equivocations, inconsistencies and lies. For the majority of Colombians, the matter is done with.

On November 2, 2009, the Colombian government releases the text of the "Complementary Agreement for Technical Assistance in Defense and Security" to the general public. The document contains 25 articles whose language is similar to previous agreements signed with Ecuador (for Manta) and Central American countries hosting FOLs. U.S. forces will have guaranteed, unhindered access to the bases, ports and facilities covered by the agreement; aircraft will be granted flyover permission for the entire country without any controls imposed on entering and leaving bases and civilian airports, and they will be exempt from paying fees for the right to land and park on runways; American maritime vessels will enjoy similar "treatment and privileges." Colombia will grant diplomatic immunity to U.S. government and military personnel, who themselves are exempt from having to apply for visas and present passports upon entering and leaving the country, as well as paying taxes (including on any property acquired). As was the case in Ecuador, the U.S. will install its own communications systems in Colombia, including an exclusive mail service, a satellite and radio and television stations exempt from outside regulation (*Semana*, 2009, November 4).

Shortly after the agreement is signed, on October 13, 2009, the Council of State rebuts the government's claim that it constitutes a "complementary" agreement "based on a previous treaty" of the 19 already signed with the United States; the Council concludes that it should be submitted to Congress as a "new treaty" (González Posso, 2009, November 16); absent congressional approval, the agreement is unconstitutional. At times it seems there is a collective stupor overtaking the country: Uribe's attempts to sidestep the constitution are just not a big deal. Uribe enjoys the support of the majorities. The nation looks on, as the government hems and haws its way around constitutional procedures, without even raising a finger in protest. The president of the Chamber of Representatives, Edgar Gómez, an Uribe loyalist, declaring himself satisfied with the government's explanations, concludes that submitting the agreement for congressional approval is unnecessary.

Third World countries that enter pacts with superpowers are playing with fire. Colombia will find itself bending to Washington's demands. Once the agreement is signed another concession will take effect: U.S. forces will be allowed to use the country's seven international civilian airports. Between the seven principal bases, the two military facilities in which the Pentagon is "interested"—Malambo and Tolemaida—and seven civilian airports, the United States will have the full run of the country, including its airspace and territorial waters. The Pentagon highlights in an internal document how the pact results in favorable conditions for carrying out operations against hostile governments. In an article titled "Yankees, Welcome!" *Semana* publishes a facsimile of the document (*Semana*, 2009, October 31). The article's title sums up the country's current submissive mindset.

To assuage fears surrounding its activities, the Pentagon asks that operations originating from Colombian bases only be referred to as "combating the drug trade." According to revelations out of the Pentagon, Palanquero is designated a CSL—that is, a training center for Latin American military personnel, to complement the former School of the Americas (which has operated since 1989 under another name in Fort Benning), in light of the Pentagon's desire to wash its hands of the unsavory practices that incite controversy at home and abroad. This training is offered in other military facilities as well (Lindsay-Poland, 2009, May 18).

When questioned about the training of military forces from around the region, a new responsibility assigned by the Pentagon to Palanquero, Fabio Valencia Cossio, the interior minister, states that Colombia is already training Latin American armies at a lower cost and of a similar quality to that offered by the United States and Great Britain (Lindsay-Poland, 2009, August 16). With Palanquero as a regional center for military training and the seven bases at the service of the Pentagon, Colombia has become like Panama in the

1960's—only in Panama American forces were concentrated in the Canal Zone, whereas in Colombia the facilities are dispersed throughout the country as well as on both coasts.

Frontier Aflame

Venezuela is surrounded by U.S. military facilities in Colombia, Curaçao, Aruba, Guantanamo and Puerto Rico. Chávez accuses the Dutch of cooperating with Washington's aggressive plots against his country. The Dutch government responds that U.S. military planes using civilian airports in Curaçao and Aruba are limited to anti-narcotics operations.

The Venezuelan government's paranoia concerning Washington's intentions is not unfounded. In 2002, Chávez was briefly ousted by a military coup supported by the Bush administration. Since then Chávez has been the most outspoken critic of the United States, promoting regional integration that excludes it, creating new international bodies to replace those historically dominated by Washington, and in general adopting policies that conflict with its interests; Washington is therefore determined to contain his influence throughout the region.

The tensions between Colombia and Venezuela, countries that are vitally important to each other, threaten regional peace and harmony and are a cause for alarm. Many fear that the continual verbal sparring between the two governments will escalate into something more serious. This much is clear:

should the hostilities intensify, the United States will not stand idlly on the sidelines. Chávez and Uribe occupy opposite ends of the political spectrum. Uribe stands in staunch opposition to the more progressive currents passing through the region. His militaristic and confrontational policies are at odds with the prevailing desire for peace and harmony. Chávez suspends relations with Colombia after its government signs the military agreement with the United States, and places the Venezuelan army on high alert.

Venezuela mobilizes against the threat posed by the U.S.-Colombian pact. On December 20, 2009, Chávez denounces the incursion of an unmanned spy plane in his country's airspace; the aircraft, which departed from Colombia, flew over the Fuerte Mara military base in the Venezuelan state of Zulia. Chávez describes the aircraft as two or three meters in length, remotely steered and capable of filming as well as dropping bombs of "Yankee" make. He calls on Uribe to act responsibly, suggesting that the Colombian president is being used by Washington, while at the same time warning that unauthorized aircraft encroaching upon Venezuelan airspace will be shot down (Toothaker, 2009, December 20).

Uribe and his defense minister, Gabriel Silva, are playing with fire by doing Washington's bidding. They grab onto the Venezuelan president's call for his armed forces to stay on high alert as evidence that Colombia is being threatened. Many believe that in relentlessly clashing with Chávez, Uribe is acting as a pawn for Washington.

The notoriously hot-tempered Uribe slings false accusations at political opponents, puts his citizens' lives at risk, makes fantastical claims and leapfrogs legal hurdles without blinking an eye. Uribe and Defense Minister Santos have no qualms representing the Colombian military's incursion into Ecuador as a "hot pursuit" and act of "legitimate defense," despite it being established that the killings took place at dawn: the guerrilla soldiers were taken out while they slept. Some corpses were discovered with a coup de grâce administered.

In November 2009, Rafael García, a high-ranking former DAS official, goes public with bombshell allegations of his agency's plot—which he claims originated at the presidential level—to assassinate Hugo Chávez along with some of his ministers. At the time, García is being confined in La Picota prison in Bogotá, charged with electoral fraud (carried out on Uribe's behalf) in coastal departments, illegal dealings with paramilitaries, and falsifying documents. His explosive revelations include claims of pervasive corruption within the DAS, which the attorney general later corroborates, leading to a slew of investigations and arrests. García also alludes to a covert DAS plot, spearheaded by the interior minister, Fernando Londoño, to assassinate Chávez and other members of his government (Fazio, 2009, November 11). These criminal schemes are reminiscent of those carried out by the Dominican dictator Leonidas Trujillo against the Venezuelan President Rómulo Betancourt, which were condemned by the OAS—not to mention innumerable CIA assassination attempts against Fidel Castro. It represents the sort of conspiracy anathema to Colombia's robust legalist and republican traditions.

Tensions Rise

Time and again Hugo Chávez has expressed his weariness with the Colombian conflict, and Uribe's bellicose posturing and stubborn insistence on militarily "defeating" the FARC, his refusal to negotiate peace and ruthless prosecution of a futile drug war.

In November 2009, the tension between the two countries spills onto the international stage, when Uribe denounces Chávez to the OAS and the UN Security Council, accusing him of threatening to use force against Colombia and providing refuge—as well economic support—to the FARC. Proof of these allegations he purports to have found in computers recovered from the bombarded FARC encampment across the Ecuadorian border. Chávez characterizes the accusations as a provocation and manipulation of the facts. In December 2009, his foreign minister, Nicolás Maduro, in a letter addressed to the President of the UN Security Council, Thomas Mayr-Harting, claims that "armed conflict that Colombia is enduring" be included on his agenda as a priority, claiming that neighboring countries are being affected by the humanitarian crisis, displacements, kidnappings and the presence of Colombian paramilitaries and assassins crossing the border illegally; he denounces the threat posed by the

U.S. military presence in Colombia to his country, as well as Uribe's warmongering and military incursion in Ecuador, and reiterates Venezuela's peaceful intentions; he alludes to the failure of Plan Colombia to reduce cocaine production, and claims that drug-traffickers and paramilitaries have penetrated the Colombian state, where they now exert influence "of an unimaginable magnitude" in the highest echelons of the country (*El Tiempo*, 2009, December 6). In Venezuela, there are millions of undocumented Colombians who have fled the violence or migrated in search of economic opportunity though the same porous border that guerrilla soldiers, paramilitaries and assassins freely pass, sowing conflict between the two countries.

Following an acrimonious media exchange, Hugo Chávez announces that he has asked the Rio Group, which will convene in February 2010, to include on its agenda the U.S.-Colombian pact. Shortly after the Venezuelan leader's denunciation of the unmanned aircraft's incursion into his country's airspace, the Colombian Ministry of Defense announces that it has created new air and special ops battalions to "reinforce the security of the country." One will be located in the southern Guaviare department, with two others in La Guajira and Arauca, departments that border Venezuela, as well as four more in the bases hosting American military personnel. Another base in La Guajira will see its capacity expanded from 50 to 1,000 troops. According to Defense Minister Silva, the addition of these new battalions solidifies the Colombian

Air Force's place as one of the largest and best trained in Latin America (*Agencia EFE*, 2009, December 19).

On High Alert!

The U.S. military has never been a popular guest in Latin America. All the arbitrary interventions, attacks, landings and invasions have taken a toll on the continent—each a new tragic episode in a living history of domination. Around the turn of the century, when left-wing governments critical of American hegemony take power in several countries, the geopolitical panorama begins to shift. Regional integration gains moment as Latin America reaffirms its independence. New Bolivian and Ecuadorean constitutions ban foreign military bases in their territories, a clear message to the old master up north: hands off.

In 2000, Hugo Chávez denies Washington permission to fly aircraft from its Caribbean to Colombian bases over Venezuelan territory, citing security concerns as well as public opposition. In 2003, Lula revokes the agreement signed by his predecessor, Fernando Henrique Cardoso, which ceded the rocket-launching base Alcántara, occupying 62,000 hectares in the Amazon, to the United States. Popular protest, coupled with pressure from several cabinet members, compel Lula to request that Congress suspend the study on that base. In September 2009, moved by the continental outrage over the U.S.-Colombian military pact, President Fernando Lugo cancels U.S. military exercises in Paraguay that were scheduled for 2010. "We don't believe it's opportune," he says, "for the U.S. Southern Command to be present in Paraguay with five hundred troops for this type of exercise." Lugo also announces that he will no longer welcome "visiting troops" for the Pentagon's "New Horizons" programs. He emphasizes that UNASUR has created a new landscape in which regional integration is the priority (*AFP*, 2009, September 19). Washington laments his decision, claiming "New Horizons"is a "humanitarian program."

In recent years Latin America has distanced itself from the United States, keeping the lending institutions through which it exerts economic control—the IMF and World Bank—at arm's length. But while many governments have broken with its neoliberal agenda, Washington continues to assert its military superiority. The latest pact with Colombia turns into a political fiasco for the White House, generating widespread protest and criticism throughout the region. Despite this tense climate and growing distrust of Washington, in April 2010 Brazil signs a military cooperation agreement with the United States to "reinforce"—both parties declare—the security ties between their countries. The news drops like a bucket of cold water over the continent: many view the agreement as a big step backwards after the recent progress made towards regional autonomy. Considering that Brazil is the regional powerhouse, and Lula the harshest critic of the recent U.S.-Colombian military pact—which he characterized as a "threat" to Latin American—around the region people ask: "Why now?" Brazil has signed no military cooperation agreements with Washington since 1977, when President Jimmy Carter suspended bilateral military cooperation in protest of Ernesto Geisel's brutal dictatorship. This new alliance, pulled out of the Pentagon's bag of tricks, demonstrates that, whatever may happen, American hegemony is alive and well. That the Pentagon has succeeded in co-opting Latin America's largest country is a major blow to all the others. The cooperation and military exchanges established by the agreement cover a broad range of areas, including arms sales. Unlike Colombia, Brazil does not cede access to its bases or agree to host foreign troops but, despite his attempts to explain it away, Lula's decision is inconsistent with the independent principles he has championed throughout his presidency. Brazil has seriously undermined regional unity.

After signing the military agreement with Colombia, in October 2009, Ambassador Brownfield announces that his country will pursue additional military cooperation agreements with other Latin American countries. He does not disclose with which, but Brazil, a symbolically powerful nation, is only the first. The second could be Uruguay: upon returning from Washington, Luis Rosadilla, its defense minister under the new president, José Mujica (a former left-wing guerrilla), informs Congress that a "security and defense agreement with the United States would be of interest to Uruguay" (Miller and Downie, 2010, April 13).

Another unexpected development takes place in Costa Rica,

a country with a strong tradition of democracy and antimilitarism, the only country in the hemisphere with no standing army (which President José Figueres dismantled, in 1948, in the name of democracy). President Laura Chinchilla authorizes 46 U.S. warships, 10 fighter planes, 200 armed helicopters and 7,000 marines to enter Costa Rican territory between July and December 2010. Faced with domestic protest, she speaks of the need to "jointly combat" the drug trade. The Legislative Assembly approves their entry, with 31 votes in favor and 8 against. Social and popular movements and organizations, including the opposition Broad Front, Citizens' Action Party, and Social Christian Unity Party, decry the presence of foreign troops in the country, which they liken to a "military occupation," an illegal violation of national sovereignty. These military exercises, however, were committed to by former president Óscar Arias (2006-2010), part of the free trade agreement he signed with the United States. Critics accuse him of joining the discredited Plan Colombia, committing Costa Rica to Washington's militaristic agenda, and aiding the aggression against Venezuela and other countries led by leftist governments. The opposition criticizes the exaggerated military deployment, supposedly to combat the drug trade. This episode can be chalked up as another victory for the Pentagon and fiasco for the region. Such a heavy military presence in Central America alarms neighboring countries but, as always, protests both domestic and international do nothing to hinder the American advance (*AFP* and *PL*, 2010, July 5). Washington installs two antinarcotic bases in Peru: one in the Amazonian region bordering Brazil and Colombia and another, to be administered jointly with the DEA, near the frontier with Ecuador (*El Comercio*, 2010, September 13).

The Pentagon's end game is to reclaim its traditional sphere of influence. Secretary of Defense Robert Gates (appointed by Bush and kept on by Obama) travels to Colombia, Peru and the Caribbean to strengthen military ties. Arturo Valenzuela, the newly appointed Assistant Secretary of State for Western Hemisphere Affairs, does the same in the Andean countries. His first official visit, in December 2009, to Argentina, turns into a disaster. In meetings with prominent opposition figures he touts the neoliberal policies of the Menem administration, which is viewed as a slap in the face to the leftist government in power. His comments are harshly criticized by the foreign minister, former President Néstor Kirchner, and other high-profile political figures and media commentators, who conclude that Valenzuela's first mission as Assistant Secretary of State for Western Hemisphere Affairs was counterproductive.

The Story Continues

Even after Obama takes office, U.S. military expansion into Latin America—under the guise of the war on drugs—continues, as does Washington's lax attitude with respect to the international pacts, treaties, and conventions it signs, only to ignore once they prove inconvenient. National borders, likewise, pose nary an obstacle when it comes to pursuing alleged terrorists. The Bush administration and legislators from both parties, including then Senator Barack Obama, applaud Colombia's incursion into Ecuador, in March 2008, to eliminate the FARC's second in command, despite the operation constituting a clear violation of territorial sovereignty.

On the domestic front, President Obama has implemented some changes to earlier drug policies. In contrast to the Reagan administration, his focus is more humane than militaristic; rather than harshly penalize all drug-related infractions, he explores ways to diminish demand for drugs and provide medical assistance to addicts. Overseas, however, his focus continues to be on military solutions. FOLs are equipped to combat drug trafficking and, in October 2009, Obama finalizes the agreement with Colombia for access to seven of its bases. The tremendous man and firepower deployed to those bases—including hundreds of marines, surveillance aircraft, and armed helicopters—suggest a motive beyond combating the drug trade: military dominance over the region.

On August 7, 2010, Álvaro Uribe's controversial presidency comes to an end, and his equally controversial military agreement endures a setback under the new administration. When Juan Manuel Santos takes office, the majority of the country believes they have voted for Uribe III; yet to the surprise—and satisfaction—of many, the new president overturns several Uribe policies and immediately reestablishes relations with

Ecuador and Venezuela. A few days after he takes office, the Court declares the military agreement with the U.S. unconstitutional, thereby rendering it void. In Washington there is revolt, but Santos promises to leave the agreement alone and not involve Congress. There will be no change in course since, as Ambassador Brownfield himself pointed out, American forces have been using six of the seven bases in question all along under Plan Colombia. The new pact only "legalized" that pre-existing arrangement to which the parties are able to return without any problem. Santos will do nothing to stop it.

Over the past twenty years the war on drugs has proven immensely costly and largely ineffective; despite being relegated to secondary importance on the White House's domestic agenda, it continues to dominate relations with Latin America, especially the Andean nations. The DEA maintains a presence in every country that plays a role in the drug trade, and the Southern Command continues to lead anti-drug operations. Bolivia and Venezuela expel the DEA and its agents for conspiring against their governments; as retribution, Washington "decertifies" those countries, suspending tariff preferences as well as military and economic aid; they are added to the black list of governments to be targeted through media campaigns and destabilizing covert operations—activities that come to light in a cable released by WikiLeaks in September 2010. Evo Morales declares that the Washington has no moral authority to criticize how the drug war is prosecuted in his country, and suggests that UNA-

SUR should "certify" whether the United States has diminished demand, "since as long as there is demand there will be cocaine" (*Semana*, 2009, September 16).

The State Department's annual report on drugs demonstrates an overt bias against the progressive governments critical of U.S. foreign policy. In September 2010the report accuses Venezuelan security forces of aiding the FARC, and the Bolivian government of allowing cocaine production to increase, and describes Ecuador as the country most vulnerable to organized crime owing to the historic weakness and pervasive corruption of its institutions (*AFP* and *DPA*, 2010, March 2). According to Evo Morales, these "decertifications" (which are, in effect, equivalent to sanctions) amount to nothing more than political retribution.

Many analysts have bemoaned the Obama administration's use of the media to disseminate falsehoods about the governments that criticize it—as well as its punitive use of economic levers against them. They point to a State Department report, which includes a list of 20 countries cited as the "largest producers of drugs and drug-trafficking routes." Fifteen are from Latin America and the Caribbean, with Bolivia and Venezuela topping the list. Suzanna Reiss, an Assistant Professor at the University of Hawaii, observes that the "political ideologies associated with governments in the hemisphere—not the actual health consequences or 'violence' emanating from struggles over control of the drug trade—have determined the certification process. If this were not the case,

Colombia and Mexico, as the major "producer" country and the largest "transit" country, respectively, would undoubtedly top the blacklist of drug war failures" (Reiss, 2010, January-February).

By the time Obama enters office, many in Washington have already written off the drug war as a failure. Presented with a startlingly bleak outlook, in December 2009 two House Representatives—Eliot Engel, a Democrat, and Dan Burton, a Republican—recommend the creation of a bipartisan commission to rethink the war on drugs. Their proposal is approved unanimously. The commission is supposed to evaluate past and current initiatives in the United States and throughout the region, and propose new strategies moving forward. The United States has made substantial cutbacks to Plan Colombia, but thus far no new policies have emerged from the commission, and things continue unchanged.

7

Against the Continental Tide: Obama and Uribe

MORE OF THE SAME?

Despite the promises President Obama made during his first meeting with regional leaders in Port of Spain, Washington's Latin American policy remains the same; relations continue to deteriorate. Cuba continues ensnared in the "historic conflict," as Raúl Castro refers to the half century of American economic and military aggression. Obama's handling of the crisis precipitated by the June 2009 Honduran coup is seen as erratic and ultimately damaging. After initially condemning the deposition—in keeping with the regional majority—the American president, without offering any explanation, reverses course and recognizes the election to be held by the de facto government; not only has the White House blocked the return of the rule of law, and legitimized a president widely rejected around the region, but he has also left the door open for future military coups in other countries. According to the *NACLA Report on the Americas*, the similarities between the military coups past and present are too glaring to ignore (*The NACLA Report*, 2011, January-February).

The military penetration of Latin America, long a staple of U.S. foreign policy, has always raised hackles around the region. Under President Obama the advance continues. In 2009, Colombia turns over seven of its bases to U.S. military personnel, and becomes the main American military foothold on the continent, and a critical strategic partner.

By the end of his first year in office the perception in Latin America of President Obama, once marked by hope and optimism, has begun to sour. The promises the president made in Trinidad and Tobago of a new beginning, of open and equal dialogue with Cuba, remain unfulfilled. And despite a campaign pledge to pull millions of undocumented immigrants (between 11-12 million, the majority Hispanic) "out of the shadows" and push through wholesale immigration reform during his first year in office, that portion of his agenda—which is of particular concern to many Latin Americans—has stalled. His promise of open dialogue with Cuba on a "broad range of issues from human rights to freedom of expression and democratic reform, drugs, migration and economic concerns" has also fallen by the wayside, despite Raúl Castro repeatedly professing his willingness to discuss "everything" (*AFP, DPA* and *Reuters*, 2009, April 18).

Obama inherits a simmering conflict with Hugo Chávez, which was aggravated by the Bush administration's support of the failed 2002 coup. Like his predecessor, Obama refers to Chávez as a threat to the region, recapitulating familiar allegations that the Venezuelan president provides aid to the Colombian guerrillas. The standoff with Caracas bears disturbing similarities to Washington's decades-long harassment and persecution campaign waged against Havana. Like his predecessor, Obama criticizes Venezuela's "checkbook diplomacy" (in the form of petroleum agreements, loans and government bond purchases), and expresses concern that Chávez is projecting his influence into other countries, such as Bolivia and Nicaragua. Despite experiencing an economic downturn in the wake of the global financial crisis (due in large part to a drop in oil prices), Venezuela continues providing assistance to allied countries. This "checkbook diplomacy," made possible by the country's vast petroleum wealth, is different from the type of influence exerted by Cuba. For decades, Fidel assumed the ideological leadership of the Third World left, supported its revolutions, and shared the advances of his own revolution with allied nations in several continents. Havana has exported doctors, educators, agronomists, athletes and experts in a variety of disciplines, assistance has been received with gratitude.

HONDURAS: ANATOMY OF A COUP

At dawn on June 28, 2009, hours before voting booths are

to open for a referendum on constitutional reform, soldiers storm the residence of the sitting Honduran president. Still in pajamas, Manuel Zelaya is taken to a military base, where he is put on a plane to Costa Rica. High-ranking military officers and right-wing elites are behind his overthrow. Two days earlier the Supreme Court erroneously declared the referendum unconstitutional, despite the fact that 400,000 Hondurans had supported it with their signatures. The current constitution was drafted in 1982 under the repressive, corrupt military dictatorship of Policarpo Juan Paz García, following decades of violent coups and sham elections.

The coup was preceded by an unusual power struggle: President Zelaya dismissed the chief of his defense staff for not following orders only to have the Supreme Court reinstate him; the Supreme Electoral Tribunal and Congress both support the Court; Zelaya ignores them and proceeds with the referendum (*El Tiempo*, 2009, June 29). The reactionary Honduran oligarchy, fearing the country will follow a path similar to Venezuela, Bolivia and Ecuador, where progressive, nationalistic constitutions have recently been ratified, opposes the referendum. The far right accuses Zelaya of seeking reelection, prohibited under the 1982 constitution, through constitutional reform.

To provide a veneer of legitimacy, the Supreme Court, the Supreme Electoral Tribunal and Congress throw their support behind the coup, accusing the Zelaya of undermining the constitution. The military, Catholic Church, principle chamber of commerce, powerful business interests and prominent media organizations also support the usurpers. In Congress, the coup leaders read a phony resignation letter, which they attribute to Zelaya, and nominate the Speaker of Congress, Roberto Micheletti, interim president until general elections, scheduled for November 28, 2009, can be held. Micheletti and Zelaya are long-standing political rivals.

During a press conference the following day Obama condemns the coup: "It would be a terrible precedent if we start moving backwards into the era in which we are seeing military coups as a means of political transition rather than democratic elections." In speaking of the past, he concedes that "the United States has not always been were it should have," and categorizes the transfer of power in Honduras as illegal, declaring that Zelaya continues to be president. "We stand on the side of democracy, sovereignty, and self-determination" (Feller, 2009, June 30) and "will not return to our dark past. We will defend democracy and fight for a peaceful resolution to the dispute without the interference of other countries" (Muñoz Bata, 2009, June 30). Obama supports the OAS resolution, a noteworthy departure from Washington's traditional unilateral tendencies; later he throws his support behind a mediation effort led by Costa Rican President Óscar Arias, a conservative U.S. ally. The OAS has too many staunch left-wing governments for Washington's taste.

Though Obama condemns the coup, he stops short of recalling his ambassador from Tegucigalpa, a measure taken by several other countries, including some regional allies. Then at a NATO summit in August, held in Guadalajara, Mexico, the Honduran crisis is not even addressed. Obama begins to stray from the pack, according to the Mexican press, after finding out that the coup originated in Washington, during the previous administration, when Zelaya, then of the center-right Liberal Party, tacked to the left: he strengthened ties to Chávez, entered Honduras into ALBA, announced the closing of the Soto Cano FOL (previously called Palmerola), which had been in U.S. hands since Reagan's wars in Central America, and initiated several projects that rankled the Honduran right, including raising the minimum wage (the lowest in Central America) and going forward with a referendum on constitutional reform (Main, 2010, January–February).

Attempts by the coup's leaders to pass off as constitutional the overthrow of an elected president fail to convince. The majority of the international community condemns the coup and demands Zelaya's immediate reinstatement. At an extraordinary OAS session, Honduras is suspended from the Inter-American System and targeted with sanctions; the UN, EU, UNASUR, CARICOM, and Mercosur likewise condemn the coup and declare the Micheletti government unconstitutional. Latin American presidents recall their ambassadors and many Western governments follow suit. Obama maintains his ambassador, he claims, "to have contact with Honduran civil society" (Thompson and Lacey, 2009, July 7).

The Honduran coup not only provokes international condemnation, but internal violence as well. Protestors loyal to Zelaya organize large demonstrations, which are suppressed with force. Micheletti supporters likewise orchestrate impressive shows of support. These clashes result in injuries and fatalities, disappearances and more than 600 arrests, including members of the deposed government and Zelaya's political party, as well as street protestors and journalists critical of the coup.

The international condemnation is intense. The president of the UN Assembly General, the Nicaraguan priest Miguel D'Escotto, convenes an emergencysession in which a resolution calling for Zelaya's immediate and unconditional reinstatement is unanimously approved. The Assembly General refuses to recognize the post-coup government and urges all countries to do the same. UN Secretary-General Ban Ki-moon condemns the president's detainment and calls for his restoration, and guarantees for his and his family's safety, and respect for human rights amid the unrest. In an extraordinary OAS meeting, called by Secretary-General Miguel Insulza, member countries—with the exception of Honduras, whose delegate abstains—approve a resolution to suspend that country from the Inter-American System (primarily affecting lending and defense), until Zelaya has been restored, and calls on Honduras to respect the Inter-American Democratic Charter, giving the government 72 hours to reestablish constitutional order. Insulza characterizes Zelaya's removal as a "coup d'état" and announces that he will accompany the deposed president on his return to Honduras. The World

Bank holds back the delivery of a 270-million-dollar loan (*Agencia EFE* and *AFP*, 2009, July 1), and the Pentagon suspends military activities in Honduras and assistance to the country (Rojas, 2009, July 1).

The international community moves to isolate the Micheletti government. José Luis Rodríguez Zapatero, Spain's president, voices his unreserved condemnation of the illegal detainment and forced exile of the president and offers his country's armed forces, should they be needed, to restore democracy to Honduras. Hugo Chávez also makes his government available to assist in any way—short of armed intervention, he makes clear—the restoration of the deposed president. The Venezuelan president pledges to respect Honduran sovereignty.

Following a meeting with Zelaya in Washington, Hillary Clinton announces that the deposed president and his post-coup successor are both prepared to accept President Arias's mediation, and her hope is that the dialogue will begin as soon as possible to restore constitutional order and democracy to Honduras (Gómez Maseri, 2009, July 8). The political rivals arrive in Costa Rica and are invited by Arias to his residence, but they refuse to meet face to face and each departs after holding private conversations with Arias. Micheletti proves to be the more inflexible of the two, announcing the continuation of his presidency until an election can be held in November. The attempts to start up talks fizzle. Arias asks the United States to use its influence to end the "stalemate" and warns the coup leaders "elections called by an illegitimate government are illegitimate" (Thompson, 2009, July 13).

Cracks begin to emerge in Insulza's leadership. He offers to accompany Zelaya on his return to Honduras, but the Honduran army prevents them from deplaning in the international airport. When the secretary-general travels to Tegucigalpa to convince Micheletti to restore Zelaya to power, he is notified that an order for his capture and arrest will be issued if he returns to the country. Honduras ultimately announces its withdrawal from the OAS.

OBAMA GETS COLD FEET

The White House initially aligns itself with the Latin American consensus on the Honduran question, which kindled fears of future coups similar to those that once plagued the hemisphere. Regional leaders demand the restoration of Zelaya as a sine quo non for their recognition of the presidential elections scheduled for November. After months of fruitless OAS negotiations and mediations led by President Arias, Obama breaks the consensus with no advance notice and, turning his back on regional leaders, recognizes the upcoming elections. This sudden reversal causes bewilderment all around. According to Lula, Obama has destabilized the region and emboldened future "adventurers" to perpetrate coups of their own.

Obama justifies his support for the elections on the grounds that they will "allow the Honduran people to exercise their free will and defend democracy" (Brooks, 2009, November 26). These elections, however, held by a de facto government, are far from legitimate. Even Óscar Arias stated in advance that to endorse the elections is to endorse the coup, to impede the return of constitutional order and leave alive—as Lula claims—the specter of future military coups, and president (Porfirio Lobo) lacking legitimacy in place. Most Latin American governments do not recognize Lobo. To international institutions (including the UN, OAS and Mercosur) the elections are unconstitutional and their victor illegitimate. Lula and Correa refuse, as a matter of principle, to recognize their outcome.

Prominent Democrats criticize the administration's handling of the Honduran crisis as "lacking in vision and tact." Senator John Kerry believes the president made a mistake, noting that the regional agreement depended on U.S. support; Robert White, president of the Center for International Policy in Washington and the former ambassador, under President Carter, to El Salvador, writes that Obama has "transformed an imminent diplomatic triumph into a negotiated defeat" (Brooks, 2009, November 29) and wasted a golden opportunity to demonstrate that relations with Latin America have truly been reset.

Obama frustrates the Latin American goal of uniting in loud opposition to military coups, and making clear, once and for all, that governments that come to power by way of force will not be tolerated in the region or world. According to Evo Morales, the American president might as well have given the coup leaders a pat on the back; the White House has allowed them to make good on their pledge to govern until elections, thereby impeding the restoration of constitutional order. According to Lula, Obama has reneged on his own promise to reset relations with Latin America, while the Venezuelan foreign minister characterizes as very "unusual" the decision of a group of countries to endorse the elections, despite the consensus reached at a recent Rio Group summit in Jamaica calling for Zelaya's reinstatement prior to holding new elections. He is referring to the conservative governments of Colombia, Costa Rica, Peru and Panama, all of which dutifully follow Washington's lead. Óscar Arias has chosen to contradict his own prior declaration that "elections carried out by illegitimate governments are illegitimate" (Thompson, 2009, July 13). Hugo Chávez finds the American position "particularly shameful" in that it accepts "the electoral fraud perpetrated by the Honduran dictatorship, before even receiving the official results of the de facto government" (*AFP*, 2009, December 1).

A senior State Department official offers a glib dismissal of the rebukes emanating from home and abroad over the administration's unexpected about-face: "We never changed policy, we always considered elections to be part of a general solution." He goes on to stress how important it is that "everyone send a signal that [a coup] is not an acceptable way to change governments." But the U.S. government is sending the exact opposite message, according to David Brooks, Washington correspondent for *La Jornada*, since supporting elections carried out by the coup leaders allows them to "wash away" their original sin. "There were negotiations," he adds, "and concessions from the White House;" the Republican Senator Jim DeMint, for instance, offered to lift his veto on Arturo Valenzuela's stalled confirmation as Assistant Secretary of State for Western Hemisphere Affairs in exchange for a "guarantee" that the victor of the elections will be recognized, regardless of whether or not Zelaya is reinstated (*AFP*, 2009, November 13).

With the green light from Washington, presidential elections are held and a right-wing agricultural landowner, Porfirio Lobo, is voted into office. His victory is met with elation by conservatives around the region, in Honduras, the United States, among anti-Castro Cubans, anti-Sandista Nicaraguans and Miami's Hispanic community. At Micheletti's invitation, some of these figures were present in Tegucigalpa as "election observers." Among Republican leaders and the conservative press, including *The Wall Street Journal* and *The Washington Times* and certain *Washington Post* columnists, the election results are hailed as "a triumph for democracy" and "defeat for Hugo Chávez." The reality, however, is something different: it's the reactionary Honduran oligarchs, supported by the American right, who have triumphed—and perhaps the biggest winner of all are military coups as a viable and tolerable mechanism for change. According to Mark Weisbrot, co-president of the Center for Economic and Policy Research, these right-wing ideologues could care less about Honduras and are merely intent on "striking down leftist democratic movements throughout the region, what they characterize as a Havana-Caracas-La Paz conspiracy, and 'Honduras was the weakest link'" (Brooks, 2009, November 29).

With each passing day, it becomes increasingly clear that the Bush administration played a role in planning the coup. This is certainly the prevailing belief within progressive circles in Honduras. *La Jornada* confirms that the perpetrators "departed from the Honduran base Soto Cano, occupied by the United States since Reagan's wars in Central America; it is approved by the Southern Command and State Department officials with complicity of the ambassador himself Hugo Llorens," a conservative Cuban-American appointed by the previous administration (Guerra-Cabrera, 2009, November 5). Evo Morales also accuses the Southern Command of having had a hand in the coup.

Eight heads of state, including those of Cuba, Venezuela, Bolivia and Nicaragua, withdraw from the December 2009 Ibero-American Summit, held in Estoril, Portugal. The frustration and anger with the Obama administration's handling of the coup is on full display at the conference, with the Honduran crisis dominating the dialogue. Divisions are deep and there are few points of convergence. The majority will not recognize the elections held under the de facto government, which Cristina Kirchner dismisses as "pantomime"; Lula predicts that Washington's blessing of these elections will serve as a green light to future "adventurers" and ferment instability in the region. From la Paz, Evo Morales declares there were no democratic elections to speak of: the Honduran government is just a dictatorship taking orders from the "Empire." He laments that Washington's outlook and policy toolkit in the region remain unchanged, and that the White House "did not know to protect democracy in Honduras." The conservative presidents of Colombia, Costa Rica, Peru and Panama follow Washington's lead in recognizing Lobo. Though no consensus can be reached in the summit's final resolution, the representatives register their unanimous condemnation of the coup, and the majority refuse to endorse the elections or recognize Porfirio Lobo and demand the immediate reinstatement of Zelaya (Urrutia, 2009, December 2).

The overwhelming majority of Latin American countries refuse to establish relations with the Lobo government and at the UNASUR summit held in Campana, Argentina, to prepare for the upcoming May 18 European Union-Latin America and Caribbean Summit in Madrid, Lula and the majority of the attendees elect to boycott the event if Lobo is invited. Rafael Correa, acting as UNASUR's pro tempore president, notifies the Spanish Prime Minister, José Luis Rodríguez Zapatero, of the collective determination, as a statement of principle, to not trivialize the constitutional violations seen in Honduras "as if nothing has happened" (Valente, 2010, May 4). Zapatero proposes a compromise: though Lobo will be invited, he will only attend the EU conference with the Central Americans.

Obama's controversial decision to recognize the post-coup election points to several unfortunate truths: the United States cares more about maintaining appearances than actually defending democracy. Though the elections provide a façade of democracy, with citizens going out and casting their ballots, Washington is ultimately unconcerned by democratic principles when its own political interests are in play. That voter abstention exceeded the level permitted under Honduran law, that the authority overseeing the elections was illegitimate, none of that matters. The overriding lesson to be gleaned is that the relationship between Obama and Latin America will follow the same dynamic as that of his predecessor. The region should expect more of the same.

URIBE: GOING AGAINST THE CONTINENTAL TIDE

Álvaro Uribe is the antithesis of the New Left in Latin America. The only other conservative heads of state are Alan García of Peru, and Sebastian Piñera of Chile, who follows Michelle Bachelet of the center-left Socialist Party (her 80% approval rating upon leaving office was not enough to secure the election of the party's nominee to succeed her).

Uribe's unilateral posturing put stress on an otherwise harmonious climate, undermining the ability of the region to act as a block, with synchronized ideas and interests, on the world stage. The most damaging blow to integration is his granting the U.S. access to seven bases. Uribe is a staunch conservative, bellicose, combative (what he himself defines as "feisty") and fully acquiescent to Washington. Surrendering seven military bases, however, represents the new nadir of dependence and subservience.

The epicenter of the drug trade and largest producer of cocaine in the world, Colombia is unquestionably a problem country for the United States; it is also, however, a strategically vital and loyal ally, a foothold in the continent. This deepening bilateral relationship comes to be viewed as a threat by the rest of the region.

WHO IS ALVARO URIBE?

The Uribe name carries considerable political baggage, not least of which is alleged ties to drug lords (including the legendary Pablo Escobar) and paramilitary commanders. Though a staunch conservative, Álvaro Uribe has held high-profile positions as a member of the Liberal Party: Director of Civil Aviation (1980-1982), Mayor of Medellín (1982-1984), Senator (1986-1994), governor of Antioquia (1995-1997), and presidential candidate. His entire public life, including his tenure as president (2002-2010), are clouded by numerous scandals, from which he somehow always manages to emerge unscathed.

As Director of Civil Aviation, Uribe is accused of granting landing permits to aircraft belonging to drug traffickers; in 1991 the Pentagon declassifies a document in which his name appears on a list of the Medellín cartel's most important associates (Hristov, 2009: 142). As governor of Antioquia, he is given the moniker "The Pacifier of Urabá" in recognition of his operations against the FARC-EP. A sub region of Antioquia, Urabá is the scene of a bloody territorial dispute between the United Self-Defense Forces of Córdoba and Urabá (AUCC)—a ruthless paramilitary association led by Carlos, Fidel, and Vicente Castaño—and the FARC-EP. General Rito Alejo del Río of the 17th Brigade leads the campaigns while coordinating with the AUC. When that corrupt union comes to light, the United States strips the general of his visa, drawing the ire of the Colombian far right as well as Antioquia's oligarchy who, to demonstrate their support, fete Alejo del Rio at the Hotel Tequendama in Bogotá, a select venue for this sort of tribute to national figures. Uribe is the banquet's host and keynote speaker.

URIBE AND PARAMILITARISM

In 1994, as guerrilla and paramilitary violence ravages the nation, the Colombian government forms peasant self-defense groups to act as informants, hoping they will help foil guerrilla attacks and increase security. The groups are christened Special Vigilance and Private Security Services (CONVIVIR). Arguing that there is already too much violence in the country, human rights leaders oppose the militarization of peasants; they predict it will leak the conflict into the civilian population. Amnesty International contends that arming citizens entangles them in the conflict, transforming victims to victimizers. CONVIVIR fails to decrease levels of violence, as had been hoped, and complaints of abuses against the civilian population persist throughout its implementation (*Alternativa*, 1996, December; *Alternativa*, 1997, March 15–April 15).

As governor of Antioquia, a department wracked by both guerrilla and drug violence, Uribe becomes one of the country's most high-profile proponents of CONVIVIR. He is responsible for establishing 70 of 500 total groups. Seventeen are installed in Medellín, Pablo Escobar's former stronghold. The project gives rise to deep unease. Uribe assures the public that these groups only use small arms for self-defense, but the magazine *Alternativa* accuses the governor of promoting official paramilitarism, claiming that the armed groups he formed operate without any reigns. According to the magazine, the department of Antioquia has acquired a military-grade arsenal that includes 422 sub-machineguns, 373 pistols, 217 pump-action shotguns, 17 Mini-Uzis, 70 rifles, 109 .38 long guns, 41 weapons intended exclusively for military use, including Galil rifles, rocket launchers, fragmentation grenades, and mortars. A major scandal ensues (*Alternativa*, 1997, March 15–April 15). Through his Secretary of Government, Pedro Juan Moreno Villa, Uribe files a defamation suit against *Alternativa's* director, María Teresa Herrán. When the attorney general calls on the parties to reconcile, she refuses, citing the magazine's right to inform the public. The attorney general ultimately discards the suit for lacking merit, a decision hailed as a victory for freedom of information and journalist rights.

"Defeating" the FARC has always been foremost on Uribe's agenda, both as the governor of Antioquia and when he assumes the presidency. Many attribute this monomaniacal obsession to a personal vendetta: in 1986 guerillas killed his father, Jorge Alberto Uribe Sierra, a cattle rancher and landowner, during a kidnapping attempt. A 1991 U.S. military intelligence document published by the National Security Archive in Washington fingers the elder Uribe as a drug trafficker with ties to the Medellín cartel, as well as personal friend of Pablo Escobar (Evans, 2004, August 2). According to the document, Uribe Sierra was once arrested and nearly extradited to the United States, only to have his release secured at the last minute by Jesus Aristizábel Guevara, Medellín's Secretary of Government (Hristov, 2009, 142).

Uribe blames the FARC for all the ills afflicting Colombia and the vast majority of his supporters, who feel insecure with the country in a perpetual state of war, seem to agree. The national ire directed at the FARC, stoked in large measure by the president's own fiery rhetoric, continues to crescendo. The government and its surrogates abroad organize large anti-FARC demonstrations in France and the United States, replete with slogans calling for the release of guerrilla-held hostages. More than disgusted manifestations against the FARC these events can be seen as plebiscites in support of Uribe and his aggressive counterinsurgency strategy. Noticeably absent from the protests is any condemnation of the paramilitary organizations cited by domestic as well as international human rights organizations—and even the U.S. State

Department—as being responsible for 90% of the country's violence, including the most killings, countless massacres and other unspeakable atrocities. To counter the onslaught of pro-Uribe propaganda, a demonstration is held against the paramilitaries in Bogotá. Despite attracting many people, it does not reach the scale of the anti-FARC government-sponsored demonstrations. This time around the government offers no support.

Negotiating peace with the FARC is out of the question. For Uribe, the only solution to the conflict is military. Many analysts come to see CONVIVIR as the government's paramilitary arm. The ties between CONVIVIR groups and the United Self-Defense Forces of Colombia (AUC), a paramilitary organization formed in 1997 by the Castaño brothers—Carlos and Fidel—to combat guerrilla movements, run deep. The relationship is even confirmed by AUC commanders. Financed by wealthy landowners, right-wing ranchers and drug traffickers, the AUC represents the pinnacle of Colombian paramilitarism, merging the Peasant Self-Defense Forces of Córdoba and Urabá (ACCU), led by Fidel Castaño, and eight other illegal armed groups from all corners of the country. The paramilitaries kill and torture thousands of peasants to seize their land, which is then occupied by settlers, landowners and drug-traffickers. It's a perverse sort of inverse agrarian reform. The number of internally displaced citizens reaches 4.7 million, the vast majority peasants; widows and orphans abound. It is the worst such crisis in the world after Sudan. The paramilitaries carry out social cleansing at the behest of their wealthy patrons. Their targeted assassinations of labor leaders is condemned by the U.S. Congress, civil and human rights activists, opposition politicians, progressives and peasant leaders. The AUC is a cold-blooded killing machine, a perpetrator of atrocities whose sheer barbarity is without precedent. Between 1998 and 2000, the number of massacres reaches 200 per year. In September 2001, the United States adds the AUC to its list of terrorist organizations.

After a scandal breaks out involving Chiquita Brands, an American banana company with operations in Urabá, over multi-million-dollar payments the company made between 1997-2003 to the AUC, *Alternativa* reports that CONVIVIR served as an intermediary. The magazine characterizes the government-sponsored groups as legalized paramilitarism, and alleges that they operate in conjunction with the AUC. The paramilitary commander known as "HH" describes CONVIVIR as a government platform for paramilitary groups in Urabá. Operating under the aegis of the AUC, the groups strip peasants of their land (Duzán, 2008, July 13). Several international human rights organizations confirm CONVIVIR's ties to paramilitarism. According to Salvatore Mancuso, the AUC's highest commander, his organization was involved in the formation of ten CONVIVIR groups in the north of the country. "We don't lie to ourselves, the CONVIVIR groups were all ours," HH admits (Comisión Colombiana de Juristas, 2008, June 20). Faced with growing unrest over allegations of human rights violations and abuses against the civilian population, the Colombian government dismantles CONVIVIR in 1997. Many of its former members subsequently join the ranks of the AUC.

In a March 2007 article, Michael Evans, an analyst for the National Security Archives in Washington, alleges that there were ties not only between Chiquita Brands and the AUC, but also between Uribe—then governor of Antioquia—and the paramilitaries. Moreover, declassified CIA documents reveal that joint operations between CONVIVIR groups and the AUC took place. This connection is significant, Evans points out, considering that it spans the period in which Governor Uribe was CONVIVIR's most vocal proponent (Evans, 2007, March 29).

PRESIDENT URIBE

The AUC leaders Carlos Castaño and Salvatore Mancuso celebrate Álvaro Uribe's 2002 electoral victory, for not only has their candidate claimed the presidency, but they also helped elect 35 congressional representatives, ensuring his government will enjoy the majorities necessary to push through its agenda (*Cambio*, 2009, May 27). Years later, the attorney for Diego Murillo (alias "Don Berna"), the extradited former commander of the AUC's demobilized Northern Bloc, then incarcerated in the United States on drug-trafficking charges, confirms to a federal judge that her client helped finance Uribe's 2001 presidential campaign.

Upon assuming the presidency, in August 2002, one of Uribe's first acts is to extend an olive branch to the country's paramilitary groups, and a large segment of the AUC demobilizes in record time. The majority of paramilitaries accept the favorable terms offered by the president. In December, Uribe sends the "Justice and Peace Law" to Congress, setting the demobilization process in motion. According to international human rights organizations, the bill practically amounts to amnesty, given the utter barbarity of the crimes committed. The maximum sentences that can be imposed—five to eight years—violate the principle of equality before the law and could very well give rise to even greater impunity than that which is already prevalent in the country.

To ensure passage of the bill, which is seen as exceedingly generous to the paramilitaries, Uribe assigns the interior minister, Carlos Holguín Sardi, the task of rallying his congressional majority. The bill's lax terms face strong opposition in Congress, but the protests gain no traction and are ultimately overridden by the president's majority. Thus Law 975 passes: in exchange for laying down their arms, voluntarily confessing their crimes and compensating victims, the 5 to 8 year prison sentences will be extremely lenient for the Colombian penal code, which typically mandates 27 to 40 years for aggravated homicide, 30 to 40 years for genocide, and 28 to 40 years for kidnapping. The Constitutional Court introduces amendments to stiffen penalties against the paramilitaries and ensure victim compensation. In July 2003, Uribe initiates negotiations for a gradual demobilization. Fifty paramilitary groups have a presence in 28 of the country's 31 departments. The process concludes in February 2006. According to the government, 31,000 paramilitaries have consented to the deal and laid down their weapons over the previous three years.

In its 2009 annual report on the armed conflict, the New Rainbow Corporation (CNAI), an NGO supporting the modernization and democratization of Colombia through peace and social development—whose board of directors is comprised primarily of former guerrillas—argues that the mass demobilization "over which the government rejoices" has left paramilitary structures in place, and the number of weapons surrendered is far lower than the number of demo-bilized fighters; the report also highlights the emergence of a new generation of paramilitaries and the FARC's recovery from a string of resounding blows dealt by the army (CNAI, 2005, November 25; *Semana*, 2009, November 25).

In a February 2010 report, the Inter-Church Commission of Justice and Peace (CIJP), which is comprised of members of various Christian denominations, criticizes the Justice and Peace Law as a recipe for impunity. Of the 35,355 demobilized paramilitaries (according to government statistics), the report contends that only 698 are being criminally tried and thus far only one has been convicted (with the sentence later annulled by the Supreme Court). The CIJP report further calls attention to the paramilitary infiltration of every sphere of government. Most of the legislators under investigation are Uribe loyalists. The Commission also criticizes CON-VIVIR. On the subject of extrajudicial executions it notes that the 1,200 killings attributed the false-positive scheme demonstrates the systematic character of that practice among members of the armed services, who are motivated by the promise of reward payments for the killing of guerrilla soldiers (Comisión Intereclesial de Justicia y Paz, 2010, February 16).

In October 2002, "Operation Orión" becomes the first military campaign carried out under Uribe's new Democratic Security Policy. The operation's target is urban guerrilla groups affiliated with the FARC, ELN and EP in Medellín's Comuna 13. General Mario Montoya, Commander of the Colombian Army, and General Leonardo Gallego of the Metropolitan Police lead the operation, while coordinating with the AUC's Cacique Nutibara Bloc, commanded by Diego Fernando Murrillo (alias "Don Berna"), who is later extradited to the United States. From an American penitentiary, Don Berna confirms his cooperation with Generals Montoya and Gallego in the operation (*El Tiempo*, 2009, June 25), which succeeded in neutralizing the guerrilla forces. Paramilitaries take control of the community and paint messages on the walls that read: "Bloque Cacique Nutibara-Orión" (*BBC Mundo*, 2002, October 17). Ignoring the paramilitary involvement, local authorities hail the operation as a spectacular success, citing it as an example of citizen cooperation (Agencia de Prensa IPC, 2009, July 16). Relieved that the deadly clashes between the army and guerrilla forces have come to an end, the community supports the government's "peace" initiative as well.

Five years later, in April 2007, *The Los Angeles Times* publishes a declassified CIA document that also establishes the cooperation between General Mario Montoya and paramilitary commanders in Operation Orión (Evans, 2007, April 4). In response to those revelations, Democratic Senator Patrick Leahy calls for the suspension of 55 million dollars in assistance to Colombia; it is to be withheld until the government presents proof that measures are being taken to punish the guilty parties (Bronstein, 2007, May 3).

PARAPOLITICS BLOWS UP

In June 2005, Clara López Obregón, the auditor general, calls on the Supreme Court to investigate the "possible" paramilitary infiltration of Congress, setting off a political scandal that comes to be known as "parapolitics." The allegations stem from declarations made by the AUC commanders Carlos Castaño and Salvatore Mancuso, following Uribe's 2002 victory, that they had a hand not only in the president's election, but in dozens of congressional contests as well. The country braces itself for the results of the Supreme Court investigation: more than a hundred legislators from Uribe's majority are discovered to have paramilitary ties. Of those, 45 wind up in prison on conspiracy charges. To block convictions of these allies, Uribe wages a relentless, destructive campaign against the Supreme Court, leveling false accusations against

Ivan Velásquez, the judge presiding over the cases, attempting to derail his inquiries. To prevent the court from leading the investigation, as the law mandates, several legislators challenge its jurisdiction and get their cases handed over to the attorney general, Mario Iguarán, whom the administration has in its back pocket. The Supreme Court reclaims those cases in November 2009, on the grounds that the accused committed the alleged crimes in their capacity as legislators, not as private citizens.

The paramilitary demobilization concludes in February 2006. The AUC leadership as well as members of several other paramilitary organizations are sentenced to prison. As is mandated under the Law of Justice and Peace, they begin providing testimony regarding their illegal activity, disclosing names of politicians, industrialists, ranchers, senior government officials, police and military officers—active and retired—with whom they collaborated over the years. The degree to which paramilitaries managed to infiltrate the government and civil society is shocking, as is the abyss of corruption into which the country's elite have fallen. Mario Uribe, a former conservative senator from Antioquia—and favorite cousin of the president—is among the 80 politicians under investigation by the Supreme Court. The vast majority of those implicated are presidential allies.

THE TEMPERATURE RISES

Uribe's presidency warps Colombian society in an unprecedented, insidious way. The vast majority of the country rallies behind the government's flagship Democratic Security Policy, a low-intensity counterinsurgency strategy against the FARC whose lone objective is defeating the guerrilla army on the battlefield. Disillusioned with the peace process, the people grow thirsty for war; nor is the domestic media immune to the unanimity coalescing around the iron fist. Masterfully manipulated by the government, the majority of the country supports the president's agenda, falling in line with newspaper headlines and opinion columns parroting official positions. This perversely uncritical environment, nurtured by the president's McCarthyesque rhetoric, in which criticism and opposition are tantamount to subversion, breeds a dangerous climate of intolerance and polarization. Never before has there been "such a large divorce between the majority opinion reflected in polls and that of the majority of the columnists," notes María Elvira Samper upon receiving the Simón Bolívar Award, the country's highest honor in journalism (Samper, 2010, October 12). Broad majorities favor the president's hard-line stances, and are impressed by his ruthless determination, his vows to never rest until the guerrilla forces are vanquished and the country rid of drug-related violence. Uribe thumps his chest and his supporters are all too happy to measure his worth in guerrilla causalities and paramilitaries demobilized, which when all is said and done turns out to be something of a smoke screen. Operations "Phoenix" (to take out the FARC commander Raúl Reyes in Ecuador), "Jaque" (in which 15 hostages, including Ingrid Betancourt, a former presidential candidate, are freed without a shot being fired) and "Chameleon" (a 2010 rescue of senior military officers), are highpoints in the government's relentless campaign against the FARC.

Uribe has weakened the FARC and driven the guerrilla forces out of several regions, and the sheepish masses sing "Hosanna." Guarded by soldiers, principle highways are once again traversable: guerrilla road attacks (known as "the Miraculous Catch of Fish"), which frequently ended in abductions, appear to be a thing of the past. After so many decades of insecurity and violence most Colombians feel safer and accept without questioning, or tolerate without criticizing, the endless scandal engulfing the presidency. For reasons inexplicable, Uribe is rarely criticized and never held accountable for his administration's misdeeds. Under his successor, Juan Manuel Santos, the lids fly off several previously contained scandals, and figures close to the former president are brought to justice. When cornered by allegations of malfeasance, the president resorts to what journalists refer to as "rearview mirror" tactics: he revives juicy scandals of previous administrations, unleashes rash accusations against political opponents, attempts to discredit Supreme Court justices, accuses human rights activists of being terrorists, intimidates journalists critical of his government, and lashes out against international condemnation. These tactics for the most part succeed in distracting—and confusing—the general public.

In mid-2009, a wide-ranging scandal involving the Administrative Department of Security (DAS), Colombia's intelligence and security agency, a sort of secret police not unlike East Germany's infamous Stasi. *Semana* reveals the existence of an expansive, illegal espionage operation: the shadowing and intimidation of Supreme Court justices, political opponents, journalists, human rights activists and even administration officials (*Semana*, 2009, February 21). DAS has been illegally intercepting telephone calls, faxes and emails and shadowed—even abroad—its targets. These spying operations come to be known as "stings" (*"chuzadas"*). The DAS director—and former campaign manager for Uribe—Jorge Noguera invokes national security in defending the campaign, claiming the surveillance was necessary to identify subversive threats to the government—individuals and organizations that are later harassed and paralyzed by trumped-up legal charges based on fabricated evidence. Even former high-ranking officials of the agency characterize it as a Machiavellian scheme.

In 2005, a former DAS technology chief, Rafael García, is arrested on charges of collaborating with paramilitaries in an electoral fraud scheme in Magdalena and other Caribbean departments (where he helped secure 300,000 votes for Uribe), aiding the congressional campaigns of candidates with ties to the AUC's Northern Bloc, and deleting databases of drug-traffickers with pending extradition requests. He is held in La Picota prison in Bogotá. The following year, García turns on "the fan"—that is, starts to air what he knows about his agency's extralegal activity: he accuses the DAS director of corruption and maintaining broad ties with paramilitary leaders and drug capos, planting them within the agency and providing them with hit lists of labor leaders and academics. Bruised by the allegations, Noguera is forced to step down and, after the attorney general initiates an investigation into the allegations, Uribe appoints him consul general in Milan: the former DAS director knows too much.

García casts new light on the extent of the corruption pervading the country. He fingers legislators, mayors, governors and businessmen—almost all political allies of the president—with ties to paramilitary organizations. The attorney general corroborates his allegations and launches an investigation of more than a hundred legislators, 45 of whom eventually receive prison sentences. The *parapolítica* and *narcopolítica* scandals rage on. García sheds light on the unholy alliance between the political class, large landowners and ranchers, industrialists, military officers and the paramilitary commanders who carry out political and social cleansing, liquidating guerrillas, labor leaders, progressive opposition figures, and peasants whose land they covet. These peasants are tortured, massacred, and more than 4.7 million people have no choice but to flee the terror—an exodus of internally displaced victims of violence that ranks among the worst humanitarian crises in the world (Fazio, 2009, November 9).

García also exposes a conspiracy, in which he himself was involved, to assassinate Hugo Chávez and other members of the Venezuelan government. It was Noguera who devised the plot with assistance from the interior minister, Fernando

Londoño, a controversial right-wing figure under investigation for the fraudulent acquisition of millions of dollars worth shares of a company called Ecopetrol, whose dividends he should return. By mid-2010, the dividends have still not been returned, no punishment has been meted out, and the minister can still be found dispensing smug opinions in respectable media outlets. Noguera forms a special group to infiltrate Venezuela with assistance from AUC's Northern Bloc, commanded by "Jorge 40." In Caracas, the Colombians collaborate with the Democratic Venezuelan Bloc (Fazio, 2009, November 11), a right-wing organization whose goal is to fight the "Cubanization" of the country. Colombia has never previously engaged in this sort of cloak-and-dagger conspiracy, reminiscent of the Dominican dictator Generalísimo Leonidis Trujillo's plot to assassinate the Venezuelan President Rómulo Betancourt in the 1960's, which earned a condemnation from the OAS and continental repudiation.

More than a hundred legislators loyal to the government find themselves tied up in court cases over their paramilitary associations, a considerable setback to the president, who depends on his congressional majorities to rubberstamp whichever bills he introduces. The prospect of losing that majority explains the tenacity with which he maneuvers to block the Supreme Court investigations, not to mention his vicious attacks on Iván Velásquez—the judge heading the proceedings against his political allies—whom he goes to great lengths to smear. From his prison in the United States, Salvatore Mancuso intimates that many more names of implicated officials will come out once the commanders decide to speak (*Cambio*, 2009, May 27).

In May 2009, two years after the DAS scandal breaks, Uribe belatedly offers a 10,000-dollar reward for anyone who can provide information leading to the capture of material or intellectual authors of the persecution of judges, politicians and journalists. The president's press officer announces the reward on television while reiterating "the government's rejection and repudiation of the deeds committed by unscrupulous former employees" and acted with the "apparent aim of discrediting the government" (Guerra, 2009, May 13). This presidential excuse is typical: full responsibility lies with a few "unscrupulous" subordinates who are always "isolated." The government denounces and insults and brands them terrorists and friends of the FARC while Uribe plays the innocent victim. As always, all the wrongdoing has transpired behind his back.

More than forty DAS agents and four former directors are arrested and investigated. At their hearings, each and every one claims to "know nothing," not even that the acts committed were illegal. Meanwhile, critical questions remain unanswered: Who ordered the operations? Who authorized the millions to fund them? And who benefited from the intelligence collected? This much is certain: the DAS serves at the pleasure of the president. The candidates vying to succeed Uribe offer their opinions. Rafael Pardo, of the Liberal Party, points out that the operation in question could not have been carried out by mid-level agents on their own, and it is yet to be determined who the real mastermind was; Marta Lucía Ramírez, Uribe's former defense minister, suggests that an investigation should be launched to find out who gave the orders from "up above"; Gustavo Petro, from the opposition Democratic Pole, accuses Uribe of giving the orders himself. Cecilia López Montaño, of the Liberal Party, is certain that the orders came from the presidential palace, given that the DAS is subordinate to the executive (*El Espectador,* 2009, August 1).

An appeal to the Inter-American Commission on Human Rights (IACHR) by the José Alvear Restrepo Lawyers' Collective, a respected human rights NGO that was targeted by the DAS, details the breadth of that agency's illegal surveillance. The Collective's president, Reinaldo Villalba, reveals that not only DAS employees took part in the operation against his organization, but also military and intelligence agents, the Directorate of Criminal Investigation (DIJN) and other state intelligence and security agencies; they intercepted phone calls, faxes and electronic communication and performed physical surveillance on targets not only within the country, but also on trips abroad; they gathered personal and professional information on the organization's members, photographed them, conducted psychological evaluations, documented their predilections and weaknesses, and dug into their personal finances. Paulo Sergio Pinheiro, a Brazilian IACHR representative, declares such practices to be unacceptable in a supposed democracy (*Semana,* 2009, November

5). The behavior of Uribe's ambassador to the OAS, Luis Alfonso Hoyos, in response to the allegations is an embarrassment: alleging procedural irregularities, he withdraws from the hearing. The IACHR representative denies any failures to follow protocol (*Agencia EFE*, 2009, November 5). Hoyos departs without offering any response to the accusations or a single argument in defense of the government he was appointed to represent.

On April 18, 2007, *The Washington Post* reports a recent denunciation made in the Colombian Senate regarding a gathering of paramilitaries, in which assassinations were allegedly plotted, at the Uribe family estate in Antioquia (Forero, 2007, April 18). To signal his disapproval, former Vice President Al Gore withdraws from an environmental conference, to be held in Miami, where Uribe will be present. Few in Washington, however, are willing to add their voices to the former vice president's rebuke; the Republicans who control Congress consider the Colombian president to be a strong leader and loyal ally. Gore's snub both humiliates and irritates Uribe, whose repeated phone calls to the former vice president go unanswered. Uribe feels the need to publicly deny the accusation so he can have, as he is accustomed, the last word. He calls two press conferences in Miami and Bogotá to tout his government's achievements, and assure that the demobilization process has resulted in sixty paramilitary leaders behind bars. Marcela Sánchez, a *Washington Post* columnist, writes that the dustup with Gore has brought attention to Uribe's dark side, of which little is known in

Washington. She describes the Colombian president as "a petty, defensive control freak," and characterizes his denunciations of Colombians that raise concerns in Washington about developments back home—critics whom Uribe accuses of "discrediting" the country—as "chilling." The president claims to be paying close attention to military intelligence on these individuals (Sánchez, 2007, May 4).

In the early morning of May 13, 2008, sixteen AUC leaders—including Salvatore Mancuso, Rodrigo Tovar Pupo (alias "Jorge 40"), commander of the Northern Bloc, and Diego Murillo (alias "Don Berna") of the Cacique Nutibara Bloc—are extradited to the United States. Accused of drug trafficking, the prisoners are transported in secret. The public is kept in the dark until these warlords, responsible for some of the most horrific massacres in the country's history, are in DEA custody on U.S. soil. The only problem is the extraditions are illegal: the commanders should have been tried in Colombia, for crimes against humanity, and forced to make reparations to their victims. But yet again, the majority of Colombians remain silent. Legal commentators criticize the extradition for preventing the paramilitaries from providing additional disclosures, under the Justice and Peace Law, in "free version" hearings. Some accuse Uribe of attempting to silence the commanders, who in Colombian custody had begun to finger his political allies with ties to their organizations. Clearly, there is a potential major scandal leading right to the doorstep of the presidency. Despite this brazen abuse of power, and constitutional violation, the majority of Colombians swallow the revelations in silence.

In the domestic media there is considerable speculation surrounding the president's motives for shipping the AUC commanders out of the country: could it be to demonstrate to Washington that he is no "friend" of the paramilitaries and does not fear them, as one columnist suggests? Bruce Bagley, a University of Miami professor who specializes in U.S.-Latin American relations, describes the move as "astonishing," and suggests it could be an attempt to prove to U.S. Congress that "the rumors of his ties to the paramilitaries are false" (Romero, 2008, May 14). No other Colombian president has ever matched the current officeholder's eagerness to extradite his own citizens to the United States. In seven years Uribe has extradited 900 alleged drug traffickers; 180 are sent north in 2008 alone, including two FARC guerrillas labeled "narco-terrorists."

At a peace conference held on April 21, 2009 at Casa de las Américas in Madrid, the renowned Spanish judge Baltasar Garzón adds his voice to those opposing the paramilitary extraditions. Uribe, he argues, is disregarding the norms of international justice with respect to crimes against humanity. "This has caused things to stall," he adds, "and left the Justice and Peace Law on hold, which should be contributing data, documents and new angles to clarify events." Eduardo Pizarro, director of Colombia's National Committee of Reparation and Reconciliation (CNRR), and Frank Pearl, the

High Commissioner for Peace—both presidential appointees—are present at the conference and defend the paramilitary extraditions, dismissing the notion that the decision will have an effect on the Justice and Peace Law. On the contrary, it will reinforce the law, Pizarro asserts (*Agencia EFE*, 2009, April 20).

From a Washington penitentiary, Mancuso declares that "by sending us to the United States, [the Colombian government] has extradited the truth." He confirms that his organization supported Uribe's presidential campaign, and recounts conversations with Juan Manuel Santos during the 1990's in which the future defense minister (who at the time held no government office) sought his support for a coup against President Ernesto Samper (*Cambio*, 2009, May 27). In a November 2008 interview with *Semana*, Mancuso's attorney, Joaquín Pérez, remarks that "there is still a lot of truth to come out," and that his client is willing to reveal what he knows. "A large segment of society is either greased by, or under the influence of, the AUC," the attorney claims (*Semana*, 2008, November 15).

In April 2008, it emerges that Uribe's 2006 reelection hinged on buying the votes of two legislators—Yidis Medina and Teodolindo Avendaño—for lifting the constitutional prohibition on a second presidential term. Uribe's supporters, who comprise a majority in both congressional chambers, approve changing that "little article," thereby paving the way for his reelection. The scandal comes to light when Yidis accuses the government of failing to deliver what it promised in exchange for her vote; the congresswoman implicates several high-ranking administration officials, including the interior minister, Sabas Pretelt, minister of social protection, Diego Palacio, former general secretary of the presidency, Alberto Velásquez, and his successor, Bernardo Moreno, whom she alleges led the negotiations. The Supreme Court confirms that Medina and Avendaño did in fact sell their votes and both are convicted (*Semana*, 2009, July 15). While the two legislators languish behind bars, however, the ministers and senior administration officials implicated in the scandal continue in their same positions. In June 2008, Uribe appoints Sabas Pretelt ambassador to Italy. Pretelt later returns to Colombia to testify before the attorney general, but back in Rome declares that he has proven his innocence and is unconcerned by the allegations against him. The investigation drags on for two years, one of those locked in Attorney General Mario Iguarán's drawer. In December 2008, Alejandro Ordóñez, the new attorney general, and an Opus Dei devotee, whose nomination is met with strong resistance, absolves Pretelt; in September 2010, however, the same office reverses course, finding him guilty of bribery and the former minister now faces potential prison time.

Though the Yidis scandal exposes the fraud behind Uribe's reelection, the revelations do not result in street protests like those in Iran. One analyst contrasts Colombia's silence with the heated demonstrations against President Ahmadinejad's 2009 reelection, which the opposition claimed was ridden with fraud. The Iranian street protests reverberate throughout the West, and in the Colombian media, which in turn barely takes note of the fraud being perpetrated in its own country. The president's congressional majorities will block any measure against him.

Three years later, the former superintendent of the Notary and Registry, Manuel Guillermo Cuello Baute, revives the reelection scandal when he testifies to the Supreme Court that, in 2007, 74 notary offices were doled out as patronage related to the president's reelection. The beneficiaries were legislators and private backers. Cuello recalls a meeting (of which he claims Uribe was aware) in the presidential palace with the secretary general of the presidency, Bernardo Moreno, and vice interior minister, Hernando Angarita to advance the president's reelection bid, in which he claims to have been pressured to turn over the notary offices they had promised to the president's supporters; Cuello also alleges the president's sons were involved in some of these transactions (*El Espectador*, 2009, July 8). Legal experts warn that Uribe has committed bribery, as the decrees granting notary offices originated in the presidential palace. The Court corroborates these allegations and orders raids on the residences of the president's supporters who were awarded notary offices. Cuello later repeats his allegations to the attorney general that Bernardo Moreno, Sabas Pretelt, and a congressman, Hernando Henríquez, forced him to assign notary offices to their political backers. Cuello recalls a "visibly shaken" Moreno accusing him of standing in the way of "fulfilling promises" that enabled the president to be reelected (Castro, 2009, June 27).

Uribe's insolence reaches new heights. In August 2008, reports come out in the national media of a rendezvous that took place the previous April between paramilitary mafiosos and drug lords and senior government officials inside the presidential palace. The paramilitary-drug gang enters the palace through a backdoor for an appointment—their third—with the legal secretary of the presidency, Edmundo de Castillo, and press secretary, César Mauricio Velásquez. The purpose of the palace visit is to supply "evidence of witness tampering" by Judge Ivan Velásquez, which supposedly occurred during his quest to inflict political damage on the president. Uribe has been trying to take down the judge and halt his investigations into paramilitary influence in government. The allegations against the judge prove to be false. Many of those present at this secret meeting have, or soon will have, a criminal record. Diego Álvarez is Don Berna's attorney; a former paramilitary commander known as "Job" represents Office of Envigado, an insidious criminal network founded by Pablo Escobar and currently controlled by Don Berna (Duzán, 2008, August 30). Job is assassinated, three months later, in Medellín. Rodrigo Zapata Sierra (alias "Ricardo") a demobilized AUC commander is captured in March 2009 in a Bogotá shopping center, and convicted of aggravated homicide and criminal conspiracy; Gustavo Tapias Ospina is later extradited to the United States and sentenced to eleven years in prison for drug trafficking. Finally,

Juan José Chaux Mosquera, an oligarch and former governor of Cauca (now serving as ambassador to the Dominican Republic) is another attendee at this highly irregular meeting at the Nariño Palace—or the "Palacio de Nari," as the mafia refers to the presidential palace (Quevedo, 2009, April 4). After the scandal blows up, Chaux resigns from the embassy and, in May of the following year, is arrested in Bogotá's El Dorado airport and convicted of participating in a criminal conspiracy. His relations with the AUC hierarchy run very deep (*Semana* 2009, May 18).

In October 2008, the massacre of 19 young men from Soacha, a working-class suburb of Bogotá, comes to light. Though the army initially presents these men, who were discovered in a common grave 500 miles north, as guerrillas killed in combat, it's later discovered that they were lured out of Soacha with promises of work, and transported to a combat zone where after being slain their corpses were outfitted as guerrillas. The assassins were motivated by the monetary reward offered by the government for the killing of enemy combatants. The scandal sheds new light on the deadly alliance between the army and the paramilitaries hired to murder innocent civilians. As an added bonus, the government can cite "guerrilla" fatalities as evidence of the efficacy of the president's signature policy. This urgency to validate Democratic Security puts even greater pressure on the army rank and file, with ghastly results. The reward system for "enemy" killings did not originate in Colombia. It can be found in the Pentagon's counterinsurgency training manuals, the same texts taught at the School of the Americas. Uribe and his defense minister, Juan Manuel Santos, apparently find the method to be very effective.

Shortly after the Soacha scandal breaks, Uribe goes on national television, surrounded by several ministers, and reads a statement announcing the purge of 28 army officers and their subordinates, including three generals. The "purge" is reported as the most extensive in years, a televised spectacle less for domestic consumption than to demonstrate to Washington the government's willingness to "punish the guilty"—never mind the improbability that the "exhaustive" investigation the president claims to have carried out could have concluded so rapidly. The sacked generals protest that the punishment was "unjust" and defend their service records and oversight of soldiers under their command. Ivan Cepeda, president of the National Movement of Victims of State Crime (MOVICE), argues that the buck should not stop with the generals, and calls for Defense Minister Santos's resignation. In December, the press reports that 3,500 servicemen are under investigation for alleged executions outside the theater of combat (*Cambio*, 2008, December 22). Never once does Uribe assume any personal responsibility for the massacre.

The U.S. Congress calls on the Colombian government to investigate the massacre and bring the responsible parties to justice. It suspends military aid, which exceeds 500-million dollars annually, until it has seen an adequate response. A year later, the wait continues.

Colombian presidents are known to sustain periodic blows to their image resulting from scandals that involve members of their inner circles, referred to locally as the "executive's children." The controversy usually involves business dealings, some less legal than others, lacking transparency and invariably yielding lucrative returns to the president's close friends and relatives, but at a political cost. When a scandal erupts, in April 2009, involving Uribe's sons, Jerónimo and Tomás, the president plays dumb, declining to comment other than: "Ask the boys [about it]." The boys, as luck would have it, have become multimillionaires in the blink of an eye after purchasing large tracts of land in the municipality of Mosquera which, by the most remarkable of coincidences, is suddenly declared exempt from taxes by José Álvaro Rozo Castellanos, the mayor of that settlement in the Bogotá savannah. The finance and commerce ministers and director of the Tax and Customs Administration (DIAN), among other high-ranking government officials, sign off on the re-designation of the land. For Uribe's sons, the return on their investment is calculated to be in the range of one thousand percent. The matter ends up before Congress, where the ministers claim to have been unaware of the relation between the proprietors of the land and the president (Cardona, 2009, April 20). Jorge Enrique Robledo, a senator from the opposition Democratic Pole, describes the deal as "thorny," and questions the judgment of the ministers for not recusing themselves from a business deal involving their boss's sons. "They cannot claim to have been unaware," he argues, "considering that before declaring the land tax exempt they had the obligation to investigate." Robledo presents detailed findings on these and several other large land acquisitions made by the president's sons (*Cambio*, 2009, May 14; Robledo, 2009, May 12).

Ethics, morality and decency are, for the most part, alien concepts to the Uribe administration. Scandal after scandal—including some yet to be sorted out—have marred Uribe's tenure in office, despite his uncanny ability to shirk any and all responsibility for them and emerge unscathed time after time. Before even completing his second term, the president has nearly secured a referendum that could allow him to seek another reelection and, despite a growing list of administration scandals, he still boasts approval ratings higher than 80%, and his loyalists continue to control the legislature.

Despite being a man of principles, who leads his life according to a firm set of values (in his best-seller *The Audacity of Hope*, the future president dedicates an entire chapter to their importance), Obama has no choice but to accept Uribe and all his baggage and unsavory associations and ignore the mounting political scandals. Bush, who himself ran a corrupt administration, had no problem looking the other way. The ever loyal and sycophantic Uribe, after all, was his only ally on the continent. Uribe's public—and perhaps private—life is documented in reports out of the U.S. embassy in Colombia, and from the CIA, DEA and military intelligence services. On occasion compromising leaked or declassified documents, prepared by senior U.S. officials, come to light. His guaranteed access to seven Colombian bases is Obama's trump card:

Uribe is a subservient toad, propped up by his country's right wing.

SECURITY TURNS TO WATER

Democratic Security is a counterinsurgency strategy focused on the military defeat of the FARC—an organization financed in large part through the illegal trafficking of narcotics—and the reassertion of state control over guerrilla-held territory. These goals, articulated during Uribe's campaign, become the focus of his presidency. His government's security achievements garner praise both at home and abroad. The aggressive campaign against the FARC succeeds in reducing violence around the country, including kidnappings and guerrilla attacks on highways (which usually end in kidnappings); no such attacks have occurred since 2008. In 2009, a State Department analysis describes this progress as "noteworthy." Between 2002 and 2005 attacks by illegal armed groups on rural populations drop 91%; from 2002 to 2007 homicides decrease 44% and, during that same period, the number of kidnappings falls 85% (U.S. State Department, May 2009).

Of all the blows dealt to the FARC during Uribe's presidency, perhaps none stings worse than "Operation Jaque," a spectacular ploy that results in the rescue of fifteen hostages without a single shot being fired. Among those freed is former presidential candidate Ingrid Betancourt, whose detainment had become an international cause célèbre with French President Nicolas Sarkozy directly involved in the negotiations for her release (Betancourt holds duel French citizenship). Also rescued are three American mercenaries, captured after their Cessna crashed in the jungle, along with eleven Colombian soldiers. The hostages were held between five and eleven years. The audacity and brilliant execution of the operation—worthy of a Hollywood film—garners worldwide attention. Only later do cables released by WikiLeaks reveal the role of César, the guerrilla-jailer, who aided the mission in exchange for money and other concessions. In 2009, he is extradited to the United States and sentenced to twenty years in prison (*El Espectador*, 2011, February 20).

In mid-2009, CODHES and other human right organizations monitoring Democratic Security report that the policy is showing signs of breaking down. In September, *El Tiempo* reports that its gains are on the verge of collapse; the official figures supporting the program's success have been inflated. "If Uribe contends that he is winning the war on crime and his Democratic Security Policy is so successful, then why are so many terrorized people fleeing the countryside?" the newspaper asks. According to the article, the year 2008 registered 380,000 new displacements as a result of paramilitary violence; peasants are driven from their land, which is then occupied by drug-traffickers and newly formed paramilitary groups—in cahoots with local businessmen and landowners—who subsequently plant oil palms and exploit the land's mineral and petroleum resources (Gómez Maseri, 2009, September 1).

A report published by the Ministry of Defense touting Democratic Security's accomplishments cites a total of 114,259 guerrillas captured, killed, or demobilized as a result of that policy—figures that CODHES contests. "If [they] are accurate, illegal armed groups are or have been far more numerous than what has been generally believed, and if indeed [the figures] are exaggerated that raises doubts as to the Ministry of Defense's effectiveness and the results of this policy." CODHES highlights the increase in violence, including 380,000 newly displaced people, and 21 labor leaders assassinated in 2009; according to the organization, impunity remains at 95% and only 16 soldiers accused of extrajudicial executions (false-positives) have been convicted (Romero, 2007, December). According to the Attorney General's Office, over the last two decades paramilitaries and guerrillas are responsible for 155,000 deaths, calculations derived from the "free version" hearingsof demobilized paramilitaries under the Justice and Peace Law.

In its November 25, 2009 annual report on the armed conflict, CNAI's critical assessment of Democratic Security unsettles the government. According to the report, the number of military operations has reached an all-time high and only two options remain: deepen the war or negotiate. The FARC has regained territory and the ELN reinvented itself in an alliance with drug traffickers. And although the government has tried to pass off its demobilization program as the definitive end of Colombian paramilitarism, and the weakening of guerrilla forces as "crushing" blows dealt by the army—achievements that have gained widespread currency in the public opinion—the report concludes that this official version does not conform to reality. CNAI reports there has been a paramilitary resurgence, with armed groups rapidly proliferating throughout the country, exercising control over 293 municipalities. The government, according to the report, does not want to acknowledge this new generation of para-militaries, referred to as "criminal bands" ("BACRIM"). As these violent organizations lay down roots in Bogotá and Medellín the homicide rates in both cities shoot up (Valencia 2009, November 26). Moreover, of 40 AUC commanders, only 19 are currently incarcerated, the report claims (Valen-cia, 2009, November 26). This critical evaluation of Demo-cratic Security infuriates the government and its supporters, who reject the findings. The data CNAI presents is favorable to the guerrillas, and therefore can be exploited by the oppo-sition in its attacks against the government. The new defense minister, Gabriel Silva, defends the president's flagship policy as the boldest and most successful ever against the FARC, and dismisses as a "fairy tale" the uptick in paramilitary violence alleged in the report. "The Justice and Peace Law, combined with the use of state force, ended that phenomenon," Silva claims (El Tiempo, 2009, November 29). The former defense minister, Juan Manuel Santos, remarks that the report's "crit-icism of the current state of government policy against sub-version leads to many voices becoming confused, which ends up strengthening the guerrillas' hand." It allows them to get a "breather," he adds (El Tiempo, 2009, November 30).

THE STORY CONTINUES

Obama relies on a small group of right-wing governments throughout the region: Felipe Calderón of the PAN in Mexico, whose six-year term ends in 2012; Alan García in Peru, who tacks to the right despite belonging to the APRA (the largest leftist party in the country) and having previously fought on the side of progressive movements; when his five-year term comes to an end in 2011 he will seek reelection; after eight turbulent years in office, Álvaro Uribe's aspirations for a third term are thwarted and he is succeeded in August 2010 by his former defense minister, Juan Manuel Santos, also a loyal friend to Washington. Santos is elected with the most votes in the history of the country. People are convinced the he will be Uribe III.

Ten days after Uribe leaves office the Constitutional Court renders his 2009 military accord with the United States void, ruling that it goes well beyond preexisting commitments. On the contrary, Colombia has acquired "new obligations" that require congressional approval (RCN-Radio, 2010, August 18).

In November 2010, at a regional forum for defense ministers—with U.S. Defense Secretary Robert Gates in attendance—Evo Morales sounds off on the recent coups in Latin America: Venezuela in 2002, Haiti in 2004, Honduras in 2009, and a coup-like police uprising that attempts to depose Rafael Correa in 2010. The White House has either engineered or supported each of those coups. According to Morales, "the people triumphed in Venezuela, Bolivia and Ecuador; only in Honduras and Haiti did the United States win." State Department cables released by WikiLeaks in September 2011 corroborate these denunciations. The same old practices continue.

8

Obama in Latin America: More of the Same?

ELECTORAL TSUNAMI

On November 2, 2010, Democrats face the dreaded midterm elections, which so often result in losses for the party holding the White House. Presidents Carter, Reagan, Clinton and Bush all fell victim to the phenomenon.

What's more, the political climate is an adverse one. Republicans blame the president for the slow economic recovery and high unemployment (both inherited problems). The Hispanic community, meanwhile, is frustrated by Obama's failure to deliver immigration reform. Still, many analysts believe that no other Democratic president, midway through his first term in office, can boast of so many achievements, some "historic" in scale.

Prominent voices criticize the White House's failure—and that of the party as a whole—to defend the administration's achievements. In a *Time* column, Joe Klein describes the White House's inability to effectively explain to the public important policy decisions—such as tax cuts for the most vulnerable segments of society, increased financial regulation and historic healthcare reform—as poor politics of the highest order. Klein goes on to criticize the president's silence regarding an important reform introduced by Democratic Representative Kathy Dahlkemper, which would allow kids under the age of 26 to be covered by their parent's healthcare plans, as well as his decision to remain on the sidelines of a reelection battle the congresswoman ultimately lost (Klein, 2010, November 4).

Obama's restraint in the face of Republican lies, taunts and personal attacks many interpret as a sign of weakness. The president rarely responds to the insults or punches back. Others, however, see in his temperance admirable qualities such as a modesty, integrity, fortitude—and faith in a higher purpose.

The president's agenda prioritizes the vulnerable majority, the middle and lower classes. His policies have improved their living conditions, surpassing in scope programs implemented by many of his predecessors.

Two months before the elections, Obama finally launches his counterattack. The president rails against the excesses of the Bush years, the misguided policies that led the country to the brink of catastrophe, and underscores the differences between the Democratic and Republican parties in defending the interests of middle- and working-class families. He also calls out the GOP for its opposition to immigration reform, through which he hopes to "bring millions of undocumented residents out of the shadows." His supporters hope that shining light on the severity of the Republican agenda will work against them in the elections.

These midterm elections are neither a referendum on the performance of the nation's first black president nor the typical partisan jousting for congressional majorities. Republicans hope to politically maim Obama and eviscerate any chance of his reelection. Noam Chomsky writes that the country has never before seen this level of discord, fear and disillusion. Moreover, he is alarmed by the country's rightward swing, with large segments of Republicans supporting the Tea Party, and dismayed that people turn to a movement of rabid extremists rather than engaging in constructive activism akin to that which emerged during the Great Depression. Chomsky goes so far as to cite the renowned German-American historian, Fitz Stern, who studies the process of resentment versus secular disenchantment, and projects an American future bearing similarities to the Third Reich (Chomsky, 2010, November 4). These Republican and Tea Party attacks reflect a racism that persists in many "shameful" forms, according to *The New York Times*. Paul Krugman cites the "ire that the presence of Obama has awoken since the day he took office" as evidence of the racism underlying Republican attacks (Krugman, 2010, September 19).

On November 2, millions of disillusioned voters—and Obama haters—from every corner of the country punish the president in the ballot box; the electoral bloodbath, which many saw coming, represents the largest shift in congressional seats of the past seven decades. Republicans gain 60 seats in the House, seizing a sizable majority (239 to 189) while in the Senate they claim six additional seats, though Democrats hold on to a slender 51-46 majority. Republicans moreover win 29 governorships (versus 18 claimed by Democrats) and register substantial gains in state legislatures (*The Washington Times,* 2010, November 3). The Tea Party manages to elect 32% of its candidates.

A humbled Obama takes responsibility for the defeat, which he himself describes as a "shellacking." The national media reports of gloom and uncertainty pervading the Democratic camp, in contrast to a Republican triumphalism and thirst for political retribution. Most commentators, however, allow for the possibility of redemption. Why couldn't the president bounce back from this resounding defeat like Bill Clinton did in 1996, two years after losing both the House and Senate? Obama's approval ratings remain higher than those of both Clinton and Reagan at the same juncture in their first terms, despite the most severe socioeconomic crisis confronting an American president since FDR.

Some commentators predict that a Republican-controlled

House could prove disastrous for Latin America. The new chairwoman of the House Foreign Relations Committee, for instance, is Representative Ileana Ros-Lehtinen, a fervent anti-Castro Cuban-American and GOP hawk; staunch supporter of the Honduran coup, regime change in Cuba, and critic of Latin America's leftist governments.

Despite his landslide defeat, Obama presses on. A few months later, in his second State of the Union, the president presents a revised agenda, one more closely aligned with middle- and working-class interests, and calls on bipartisan cooperation despite an emboldened GOP determined to thwart his policy objectives. The Republican opposition remains bent on repealing the Affordable Care Act, despite the fact that millions of Americans will receive coverage for the first time, an unprecedented achievement.

AND LATIN AMERICA?

Obama's Latin American policy leaves much to be desired. In a January 2011 press conference, held just prior to leaving office, Lula da Silva laments that Obama has done "nothing" for Latin America. He barely knows the region, which no longer behaves like the subservient, self-defeating vassal of decades past. The majority of its governments are leftist; critics of the neoliberal model, many sever ties with the World Bank and IMF. Mexico and Ecuador withdraw from the TIAR, another of Washington's mechanisms for regional control. The integration movement marches forward.

The decline of American hegemony in its traditional sphere of influence is the focus of an article titled "Nobody's Backyard" published in *The Economist* on the bicentennial of Latin American independence (*The Economist*, 2010, September 9). The OAS, dominated by Washington since its inception in 1947, has also been pushed to the margins by new regional organizations, such as UNASUR and the Council for South American Defense. Obama surprises some by declaring his intention to listen and exchange ideas, but not give orders to the region. He is aware of the shifting landscape.

Latin America's self-assurance continues to grow. It is the first region to emerge from the 2008 global recession, boasting an average annual growth rate of 5.5%. Several countries broaden economic and political relations with other continents; they deepen ties with China, Russia, India and the Middle East, upending the U.S. from their markets. Emerging economic powers such as Brazil and Mexico are invited to participate in high-profile economic summits alongside the great powers. And several Latin American governments cultivate relations with Iranian President Mahmud Ahmadinejad in direct defiance of U.S. policy.

The political clout of Hispanics in the United States has also increased. Their votes proved decisive in both of Obama's national campaigns, demonstrating they are capable of tipping the electoral balance one way or the other. Frustration with the president's inability to make real progress on immigration reform, however, may work against him in the 2014 mid-term elections.

Latin America's leftward drift continues. In 2010, Uruguay elects a former Tupamaro guerrilla, José Mujica. The following year, Dilma Rousseff, Lula's handpicked successor, is voted into office while the Chávez camp triumphs once again in Venezuela's congressional elections; both countries wield considerable influence in the region, and thus are of special interest to Washington. In 2011, Argentina reelects Cristina Kirchner by an overwhelming margin, and in Peru Ollanta Humala, who is on record as a critic of the neoliberal model, triumphs over the incumbent Alan García. Despite having raised the possibility of modifying his country's free trade agreement with the United States, Humala, distances himself from his combative friend, Hugo Chávez, likening his foreign policy to that of Lula da Silva, who tended to adopt measured stances in order to avoid friction with Washington.

The June 2012 impeachment of Fernando Lugo, Paraguay's democratically elected president of the leftist Guasú Front (FG) is an example of a new method of regime change: the institutional coup. Parliament votes to remove him from office in an astonishingly hasty proceeding in violation of constitutional law. Vice President Federico Franco takes office and in presidential elections the following April Horacio Cartes, of the far-right Colorado Party, triumphs.

Though a conservative, Chilean President Sebastian Piñera is respectful of the continental amity prevailing during his time in office. A constructive member of UNASUR, he governs, for the most part, as a moderate, and the Chilean economy flourishes; his approval ratings fluctuate in accordance with his handling of student and indigenous protests, and the rescue of trapped miners. Piñera is succeeded in office by the woman he replaced, Michelle Bachelet. Her opponent in the 2013 presidential election was also a woman, Evelyn Matthey. Bachelet describes their respective visions as vastly diverging.

Obama's lack of attention to Latin America gives rise not only to frustration and disillusion, but also alarm. Despite his promises of change, Cuba continues to be the target of an economic embargo and myriad other aggressions. His misguided validation of the Honduran coup leaves the door open for the unconstitutional removal of democratic leaders down the road. And militarism makes a dangerous advance with the controversial agreement Colombia signs with Washington, granting American forces access to seven key military bases and airports, a stinging setback for regional integration. A year later, the Pentagon pushes through a military agreement with Brazil, the first such bilateral pact since President Carter cut off military cooperation with the Brazilian dictatorship three decades earlier. The politics of change promised by Obama have not come to bear in his own backyard.

THE WIKILEAKS SCANDAL

In September 2010 *The New York Times*, *The Guardian* and

Der Spiegel publish bombshell reports exposing secrets of U.S. foreign policy taken from classified government documents. The documents were obtained by WikiLeaks, an organization founded by the Australian Julian Assange, which has amassed some 250,000 government documents, a large portion of which were leaked by Bradley Manning, a 22-year-old army intelligence analyst who is subsequently charged with twenty criminal counts, including violation of the Espionage Act. Manning is arrested, subjected to nine months of solitary confinement and eventually sentenced, in 2013, to 35 years in prison. Having had its clothing ripped off, the Empire sets its sights on Assange who, in June 2012, seeks asylum in the Ecuadorian Embassy in London, where he remains to this day.

Among the trove of leaked documents is the military agreement with Brazil, revealing Washington's goal of undermining continental unity and weakening or toppling leftist governments. Also leaked are classified memoranda from Secretary of States Condoleezza Rice and Hillary Clinton instructing diplomats posted abroad to carry out acts of espionage ("Democracy Now," 2010, November 26). Clearly, Washington continues to meddle in the affairs of other nations, albeit in a less overt manner. Bolivia and Venezuela expel diplomatic officers, USAID and CIA agents for attempting to destabilize their governments.

THE SECOND TERM

On November 6, 2012, Obama and Joe Biden are reelected with strong Hispanic support. They win a solid majority of delegates in the Electoral College (312 to 226), and 51% of the popular vote (though 10 million fewer votes than in 2008). The question of Latin American policy, however, is all but absent from the campaign. Obama doesn't bring it up, and his opponent, Mitt Romney, only mentions that the country is missing out on economic opportunities in the region.

To mark his second term in office, David Remnick, editor of the *New Yorker*, pens an in-depth profile of President Obama and his administration, which he describes as one of the most ambitious and "liberal since the nineteen sixties." He hails the passage of the Affordable Care Act as a "major advance in the history of social justice" and "the most ambitious social legislation since the Great Society half a century ago" (David Remnick, *New Yorker*, 2014, January 24). Nevertheless, Hispanics are frustrated that the president has not moved on immigration reform, despite citing it as a priority on multiple occasions.

For Obama, the political climate should, in theory, be more favorable than four years earlier. The economy is recovering, having jobs for 44 consecutive months, and Wall Street firms are reporting record profits; the country has reduced carbon emissions and shown progress in developing clean-energy alternatives (*The New Yorker*, "Going the Distance," 2014,

January 24). The national mood improves even further with the news Americans have been waiting a decade for: Osama Bin Laden is dead. Obama announces the lightning strike in Pakistan, where the 9-11 mastermind had been hiding out, on May 1, 2011. The president's approval rating breaks 60%.

Owing to implacable Republican opposition, however, Obama has been unable to pass wholesale immigration reform, gun control (despite public outcry following the 2012 massacre of 20 children and 6 adults in Newton, Connecticut), and reduce the budget deficit.

2013: THE LONGEST YEAR

The year 2013 is, by most measures, the most difficult of Obama's presidency. His most serious challenge stems from former NSA-employee Edward Snowden's revelations regarding Washington's domestic and overseas spying operations, which bring on scandal at home, embarrassment abroad, and strain relations with European allies and Latin American governments, including Brazil, Ecuador, Colombia, Mexico, Panama, Peru and Uruguay. Harsh rebuke comes from all corners, including heads of state, most notably Angela Merkel and Dilma Rousseff. Telecommunications networks in their countries, including their personal mobile phones, were compromised. Unusually harsh in tone, Merkel emphasizes the loss of trust arising from spying between allies; Rousseff decries the espionage as "lack of respect for Brazilian sovereignty and a grave crime against civil and human rights," and demands explanations (*El Espectador*, 2013, September 6). Though Obama promises answers, Rousseff cancels her much-anticipated state visit to Washington.

Accused of espionage and theft of government property, Snowden is forced to seek asylum or face the possibility of life imprisonment or capital punishment. He requests asylum in 15 countries, but receives no response. Russia and China, however, deny Washington's extradition requests. Snowden travels from Hong Kong to Moscow's international airport. After remaining more than a month in its transit section, Putin grants the former spy temporary asylum on the condition that he tone down his denunciations of the U.S. government. Venezuela, Nicaragua and Bolivia each offer asylum, and Snowden requests it from Ecuador as well. To preemptively neutralize pressure from Washington, Correa unilaterally and irrevocably renounces preferential tariffs from the United States. In February 2014, he signs a decree withdrawing Ecuador from TIAR, a security treaty dominated by the United States. Mexico did the same in 2002.

Obama wants to put Snowden on trial in the U.S. and warns countries against offering him asylum. Suspecting that Evo Morales might be transporting Snowden aboard his presidential jet, Washington convinces Portugal, Spain, France and Italy to bar the the plane from landing or even accessing their airspace on its return from an energy conference in Moscow—a clear violation of diplomatic immunity laws. In

Vienna, where Morales eventually lands, the plane is detained for 13 hours while the Spanish ambassador attempts to persuade the Bolivian president to consent to a search of his plane. Morales refuses.

Latin America regards the incident as just the latest in a long line of imperial transgressions. Cristina Kirchner describes it as "a vestige of the colonialism we thought had been overcome." Regional leaders view the episode as blatant violation international law, no less one that endangered a head of state. UNASUR, CELAC, Mercosur, ALBA, the Non-Aligned Movement all express solidarity with Morales. A unanimous OAS resolution, also supportive of Morales, demands apologies from the four European nations (but not the United States). "More than one hundred UN member nations collectively denounce the incident, bolstering Bolivia's complaint to the UN High Commissioner for Human Rights" (*The NACLA Report on the Americas*, July 12, 2013).

This same year, Congressional Republicans, for partisan reasons, shut down the government for 15 days, halting payments of domestic obligations—including the salaries of 800,000 government employees—and disrupting service at train stations, ports, and airports; several sectors of the economy are impacted, and the federal government's obligations to the rest of the world are put in jeopardy.

Obama's most noteworthy and far-reaching accomplishments, however, transpire in the diplomatic arena: the agreement reached with the Syrian government to surrender its chemical weapon arsenal and the initiation of negotiations with Iran concerning its controversial nuclear program. For once, the United States and other permanent members of the UN Security Council opt for dialogue rather than the usual threats of force (nonetheless all options remain on the table). These policy decisions have enormous geopolitical import. The military actions that had been threatened against those countries are put on hold. In August, UNASUR expresses its opposition to outside intervention in Syria including the potential military strike, threatened by Obama, against that country.

Though most governments praise Washington's good-will gesture towards its adversary of many years, Israel grows alarmed, fearing that American commitment to their bilateral alliance could waver. Israeli Prime Minister Netanyahu threatens a preemptive strike against Iran. Concerned, in part, that an ascendant Iran could reemerge as the primary US ally in the region, Saudi Arabia also opposes the negotiations. Two former Defense Secretaries, Robert Gates and Leon Panetta, are among the domestic critics of the president's diplomatic outreach. Republicans, as well as some Democrats, accuse Obama of demonstrating weakness—weakness that will be exploited by future rivals.

It has been a terrible year in the capital concludes Kimberly Halkett of the Al Jazeera news agency. Astonishingly little in the way of important legislation was passed, and the shutdown hurt the country and damaged its image abroad. The GOP's approval rating has fallen to 28%.

INSTITUTIONAL COUPS

Obama's controversial handling of the Honduran coup raises the question: what are Washington's true intentions regarding the region's other leftist governments? The new administration has now, in effect, endorsed regime change as an acceptable policy tool. "When is it considered legitimate," asks Mark Weisbrot, "to try to overthrow a democratically elected government in Washington? The answer has always been simple: when the U.S. government says it is. Not surprisingly this in not the way Latin American governments generally see it" (*The Guardian*, February 18, 2014).

In the 21st century, however, methods have changed. No longer cooked up in the White House and Pentagon, coups are now institutional, parliamentary, carried out in the name of "democracy." They tend to follow the "soft coup" model, formulated by the American political scientist Gene Sharp. According to Sharp's manual, institutional coups come about through protests and persuasion, civil disobedience, workers' strikes, political non-cooperation, and other methods of non-violent intervention.

In January 2011, less than two years after the Honduran coup, a police uprising in Ecuador results in a kidnapping and assassination attempt against Rafael Correa. Following a review of intelligence reports, the president subsequently declares: "After Zelaya, I will be second." Few American news outlets cover the incident, and those that do give it second billing. Mark Weisbrot, who has argued that Obama's mismanagement of the Honduran crisis will serve as impetus for future coups, characterizes the Ecuadorian police incident as a "coup attempt." In June 2012, there is another police uprising against Evo Morales in Bolivia. His government can provide evidence of U.S. involvement.

The second institutional coup takes place in Paraguay, also in January 2011, when Parliament accelerates impeachment proceedings against the former bishop and democratically elected president, Fernando Lugo. The process by which he is removed from office is illegitimate, as no constitutional grounds for impeachment have been met. Vice President Federico Franco, a member of the right-wing Paraguay's Authentic Radical Liberal Party (PLRA), assumes the presidency. The United States immediately announces its intention to cooperate with the incoming government. UNASUR, Mercosur and Latin American governments, on the other hand, are leery of the official explanation given for Lugo's abrupt removal and several countries suspend diplomatic relations with Paraguay.

The massacre of landless peasants who had occupied a rural estate in Curuguaty, near the Brazilian border, is the reason cited for Lugo's impeachment. Disproportionate force, including 324 policemen and a helicopter, was called in to clear the estate out. Eleven peasants and six police officers were killed during the operation. The UN Human Rights Committee finds the government's investigation of the incident to be superficial, inadequate, and biased, and categorizes the peasants' violent expulsion as a "political crime" (*Bolpress*, 2012, June 22). The strange circumstances surrounding the massacre, including police manipulation of the crime scene and USAID's continued support of opposition organizations, explain the coup's motives. A diplomatic cable released by WikiLeaks, revealing Washington's behind-the-scenes machinations against Lugo from the day he took office, offers further clarification (*The NACLA Report on the Americas*, 2013, April 10).

Running on the Colorado Party (PC) ticket, Horacio Cartes wins the 2013 presidential election. The conservative PC previously governed for 60 years, 35 of those under the dictator Alfredo Stroessner. Lugo's stint in office proved to be just a brief time out. A wealthy businessman, Cartes has been arrested for currency exchange fraud and investigated for money laundering and affiliations with drug traffickers in Brazil and other countries (Urgente24.com, 2014, April 2). The election is monitored by UNASUR, which certifies them as clean. Paraguay is reintegrated into international bodies and the governments that cut ties reestablish them.

Were there stirrings of a coup in Colombia? In December 2012, the Attorney General's Office orders its Technical Investigation Body (CIT) to analyze an email chain, in which a group of retired generals discuss the state of security and public order in the country, to determine whether the exchange reveals any intent to orchestrate a coup. Jaime Ruiz Barrera, President of the Association of Retired Officials of the Military Forces, himself a retired general, acknowledges the existence of the emails in question, but reassures the public that they in no way constitute any form of rebellion and have been "misinterpreted" (*El Espectador*, July 12, 2012). The supposed coup amounts to nothing.

THE STORY CONTINUES

On January 1, 2014 the Affordable Care Act, which was passed by Congress four years earlier, takes effect; this landmark legislation is the cornerstone of the president's domestic agenda, and has already benefited millions of Americans. The absence of immigration reform, however, limits the law's effectiveness. Many Hispanics don't sign up out of fear of putting undocumented family members at risk. During Obama's time in office, two million immigrants have been deported—an average of 1,100 a day—the highest such figure in the country's history; thousands more are being held in private detention centers. Discontent among the Hispanic electorate could tilt the balance against Democratic candidates in the 2014 midterm elections.

Later in the month, Obama delivers a State of the Union that is "heavy on political theater, low on substance," according to *The Guardian* (*The Guardian*, 2014, January 29). In an editorial titled "The Diminished State of the Union" *The New York Time* once again calls for GOP cooperation while acknowledging the obvious: Congress has become a "dead end," and Republican opposition is "implacable." The editorial cites the president's bold declaration: "America does not stand still, and neither will I. So wherever and whenever I can take steps without legislation to expand opportunity for more American families, that's what I am going to do." Obama calls for a "year of action" to tackle growing inequality. The editorial concludes: "As important as executive orders can be, they should not replace showing that Republicans are voting against the public wishes" (*The New York Times*, 2014, January 28). According to Jon Stewart, host of "The Daily Show," "President Obama is now in the 'Fuck It' stage of his Presidency" (The Huffington Post, 2014, January 29).

Hispanic leaders criticize the president for devoting only a brief portion of the speech to immigration. A DREAM activist invited by Michelle Obama to attend the address remarks: "This is the same rhetoric that we've been hearing for the last five years. President Obama getting up and saying, "It is time for immigration reform. I am committed to make it happen. We have been waiting," he adds, "and fighting to get something done [...] I think the president didn't do enough in this year's State of the Union, especially given that he says immigration reform is his top domestic priority" ("Democracy Now", 2014, January 29)

IN LATIN AMERICA: THE GOOD AND THE BAD

With or without Obama, Latin America is getting along just fine. Peace and harmony reign over the region and national economies, for the most part, are growing. According to the UN Food and Agriculture Organization (FAO), eleven Latin American and Caribbean countries surpassed their UN-set goal for combating poverty, including Cuba, Brazil, Venezuela, Nicaragua, Dominican Republic and some Caribbean states.

After getting off to a rocky start with UNASUR, Colombia changes course with the election of Juan Manuel Santos, who immediately goes about mending damaged relations with neighboring leaders, most importantly Rafael Correa and Hugo Chávez, whom Santos refers to as his "best new friend." Despite the heavy U.S. military presence, Colombia is no longer seen as the region's problem country. The U.S.-Colombian military pact, once the source of such widespread controversy, rarely comes up at home or abroad.

The continent enthusiastically welcomes Santos's unexpected change of course. Though his rapprochement with two staunch regional critics is not to Washington's liking, the super power remains silent.

Despite peace negotiations initiated by Santos, the armed conflict in Colombia continues to rage. And though some 30,000 paramilitaries (according to the previous administration) have demobilized, a new generation of criminal bands, referred to as BACRIM, continue to perpetrate crimes against the civilian population.

Undeterred by the failures of previous administrations, Santos embarks upon peace negotiations with the FARC, and initiates a restitution program to restore land and provide compensation to tens of thousands of peasants displaced by paramilitary and guerrilla violence. These restitutions—which have been granted in 15 of the country's 32 departments—include low-interest loans and technical assistance geared toward increasing production.

Colombia is not the only country in the region with an alarming internal crisis. A major transit country for South American narcotics, Mexico is also wracked by drug-related violence, much of it stemming from territorial disputes between rival cartels.

Venezuela has no armed conflict, and is not a major producer of illicit drugs, yet its levels of everyday crime continue to soar. Some 18,000 homicides are registered in 2010 alone. Venezuela has also become a transit country for Colombian cocaine destined for European and U.S. markets.

A "SOFT COUP" IN VENEZUELA?

The March 2013 death of Hugo Chávez is a great loss for the entire continent, as the Venezuelan leader had devoted himself heart and soul to the cause of regional unity and, along with Lula da Silva, led the effort to establish mechanisms for integration; he also created programs to help out friendly countries, which included supplying Venezuelan petroleum, via barter exchanges, at below-market rates. This program was particularly vital for Cuba.

Major changes occur in Venezuela as well. In April, presidential elections are held. Nicolas Maduro, the late president's handpicked successor squares off against Henrique Capriles, the candidate representing the Democratic Unity Roundtable (MUD), a coalition of 19 opposition parties. A vocal dissident, Capriles played a role in the 2002 coup. He also led the illegal incursion into the Cuban embassy. Maduro wins the election by a margin of 1.5%. Capriles challenges the results. The Electoral Council grants a recount request, which Capriles subsequently dismisses as "farce" after it confirms Maduro's victory

Capriles proceeds to organize large-scale demonstrations throughout the country, and dial up the anti-government media campaign both in Venezuela and abroad. The opposition accuses the government of conducting itself dictatorially, despite 19 elections having been held—and certified as legitimate by neutral observers like the Carter Center—over the fifteen years since the advent of the Bolivarian Revolution. It couches the crisis in terms generally reserved for civil war, and condemns government violence against protestors. Washington, which has not recognized the Maduro government, threatens sanctions.

Attempting to delegitimize the Maduro government, Capriles travels to Chile, Peru, Brazil and Colombia to meet with government leaders. His visits are met with resistance in some political circles, and his efforts to destabilize a democratically elected leader criticized. Governments accept his visits with reservations. Relations with Venezuela are important.

The conflict continues to simmer and exhibit disturbing optics of a coup. The demonstrations go on for several months, resulting in injuries and fatalities—the majority opposition—and hundreds of arrests. A Mercosur declaration, signed by Brazil, Argentina, Uruguay and Paraguay, categorizes the protests as "attempts to destabilize the democratic order" (Weisbrot, op. Cit.). Mercosur accepts Venezuela's request for full membership, despite Paraguay's attempts, under President Franco, to block its entry.

Venezuela severs diplomatic and economic relations with Panama after its president, Ricardo Martinelli, requests a meeting of the Permanent Council of the OAS on the Venezuelan crisis. Venezuelan foreign minister, Elias Jaua, denounces the psychological warfare being waged through the media to justify foreign intervention to the UN Human Rights Committee (*Granma*, 2014, March 4). All signs indicate a "soft coup" is in the offing. Around the continent, political leaders voice their opposition to the violence and support for conciliatory dialogue between the government and opposition leaders.

BACKYARD FULL OF SURPRISES

When Hugo Chávez and Lula da Silva set out to build the institutions for regional integration they left Central America out for an obvious reason: its historic subservience to Washington. Nonetheless, as *The Economist* reports, the region is now "nobody's backyard." Little by little, Central American countries are starting to gain independence. In recent presidential elections, several leftist candidates have triumphed over conservative opponents. Only Honduras and Guatemala continue to be led by right-wing governments.

In one of the region's strongest democracies, Luis Guillermo Solis Rivera, of the leftist Citizens' Action Party, the largest political party in Costa Rica, triumphs in the February 2014 presidential election over the conservative National Liberation Party candidate, Johnny Anaya Monge, who withdraws before the second round of voting, his defeat all but certain. Supported by the leftist Broad Front, Solis garners the highest vote tally in history. In El Salvador, the following month, the ex-FMLN guerrilla Salvador Sanchez wins the presidency. He replaces Mauricio Funes, the country's first left-wing president, who reestablished relations with the Cuban government, which had been broken for half a century.

In January, *Semana* magazine publishes an article titled "Ortega For a While" after the Nicaraguan National Assembly passes a constitutional reform lifting presidential term limits and eliminating the minimum number of votes necessary for reelection, a measure expected to favor the Sandinista leader (*Semana*, January 2, 2014). Other Western newspapers emphasize his abuses of power, and question his personal integrity and Nicaraguan democracy.

The celebration of the Second Summit of the Community of Latin American and Caribbean States (CELAC) in Havana is a bitter pill for Washington. Thirty-three heads of state take part in the January summit, along with the UN and OAS secretary-generals. While the summit is in progress, an anonymous State Department official accuses the participants of "betraying" democratic principles by "supporting the one-party system of the Cuban regime [...] particularly inexplicable for an organization whose supposed support for democracy was declared in the First Summit" (*El Universal*, 2014, January 30).

"Let them eat their declarations" is Nicolas Maduro's response. The Venezuelan president senses "bitterness" in the anonymous barb and suggests that the United States must feel "defeated" by the region's "united spirit." Raúl Castro, presiding over the summit, hails the unity among the countries in attendance, and calls for a coordinated response to Washington's espionage; he declares the region a zone of peace, reaffirms his dream of nuclear disarmament, defends regional integration ("a strategic concept for the future") and national sovereignty of territory and natural resources (*Granma*, January 29, 2014). The summit includes a tribute to the late Hugo Chávez, one of CELAC's early champions. Weisbrot considers CELAC the greatest expression of Latin American independence with respect to Washington. Mexico, Colombia and Guatemala agree to integrate their anti-drug campaigns.

Epilogue

THE STORY CONTINUES

This book concludes midway through Barack Obama's second term in the White House, with the nation more polarized than ever. In Latin America and the Caribbean the political panorama presents challenges for fluid relations; regional integration continues to consolidate. In 2014, the Bank of the South—an institution conceived by Hugo Chávez to counter the IMF and World Bank—launches and, in presidential elections, Central American nations join ranks with the continental left. Washington's isolation, which Obama feels most acutely during the Fourth Summit of the Americas in Cartagena, grows.

Under President Santos, Colombia's bilateral relationship with the United States continues to flourish. As a result of the military agreement negotiated under the previous administration—which Santos, as defense minister, helped author—Colombia has become Washington's primary military enclave in the Americas. In 2010, however, the agreement appears to be in danger after Colombia's Constitutional Court voids it on the grounds that congressional approval should have been sought. Santos brushes off the Court's ruling, with nary a protest. American troops continue to enjoy access to Colombia's military bases and the extradition of drug traffickers to the United States proceeds, albeit at a slower rate—perhaps—than under the previous administration.

The challenges facing Obama in Latin America are hardly new ones. The drug war continues to be a primary focus of Washington's hemispheric policy, and the inability to pass wholesale immigration reform many consider the president's most glaring failure. The question of Cuba continues to be a thorn in his side. The overwhelming majority of the UN General Assembly, in addition to UNASUR and CELAC call for an end to the economic embargo, and several Latin American heads of state pledge to abstain from hemispheric forums to which Cuba is not invited.

Immigration reform is a touchstone issue for Hispanics living in the United States, particularly Mexicans. Around 70% of undocumented immigrants living in the United States are Mexican. Likewise, Mexicans comprise the majority of deportees. Their presence in such large numbers, some contend, aggravates unemployment and poverty throughout the country.

Mexico is the United States' third largest trade partner, and represents for Washington one of its most complicated bilateral relationships. Despite measures taken to enhance border security, undocumented immigrants continue entering the country in search of economic opportunity. And despite an intense military crackdown, Mexican cartels continue to smuggle countless tons of narcotics across the border, with a steady flow of illegal arms and drugs money moving in the opposite direction. In the two decades since it took effect, NAFTA has proven disastrous for small farmers in Mexico, and certain controversial terms of the pact have not been revisited despite the pleas from several heads of state to Obama.

Perhaps, in part, to mollify Hispanic voters prior to the upcoming election, in June 2012 Obama issues an executive order, the DREAM ACT, granting conditional permanent residency to the children of undocumented immigrants who arrived in the country as minors. Though a far cry from legalization, it is at least a step in the right direction. In announcing the decree, Obama declares the need to "lift the shadow of deportation for these young people," and make immigration policy "more fair, more efficient and more just" (*The New York Times*, 2012, June 15). A few months later, Obama wins 71% of the Latino vote in his successful reelection bid.

Fifteen states with large Hispanic populations—including Texas, New York, California and New Jersey—subsequently pass their own versions of the DREAM Act, granting legal residence to the children of undocumented immigrants who are born in the country or arrive under 16 years of age. For

Latinos, this measure does not go far enough. Their goal is full legalization.

In June 2013, the U.S. Senate passes an immigration reform bill—with 14 Republican votes in favor—paving the way for the legalization of 11 million undocumented immigrants; the bill, however, must first pass the Republican-controlled House. Immigration activists criticize the proposed legislation for its focus on the militarization of the border, a Republican demand. The American Civil Liberties Union (ACLU) praises the Senate for passing the bill—which it hails as "historic"—with bipartisan support (*El País*, 2013, June 27).

Despite intense pressure from immigration activists, the House does not pass the bill. Across the nation there is a groundswell of support for reform, and outrage at the spike in deportations. Under the Obama administration, the federal government has deported a record two million immigrants—1,100 a day on average. In Washington and other major cities there are almost daily protests, marches and acts of "civil disobedience;" activists form picket lines in front of the offices and the homes of some of the reform's high-profile detractors and immigrants stage hunger strikes in front of the White House (*HOY Digital*, 2014, September 11).

The war on drugs continues to dominate Washington's agenda in several Latin American countries. Though it may receive scant or no mention in State of the Union speeches, the battle continues to be fought on Latin American soil as a pretext to expand U.S. military presence in the region.

Guatemala's president, the ex-colonel Otto Perez Molina, is the first Latin American head of state to raise the possibility of decriminalizing certain drugs as an alternative to full legalization. At the VI Summit of the Americas, Obama discusses the issue with Presidents Santos and Rousseff, but ultimately discards the possibility. Legalization, he declares, is not a viable solution to the drug crisis, and as an alternative promotes an economic development plan that would create greater work opportunities. Given the staggering levels and of poverty and inequality throughout Latin America, many dismiss the proposal as a pipe dream.

Despite the Obama administration's official opposition, the movement to legalize marijuana gains traction. In three states—Colorado, Washington and Alaska—the use of marijuana is legalized. And in December 2013, President José Mujica sees through legislation making Uruguay the first country to fully legalize the drug—a turning point, perhaps, in its decades-long worldwide prohibition.

In March 2014, the Pentagon releases its Quadrennial Defense Review (QDR), outlining strategic priorities in the region. Predictably, combating the drug trade is foremost among its declared concerns. "Today's threats," the report states, "stem from the spread of narcotics and other forms of transnational organized crimes [...] U.S. engagement in the Western Hemisphere is aimed at promoting and maintaining regional stability [...] we will emphasize building defense institutional capacity, increasing interoperability with the

U.S. and other likeminded partners, and supporting a system of multilateral defense cooperation such as the Conference of Defense Ministers of the Americas and the Inter-American Defense Board to respond to shared challenges (QDR, 2014, March 4). These forums are designed to bolster U.S. military control in the region.

The continental mood, however, is moving in the opposite direction. The 2009 U.S.-Colombian pact is met with harsh rebukes from UNASUR members. In their new constitutions, Bolivia and Ecuador prohibit foreign bases in their national territory. In 2009, President Correa declines to renew the American lease of the Manta military base.

Even the U.S. Congress acknowledges that militaristic, repressive anti-drug policies have, for the most part, failed. Despite countless billions in funding over the previous four decades, they have not achieved their primary objectives: stemming drug production, consumption and violence. The United States is not only the largest consumer of narcotics in the world, but the country with the highest incarceration rate. With over two million people behind bars, the U.S. is home to around a quarter of the world's total inmates, and of those 500,000 are serving drug-related sentences.

Evo Morales is one of the most vocal critics of U.S. drug policy, and its politicized "certification" process. Following its decision to expel the DEA, Bolivia is decertified. Citing his government's success in reducing coca production, Morales claims the decertification is political retribution. In May 2013, he expels USAID for meddling and conspiring against his government (Telesur, 2013, May 1). Morales points out that The International Narcotics Control Board has certified the United States as the world's largest recipient of illicit drug money, which circulates throughout its banking system, and calls for the elimination of banking secrecy. The Bolivian president takes Washington to task for failing to taper domestic demand for drugs (*Granma*, September 18, 2012).

Popular sentiment in Latin America increasingly favors the revision of existing drug policies, including the decriminalization of consumption and reframing the problem as a public health crisis with increased focus on diminishing demand through rehabilitation and education programs. This is the approach advocated by Gil Kerlikowske, the former Director of the Office of National Drug Control Policy; undeterred, Washington continues to implement military strategies throughout the region.

In 2009, former presidents Fernando Henrique Cardoso of Brazil, Ernesto Zedillo of Mexico, and César Gaviria of Colombia administer a study for the OAS Latin American Commission on Drugs and Democracy. Requested by Juan Manuel Santos, Colombia is among the eight countries funding the research. These former and current heads of state can be seen as pioneers for questioning, at such a high level, the effectiveness and human cost of the drug war, and pushing for a revision of current policies, which have borne few positive outcomes while spawning countless human rights violations and staggering levels of violence—aggravated by corruption, poverty and social inequality. They cite the tens of thousands of lives that have been lost, including 130,000 in Colombia alone.

José Miguel Insulza, secretary-general of the OAS, delivers the report to President Santos at the VI Summit of the Americas in Cartagena. The report confirms the disillusion throughout the region with prohibitionist policies, and the growing desire to explore intermediary solutions. One potential solution is the decriminalization certain drugs, in particular marijuana; another is approaching the crisis as a public health—rather than criminal—problem.

The human cost of the war on drugs is a major concern of the Inter-American Commission on Human Rights. In April 2014, for the first time, a public hearing is held to address the war's consequences in Latin America; front and center are human rights violations, the result—the commission claims—of "the extreme militarization of the state response." Several human rights organizations had called on the IACHR to organize this event, hoping to spur on new approaches to the problem.

The question of drug trafficking is addressed in the framework agreement leading up to formal negotiations between the Colombian government and FARC in Havana. Juan Manuel Santos is the first head of state to call for a global debate on drugs, with the participation of the entire continent and, principally, the United States. Though the official debate has yet to begin, at least the issue is on the table. It is a crisis the United States and its regional allies have no choice but to address.

Obama's foreign policy in Latin America and the Caribbean has been, on the whole, a disappointment. At the beginning of his term in office the president paid lip service to peaceful coexistence, dialogue on equal footing, and a new start with Cuba, but none of these promises have been fulfilled. Washington's isolation grows, which is most evident during the VI Summit of the Americas in Cartagena, whose participants "openly defied the United States in a way that was unprecedented and invigorating," with the debate focusing on Cuba's exclusion from hemispheric conferences and controversial drug policies. In past years, Washington had set the agenda and limited the parameters of discussion. This is clearly not the case in Cartagena (Oliver Stone y Peter Kuznic, *The Untold History of the United States*, 2012). Mexican President Felipe Calderón describes what transpired at the summit as "radical and unthinkable," a sentiment reflected in a *Jamaica Observer* headline: "Summit shows how Yankee influence has waned." The region views current U.S. foreign policy as a continuation of "gunboat" and Cold War-era diplomacy (Stone y Kutznic. Op cit).

Despite its diminished soft power, American military might is as incontestable as ever. Washington secures its empire through military bases that span the globe. Though the exact number remains unknown, according to a 2008 study the

Pentagon has specifically referred to 860 bases in 46 countries. Experts, however, claim there are 1,250 in 100 countries. Of those, 36 FOLs and authorized landing strips are located in Latin American and the Caribbean. The Independence and Sovereignty Committee for Latin America (CISPAL), an organization comprised of respected analysts from around the world, characterizes these bases as a threat to peace, democracy, sovereignty and independence in the region (CISPAL, 2013, December 31). Of Washington's meddling in the domestic affairs of other nations, and its track record of toppling democratic governments deemed inconvenient, much has been written.

About the Author

Clara Nieto is a Colombian journalist and diplomat who served for eleven years as a delegate to the United Nations, and later as Colombia's representative to UNESCO in Paris, chargé d'affaires in Yugoslavia, Ambassador to Cuba, as well as UNESCO's regional director in Havana. She is the author of *Masters of War*, first published in Colombia by Uniandes-Cerec (1999), and later in the United States by Seven Stories Press (2003), in Italy by Nuovi Mundo Media (2003), and by Random House-Mondadori (2003).

www.ingramcontent.com/pod-product-compliance
Lightning Source LLC
Chambersburg PA
CBHW060231290526
45789CB00001B/1